BUILDING WEALTH

BUILDING WEALTH
Achieving Your Financial Goals

Gordon Pape

Prentice-Hall Canada Inc., Scarborough, Ontario

Portions of Chapters 6 and 7 originally appeared in Canadian House and Home
Portions of Chapter 9 originally appeared in Flare Magazine
Portions of Chapters 11, 16, and 18 originally appeared in Ontario Living

Prentice-Hall Inc., Englewood Cliffs, *New Jersey*
Prentice-Hall International, Inc., *London*
Prentice-Hall of Australia, Pty., *Sydney*
Prentice-Hall of India Pvt., Ltd., *New Delhi*
Prentice-Hall of Japan, Inc., *Tokyo*
Prentice-Hall of Southeast Asia (Pte.) Ltd., *Singapore*
Prentice-Hall do Brasil Ltda., *Rio de Janeiro*
Prentice-Hall Hispanoamericana, S.A., *Mexico*

Canadian Cataloguing in Publication Data

Pape, Gordon, 1937-
    Building Wealth

Includes index.
ISBN 0-13-154295-8

1. Finance, Personal.   I. Title.

HG179.P365 1988   332.024   C88-093008-X

Cover design: David Montle
Manuscript editor: Jessica Pegis
Coordinating editor: Sharyn Rosart
Manufacturing buyer: Don Blair
Composition: ISIS Communications Limited
Printed and bound in Canada by GAGNE

1 2 3 4 5 G   92 91 90 89 88

TABLE OF CONTENTS

To my children: Deborah, Kendrew and Kim

*With the hope this book will help them
enrich their lives.*

ACKNOWLEDGEMENTS

There are a number of people and organizations I would like to thank for their assistance in making this book possible. They include: Ron Hume and Hugh Furneaux for giving me the opportunity to spend some years at Hume Publishing, where I gained many insights into investing and wealth building; David Louis, one of Canada's foremost tax experts, who inspired me to look at taxation in a different way; the Canadian Broadcasting Corporation, especially the Infotape section and the Business World group, for giving me access to a national radio audience, thereby providing a unique opportunity to gain insights into the real financial needs and concerns of Canadians; *The Financial Times of Canada* for their excellent mutual funds information; the Bank of Montreal for their assistance in complex mortgage calculations; and, finally, my family — they always manage to put up with the sometimes unreasonable demands of having to live with a writer.

Gordon Pape
August, 1987

Wealth is Not Money

I DON'T KNOW MANY people who wouldn't like to be wealthy. The few exceptions tend to fall into one of three groups:

They're already super rich and don't need any more.

They're political radicals who believe everything belongs to the state anyway.

They're religious fanatics who are hung up on the rich man and the eye of the needle bit.

If you fall into any of these groups, this book is NOT for you. Close it right now! Don't read another line! Go and demand a refund from your bookstore! Hurry! Don't wait!

Now, for the rest of us, let's get on with building wealth.

First, though, I have a confession to make, in the interests of full disclosure. I am not a millionaire. Not yet, anyway. I am more than halfway there and I expect to reach the million dollar net worth figure within a couple of years. But you should know it hasn't happened yet.

So why bother to read wealth-building advice from someone who isn't genuinely wealthy? Why not find a book by a real multimillionaire and read it?

I'll tell you why. Because if I had known 25 years ago what I know today, I'd have been a millionaire many times over by now. But I didn't begin to learn about wealth building until my late forties (I'm in my early fifties now). That's relatively late in life to get started. The fact is, the younger you are when you begin, the more wealth you'll be able to build and, more importantly, enjoy over your lifetime.

That's what gave me the idea to write this book in the first place. My children are now in their late teens and early twenties. They're approaching the point in life where they'll leave school and begin to make their own careers. That's one of the most critical times in the whole wealth-building process. You're free from parental ties, you're on your own for the first time, and you're earning more money than you ever dreamed possible. The natural temptation is to live it up. Get that car you've always wanted. Go on an expensive holiday. Buy a wardrobe full of new clothes. If you go into debt in the process, so what? You have lots of earning years ahead of you.

I don't blame young people for thinking that way. It's natural. But there's an alternative. Give up a little bit now—and get it back a thousand-fold later. Instead of spending everything that comes in, use some of that money to set up a lifetime wealth-building program.

One thing I've observed is how much more mature and sophisticated young people are today then when I was starting out in life. I'm not sure what's responsible for that, but I suspect television has played a major role. Whatever the reason, I find that people in their teens and twenties today are more aware of the world and their place in it. As such, many of them are interested in a sensible approach to building comfortable lives for themselves.

They're the people for whom this book is primarily intended —they're young enough to get the most benefit from the ideas that follow, and smart enough to know that they have to put in some effort to make it all happen.

That doesn't mean that if you're over thirty this book has nothing for you. Quite the contrary. You're never too old to become a wealth builder. No matter what your age, if you haven't made a serious start until now I believe what I have to say will be helpful. The major advantage younger people have is more time—and as we go on, you'll understand why that's important.

There is one other point I should make. This is a book for people who are just beginning the wealth-building process. The advice and techniques I suggest are best suited to their needs. If you've been a dedicated wealth builder for years, you may find a few interesting ideas. Look especially at Chapters Ten (bonds), Fourteen and Fifteen (RRSPs), Seventeen and Eighteen (mutual funds), Twenty (brokers), Twenty-one and Twenty-two (tax), and Twenty-three (financial services). But much of the information may seem rather basic. If that's your situation, I suggest you skim the chapters that might offer some helpful ideas. Then pass the book along to a relative or friend you think would benefit from it. You'll be doing him or her a favour.

I often find myself wondering why I didn't learn much of the information in this book earlier in my life. I guess it was for the same reason most of us don't: nobody took the time and trouble to teach me. The school system showed me how to bisect angles and scan poems, but offered absolutely zilch when it came to building wealth. (Judging by my children, things aren't much better today, a generation later.) My parents were hopeless when it came to building wealth—in fact, my father seemed to be inclined in exactly the opposite direction. He was a wonderfully talented man in the laboratory—he developed a process for artificially drying prunes and apricots in the early 1930s. But he was totally lacking in wealth-building skills. That process, on which he held the patent, eventually became the cornerstone of a multimillion dollar industry. But he sold off his rights at the height of the Depression for $5,000.

I suppose I could have learned the skills myself but, like most of us, I was always too busy. There were other priorities in life, like getting through school, travelling in Europe, finding a job, getting married. Who had time to worry about such esoteric matters as wealth building?

Sound familiar?

I come in contact with a lot of senior business and professional people in my work—men and women at the top of their fields, highly respected among their peers. They are smart, articulate, fun to be with—and most of them haven't the faintest idea how to handle money intelligently or build wealth.

I'll never forget the time I was having drinks with a friend after a curling game—a successful sales manager in his fifties. It was RRSP season and he'd heard me talking about the subject in a radio broadcast. He saw a chance for a little free advice and asked what he should be putting his money into. The conversation went something like this:

ME: Do you have an RRSP now?

FRIEND: Yes.

ME: What type?

FRIEND: Well, gosh, I'm not sure.

ME: Well, what kind of return are you getting?

FRIEND: Uh, well, I really don't know.

You don't need to hear any more. Can you imagine where he'd be if he ran his business that way?

Ironically, the more successful people are professionally, the worse they tend to be as money managers. Some of the most naive people I know, from a financial point of view, are well-respected doctors, lawyers, dentists, and corporate vice presidents—most of them with six-figure incomes.

Makes no sense, you say? Actually it does, if you stop and think about it a moment. What made these people so successful in the first place? To start with, a long period of education—law school, dental college, medical internship, M.B.A. studies. Total immersion in the disciplines of their chosen fields. And then what? Establishing a practice or setting up a partnership or climbing the corporate ladder. Hard work, long hours, learning how to be the best at what they do, coming home at night exhausted, with about enough energy left to eat, watch some mindless TV, and fall into bed.

When did they have time to learn about handling money and building wealth? They didn't. They were too busy launching careers, often getting married and starting families at the same time. Wealth building seemed like taking a year off to sail around the world—something everyone would like to do but no one had time for.

So what happens? Many of these people reach mid-life with big incomes, but no wealth to speak of. They're still in debt, live beyond their means, and dream of the day when they'll have some time to themselves to enjoy life. Too often, that day doesn't come.

I once heard Dr. Morton Shulman make a comment that really hit home. The purpose of acquiring wealth, he said, was to enjoy life more.

It sounds so simple. But it's the key to understanding what wealth is really all about.

As you read this book, I implore you to keep Dr. Shulman's thought in the front of your mind. You are not building wealth for wealth's sake. There is no joy in adding up the value of your investments each month and discovering you're 5% richer. The joy is in the use you can make of that wealth—whether to have a larger home, or drive a Jaguar, or own a condo in the Laurentians or Hawaii, or send your kids to the best universities in North America, or give large amounts of money to worthy causes—whatever appeals to you. The joy in wealth is in the pleasures it can bring—and they can be pleasures of the spirit as well as the flesh.

Where do you start? Well, it helps to have certain advantages. One is education. There's no question that the greater your income potential, the easier wealth building becomes. Another, as I've already indicated, is youth. The younger you are when you begin, the greater your chances of acquiring very substantial wealth over your lifetime. That's why I'm doing everything possible to make sure my children learn about money management and investing at an early age. I don't want them to go through what I did: losing major wealth-building opportunities when I was young because I didn't have the faintest idea how to go about creating a coherent plan or what to do with my money.

Does that mean if you don't have education and youth on your side you're out of luck? No, it just means wealth building will be harder. You'll have to work more and be more disciplined. It's rather like the situation with my oldest daughter. She's profoundly deaf and, although she has learned to speak, she's often hard to understand, especially by people who haven't been exposed to the hearing-impaired. It's a major disability by anyone's standards. Yet she completed high school with an 80 percent-plus average, won several scholarships, and is now a successful university student. Why? Because she was prepared to work doubly hard to overcome her handicap, and had the self-discipline to stick to it.

That's not easy—for any of us. It's always more convenient to find an excuse for putting off something—going on a diet, painting the bedroom, taking an adult education course. But the hard fact is that if you want to build wealth, you have to develop the self-discipline to learn how to do it properly, and then to apply what you learn. It's a lifetime commitment—like having a child, or making a marriage work, or being first-rate at your work. If you aren't prepared to make that commitment, the odds are you will never become wealthy.

As part of that commitment, you have to be prepared to acquire some knowledge and to keep that knowledge current. That's going to take some of the most precious thing you have—time. Not just at the outset, but all the way along. If you don't know what's going on in the world and how to relate that information to the wealth-building process, you're not going to do well.

Where do you start? Books like this one are a good beginning. (That you have read this far is also a positive sign.) Find a couple of others that are designed to provide basic information and browse through them as well. There are a lot of different ideas about wealth building; it pays to know a number of them.

If you're really interested, you might want to consider taking a course. In my view, the best starter course in Canada is Hume Publishing's "Successful Investing & Money Management" program. However, I could be biased—I coordinated a major rewriting of that program a few years ago.

You must—and I stress *must*—become a regular reader of the financial pages in your newspaper. You may not understand a lot of it at first. But as you read through this book, more and more of what seems like financial and economic gobblydegook may start to make sense. Even more important, you'll begin to understand how to use the information on the financial pages to your own advantage.

The next step is to start reading the financial press. The *Globe and Mail*'s *Report on Business* is a must. One or both of the *Financial Times* or *Financial Post* should also be on your list. Magazines such as *Your Money* are useful, as are some of the better investment newsletters, such as *The MoneyLetter*. The important thing is to keep yourself informed. Self-education is one of the cornerstones of successful wealth building.

There is something else you need: patience. Unless you become a rock star or win a lottery, you will not get rich overnight. Wealth building takes time. Years. Skill and luck will play a role in how much time it takes *you*. Perhaps you can manage it in ten years, perhaps it will take 25. But it is not going to happen in one year, or two, or probably even five. You must have patience, you must be willing to accept temporary setbacks. As long as you remain committed and follow the advice in this book, you'll make it.

Make it where? What kind of wealth is this guy talking about, you may ask? In fact, wealth is a relative concept. To a destitute person living in the streets, "wealth" is eating regularly and having somewhere warm and dry to sleep. To a young couple with two babies, it may be simply getting out of debt. To the newly retired, it may mean being able to maintain the same lifestyle they've enjoyed for the past decade.

Wealth is a personal concept. You have to decide for yourself what the word means to you—what it is you're aiming to achieve as you begin to apply the information you find in this book.

I have my own personal definition: wealth is the ability to do whatever I want in life without compromising my standard of living. In other words, comfortable independence. If I am able to quit my job because I don't like it any more and not worry about the impact on my income, I'm wealthy. If I can take a year off and sit on a beach writing a novel, I'm wealthy. If I can go to Venice and stay at the finest hotel in the city without worrying about the expense, I'm wealthy. That's my personal wealth objective. You have to decide yours.

Of course, your wealth objective will change as you grow older and your asset base grows. You may start by wanting to get out of debt. When you achieve that goal, your new wealth definition may be owning your own home. When that's accomplished, it may be to own a summer cottage or a winter condo. And so it goes. Just remember, your wealth definition must relate to something that will make your life more pleasant and enjoyable. It should never be thought of as the amount of money you're going to stash in some vault (unless, of course, that would please you the most).

One other thing before we start. You should know that I'm very conservative by nature. The advice in this book will obviously reflect that—it couldn't be any other way. The techniques I describe may be a bit too cautious, too slow, if you happen to be a more aggressive type of person. But before you decide to become a high roller, think about this: every investment professional will tell you that the cardinal rule of building wealth is NOT TO LOSE YOUR CAPITAL. Surprised? I was when I first heard it. But it makes sense. It's easy to lose money—anyone can do it. What's hard is to retain what you have and to build on it—especially in tough economic times. That's when prudence and patience will pay off.

That's about it for openers. Turn to the next chapter and let's get started.

The Arab Bazaar

H AVE YOU EVER wondered why more people aren't wealthy? Have you asked yourself what it takes? Special skills? Connections? Luck? Knowledge?

Well, none of those hurt. But it takes something else as well—determination. If you *really* want wealth, you have to be prepared to work at it.

That may sound too obvious. But the fact is that if you want to build wealth, you have to be prepared to devote at least as much time to it as you would to learning how to cook, or play the piano, or master tennis. It doesn't come overnight.

Let me give you an example. Very few people, even the pros, can tell you all the different ways in which you can invest money today. The financial marketplace has become the modern equivalent of an Arab bazaar—complex, colourful, filled with mysterious, eye-catching products that vendors are hawking as once-in-a-lifetime bargains.

The number of places to put your money is truly astounding, and dozens more are appearing every year. You have to know which ones are good, and which will devour your funds and not even spit back a chicken bone in return. And you have to know whom to buy from. After all, would you purchase a genuine diamond ring in a 24-carat gold setting from a street vendor in a Cairo bazaar? Maybe you would. I sure wouldn't.

Let me offer another example—taxes. Earning money is obviously important. But it's even more important to keep it—not to have it all taxed away. We live in a country that is tax-oppressive. In a later chapter I'll explain in greater detail why this is so. For the moment, just take my word that as things stand now, you cannot build wealth in Canada unless you take advantage of some of the opportunities in our quirky tax laws. Another reality is that the tax rules are constantly changing—no sooner do you figure out one way of getting around them than the government amends the law. It's like building a house on quicksand. Nevertheless, you have to try.

I occasionally get letters from people who suggest it's somehow immoral to plan your financial life so as to reduce taxes. Well, if it's immoral, it's the government's fault, not mine. Our government—or, more correctly, successive governments—have created a tax burden that dulls initiative and destroys incentive. But those same governments have built all sorts of weird and wonderful incentives into our tax laws to encourage us to invest our money in particular ways—and to ensure that, if we do as they wish, we can keep more wealth for ourselves. Until that situation changes, the true wealth builder will seek out every possible way to take advantage of it. That's not immoral. That's simple common sense.

Let me go back to where I started. To learn all these things obviously takes time. If you're not prepared to commit that time, don't start. It also takes some experience—you're going to make mistakes along the way. When you do, try to limit your losses and learn from them.

That's enough preaching. Let's begin.

You have to start with some basics—principles that you establish for yourself and stick to. You may find these are as basic as brushing your teeth. You're right, they are—and you'd be amazed at the number of would-be wealth builders who fail to apply them and end up in all sorts of trouble as a result.

Principle One: Establish an objective. It's much easier to begin a wealth-building program if you have a specific reason for doing it. Remember what I said in Chapter One about defining wealth for yourself in terms of things you can enjoy? That's what this exercise is all about. Set an objective and view that objective as a reward. It can be anything. Maybe it's a short-term goal, like buying a house or paying off a car loan early. Maybe it's more long-term, perhaps setting up a plan for your baby's university education. It doesn't matter what you choose. The key is to establish the motivation and the self-discipline that will be needed to set up your wealth-building plan and keep it going.

It's important that your first objective be something that's attainable within a reasonable time. If your first wealth target is something you have no hope of achieving for five or ten years, the odds are you'll soon become discouraged and lapse into your old ways.

Once you've chosen your wealth objective, put a dollar value on it and attach a time frame. That eliminates the vagueness that so often ruins the best intentions.

But remember—and I can't stress this enough—don't set your first objective too high. Make sure it's attainable. On the other hand, don't make it too easy. You should be prepared to sacrifice something to get what you want.

Principle Two: Keep things simple. Don't try to run before you can walk. If you do, you're almost sure to fall flat on your face.

Occasionally, I'm a guest on telephone hotline shows in various parts of the country. Almost every time I get at least one call from someone who says something like: "I don't know a lot about investing and I've just bought some shares in Moose Pasture United Mutual Fund. What can you tell me about it?"

That kind of question really bothers me. The caller has just bought a diamond in a Cairo bazaar and now wants to know if it's real!

The most common mistake made by beginning wealth builders is to put money into something they don't understand and know nothing about. My first response when I get a question like that is to ask the caller what he or she can tell me about Moose Pasture United Mutual Fund. If the answer is "nothing"—and it usually is—then I know the caller has a serious problem. And it's one I can't do very much about.

There's a golden rule when it comes to wealth building: IF YOU DON'T UNDERSTAND IT, DON'T PUT YOUR MONEY INTO IT! It's so basic, yet it's violated all the time—often by people who would never dream of spending a few hundred dollars on a new appliance without investigating it thoroughly and satisfying themselves they were getting the best possible deal. I know. I've done it. Never once has it turned out right.

Making an investment is like buying something. It's strictly *caveat emptor*—let the buyer beware. There are a lot of high pressure sales types out there who will call you on the phone or, even worse, come to your door trying to get you to sign up for a particular investment. And they can be very persuasive, believe me. I've had people from brokerage firms I've never heard of call me and describe in glowing terms all the money I can make by getting in on the ground floor of some obscure gold mine in northern Quebec. When you get such calls, just remember the Cairo bazaar.

That's why you never try to build your wealth on something you don't understand. Sure, that means you're going to have to take time to do some research into an opportunity that sounds good. I never said building wealth was going to be easy. If you don't want to take the time, then pass, tempting as the offer may sound. There's always another bus.

Principle Three: Start small. Don't get in over your head before you know what you're going. When you're ready to begin investing, pick something that doesn't require a large cash outlay and get a feel for what you're doing. Once you're comfortable, you can commit more funds or move on to something else.

Principle Four: Don't be afraid to build your wealth on borrowed money. Just be sure you go about it in a sensible, organized way and don't leave yourself so far out on a limb that you risk falling off if things go wrong. I'll have more to say about building wealth with other people's money later in the book.

Principle Five: Look for investments you can enjoy. As I said earlier, that's what wealth is all about. Try to hold as large a part of your assets as seems reasonable in investments that give you personal pleasure. A family home. A cottage on a serene lake. An antique car. A fashion boutique. Wealth building isn't accumulating cash so you can buy something you want later. It's obtaining the things you want as you go along—just as long as those things are genuine assets and not liabilities.

How can you tell the difference? Real assets will appreciate in value because of certain inherent characteristics. These include top quality, scarcity, high demand, and revenue potential. Not every asset will have them all—but it should have at least one and preferably, two.

Liabilities, as you might expect, have exactly the opposite characteristics: indifferent or poor quality, abundance, low demand and on-going cost.

The family Chev is a liability because there are a lot of them around, they're built to last for a limited period, maintenance and depreciation costs are high, and no one in their right mind is going to take it off your hands for more than you paid for it. On the other hand, a classic Packard is an asset because of its meticulous construction, scarcity, and desirability for antique car buffs.

So what material investments are most likely to appreciate in value? Start with real estate—a quality home, condo or cottage in a good location. I'll have more to say about that later. Fine art is a good bet—as long as you're able to recognize it and acquire it at a sensible price. That's true of any type of collectible: rare books, stamps, antiques, old wines. You have to know what you're doing.

A family business with strong profit potential is another type of material investment that can combine wealth building with personal satisfaction.

In the end, it comes down to what you know well and are most comfortable with—as long as it meets the basic asset criteria outlined above.

Principle Six: Remember that prices don't always go up. That applies to anything you can think of. Some assets do have a

13

stronger tendency to resist price declines in bad economic times—prime residential properties in desirable cities, for instance. But there are no absolutes. Under the right (or, more correctly, the wrong) circumstances, anything can drop in value. Hold that thought in the back of your mind as you embark on your wealth-building adventure.

Final Principle: Begin. That sounds simplistic, but many people don't ever get started. They have great intentions, but they keep putting things off. Next month they'll get going. But next month something comes up. That's the worst enemy of the beginning wealth builder—the "Oh, I'll get around to it sometime" syndrome.

If you're determined to start a wealth-building program, then do it! Don't make up excuses for waiting. That's a game for smokers who don't really want to quit. I don't care if it's only $5 a month—the important thing is to get into the habit of putting some money aside. Once you start you'll find it's not as difficult as you thought. And you'll find it easier to add a little more to the wealth-building program whenever your household income goes up.

Those are the seven basic principles for building wealth. Establish objectives. Keep things simple. Start small. Use other people's money, with discretion. Select investments that give you pleasure. Remember that prices don't always go up. And, above all, begin. Never lose sight of those rules and the odds will always be in your favour.

One other point I want to make before we finish this chapter— the importance of timing. I'm sure someone must have said this before but I couldn't find it in my dictionary of quotations so I'll pretend I made it up. It's this: every prediction about money comes true eventually. The problem is that you can go broke waiting for it to happen.

Building wealth is like anything else in life: good timing plays a key role in your success. That applies to everything from buying a house to investing in the stock market. If you get the timing wrong it can end up costing you a lot of money. Get it right more often than not and you'll do very well for yourself.

Just think about the gold panic a few years ago. People were actually lining up to buy the stuff for over $800 an ounce! It seemed like a good idea at the time. But in retrospect it was crazy—a classic example of bad timing. The price hasn't been back near that point since.

Or what about the housing panic of the early 1980s? Remember that? People were bidding unheard-of-prices for property in many cities. No sooner did a house go on the market than potential buyers were fighting over it, actually bidding up the asking price. Great if you happened to be the seller. Not so great if you were buying.

I have a close friend who got caught up in this mania. He sold his family's comfortable home in a good district in Toronto at a profit, and then turned around and bought a more expensive property at an inflated price. The idea was to resell the new house for an even bigger profit. It never happened. The boom collapsed as quickly as it had started. My friend ended up with a terrible loss when he had to resell the property in a down market because rising interest rates made it too expensive to carry. Talk about bad timing! He ruefully admits today it was the worst investment decision he ever made.

Obviously, no one is going to get it right all the time. We aren't soothsayers. Even the most sophisticated money managers frequently misread the signs. (In fact, I suspect they do so more often than people who use good old common sense.) There is probably nothing more difficult in the process of wealth building than getting the timing right.

I have a few thoughts that may help, though.

The first is, don't run with the herd. As often as not, the herd is wrong. Think of lemmings. When everyone wants to buy, prices often get bid up to unrealistic levels. That's when you should be selling, if you have something to sell. If not, stay on the sidelines and wait. If you get caught up with the herd, chances are you'll end up drowning.

The time to buy is when everyone's gloomy and wants to unload. As long as you buy good quality and are patient, you'll be rewarded.

Look what happened when oil prices plunged in 1986. Prices of the stocks of some of Canada's premier oil companies plunged too. You could have bought shares of Imperial Oil in the spring of '86 for around $35 a share. A year later it was trading at over $70. Sure, it took guts to buck the general consensus that oil prices would fall to below $5. But common sense said that even if that happened, things wouldn't stay that way very long. After all, they're not making any more oil and the world still needs a lot of it. The Imperial Oil rebound might have taken longer. But it had to happen, and the odds were that it wouldn't take five years.

The second point about timing is: don't be greedy. If you have a nice profit, take it. Don't hang on in hopes of more. Sure, you may miss the occasional spectacular gain. But the more modest profits will add up quickly—and you'll sleep better while they do.

For instance, I bought and sold a particular gold stock—Lac Minerals—three times over the space of about 18 months. When it went down to the $25 range, I would buy. When it got over $35, I would sell. Because of the volatility of gold, this pattern kept repeating itself—and I kept making nice profits.

Then, at a time when I wasn't holding the stock, Lac lost a highly publicized court battle. Share values plummeted to below $20. Time to buy again—but in this case, I let fear overcome common sense and didn't get back in. Within a year the stock was back around $35, and I'd let a great profit opportunity pass by.

The third rule about timing is to be flexible in your thinking. Change your wealth-building program to meet changing conditions. It wasn't too long ago that carrying a large mortgage on your home made good financial sense. All the financial experts were advising it, because you could pay off the debt in rapidly depreciating dollars due to high inflation. The idea was fine at the time. Then came the era of disinflation—declining inflation rates—and anyone who adopted that kind of strategy was in deep financial trouble.

Finally, don't try to call everything on the nose. The chances are pretty slim that you'll be able to renew your mortgage just as interest rates hit their low for the decade, or sell your stock at what turns out later to have been its all-time high. You want to avoid being caught at the wrong end of any cycle—locking in long-term mortgages when rates are at record highs, for instance, as many people did in 1981-82. Believe me, that is not a way to build your wealth. Just ask the folks who finally got out of their 16% and 17% mortgages in 1986-87.

To avoid that kind of situation, it's essential to stay informed on what's going on in the world around you—and to understand what the likely consequences of current events will mean to your money. It was obvious in 1981-82 that those crazy interest rates could not be sustained for very long without completely wrecking our economy. But in the trauma of the time, many people lost sight of that reality. Unfortunately, they paid a high price for their short-sightedness.

Wealth building does not take place in isolation. The degree of your success will be influenced, at least in part, by your ability to understand the significance of national and international events and relate them to your decisions and your timing.

"No man is an island," wrote the great English poet and essayist, John Donne. The successful wealth builder needs to understand that better than anybody.

There's No Such Thing as Riskless

I F YOU'VE EVER read anything about making money, you've probably been told that the place to start is with riskless investments. Well, I hate to disillusion you—but there's no such thing.

There are low-risk investments, investments that guarantee capital, and investments that provide a steady income flow. But risk-free, no. I only wish there were.

But wait a minute, you say. What about a home? Surely that's a riskless investment. Real estate prices don't seem to go anywhere but up.

It's true, a home classifies as a low-risk investment. But it's not risk-free. Just ask the folks in Calgary and Edmonton who bought their dream home in the late '70s or early '80s when oil was king and property values in the West were skyrocketing. It seemed like a terrific investment at the time. Alberta's economy was booming and there was nowhere to go but up.

Except down. And that's what happened. I'll describe the events in more detail in Chapter Six. But in a nutshell, The National Energy Policy took the steam out of Alberta's oil boom. Then the 1981-82 recession ended the dream of massive energy megaprojects that were going to turn the province into North America's Saudi Arabia.

Population inflows turned into outflows as people drifted off to other parts of the country in search of jobs. The housing market went from famine to glut in the space of a few short months, sending property values tumbling.

While all this was going on, interest rates were soaring. Mortgages were going for 16% and up. The cost of carrying that Alberta dream home escalated far beyond the capacity of many owners who suddenly found themselves facing pay cuts or, even worse, lost jobs.

The result? Thousands of Albertans simply turned the key in the lock and walked away from their homes. Their houses were worth less than the outstanding balance on the mortgage, and the monthly payments were beyond their means. It made more sense to sacrifice the downpayment and any equity they had built up in the home than to struggle on.

That's why a home is not a risk-free investment. A combination of personal misfortune and economic circumstance can result in a loss of many thousands of dollars.

Don't misunderstand me. In most circumstances, owning your own home is an excellent wealth-building technique and one which I highly recommend. But there are no guarantees. As with any other investment you make, you must be prudent and sensitive to the downside potential.

Well, that may be so, you say. But what about good old, rock-solid Canada Savings Bonds? The principal is guaranteed and you can cash them in at any time. And if interest rates rise, the government increases the rates on CSBs to keep pace. Surely there's an example of a risk-free investment?

Sorry, no. I saw a television program recently that illustrated vividly the truth of the ancient admonition: "Put not thy trust in princes"—or, in this case, governments.

The show dealt with Russia at the turn of the century. The czars were in power, the country was stable, and the economy was growing faster than that of any other European nation. To accelerate growth, the government issued high-interest bonds to attract foreign investment. British investors snapped them up, in some cases heavily mortgaging their stately homes to raise the cash. Then came the Revolution and we all know what happened to those high-interest bonds. They became worthless pieces of paper. It was pathetic to see the descendants of the original investors ruffling through stacks and stacks of the colourful script, musing whether, after all these years, the Soviet government might concede to pay as much as 10% of the original value for the old bonds.

I'm not suggesting that we're about to experience a takeover of the Canadian government that will lead to the renunciation of all outstanding debt. That's patently absurd. Of course, British investors at the turn of the century probably felt the same way about the prospects of a radical takeover of the Russian government. You get the idea. Nothing is risk-free. The improbable does occasionally happen.

But there are more realistic risks to consider in investments like Canada Savings Bonds. Many people—perhaps the majority of CSB purchasers—buy them for the long haul. They see these bonds as a bedrock investment, one of the foundation stones in a wealth-building program.

Well, they can be that. But, again, economic circumstances can create a different scenario.

Suppose you bought CSBs when interest rates were low. The return you were offered at the time of purchase seemed fair. But then rates started to move up. You could invest your money in equally low-risk Treasury bills and receive a better return. And then suppose the government decides on only a token increase in the interest rate it's paying on the CSBs. You're left with an investment that pays you significantly less than if you'd put your money elsewhere.

If you think that's an unlikely situation, you should be aware that it's exactly what happened in the spring of 1986.

Nor was that an isolated case. In the summer of 1987, interest rates suddenly took an upward jump. The Canada Savings Bond issue that had come out the previous fall at 7¾% suddenly was returning investors more than a full percentage point less than 91-day Treasury bills. And in this case, the government didn't even bother to raise the CSB rates to compensate.

In those circumstances, you should seriously consider cashing in CSBs and reinvesting the money elsewhere to improve your return. And the higher interest rates go, the more attractive that alternative becomes.

Since you can do exactly that—cash in the bonds any time—where's the risk?

Inertia. A risk you create yourself. Most beginning wealth builders suffer from it. They put their money into something, often after having agonized for days over the decision, and they're reluctant to move it out. So they sit on the investment, long after they should have dumped it and moved on. Canada Savings Bonds provide the classic example. Once you buy them, you tend to keep them—even when you shouldn't. Some people call it falling in love with your investments. It might be more accurately described as the Investor Inertia Syndrome. Whatever you choose to call it, it's one of the risks of owning safe, solid Canada Savings Bonds. Don't fall victim to it.

Okay, so why not just hold cash? Surely that's risk-free.

Nope. Remember inflation? That chronic eating away of the purchasing power of your money? If you want to really see it at work, just try this test. Put aside $1,000. Stuff it in your mattress or bury it. Include a note of what it will buy today—how many bottles of your favorite wine, or how many litres of gas, or how much fertilizer for your lawn. Then forget about it for ten years.

I don't need to go on. You know what will happen when you finally retrieve that money. Cash risk-free? Not on your life. Its purchasing power will erode every year, unless there's a major depression in the meantime. You won't have built wealth by keeping your funds in "risk-free" cash; you'll have diminished it.

I hope I've made my point. Nothing—absolutely nothing—is without risk when it comes to building wealth. The key is to manage risk effectively. To know the level of risk in any wealth-building decision. To know when to take a risk, and when to pass. To diversify risk.

It follows that in order to build wealth, you have to be prepared to accept some level of risk. The amount that's tolerable is a personal decision.

When you're just starting out, you're better off aiming for minimal risk. A big loss at that stage could spook you for life.

I have a golfing buddy who's a very successful professional. He's built an excellent practice and makes a fine living from it. We have a lot of things in common—but investing is not one of them. He's scared to death of it. Several years ago, he put money into a business venture—a high-risk deal that seemed to offer the prospect of good returns. It went sour and he got burned. Now he doesn't want to hear about the stock market or bonds or anything else. He's gunshy.

That's why it's wise to minimize your risks during the early years. Stick with wealth-building techniques you're comfortable with and which have low downside potential. And never, never put all your eggs in one basket, even if that basket is your own home.

As you start to accumulate wealth, you can accept a higher level of risk if you want to try getting rich sooner rather than later. Higher-risk investments should, by definition, offer the potential for higher returns—otherwise why would you be in them at all? This relationship is known as the *risk/return ratio*. It simply means that the more risk you assume, the greater the rewards of success should be. But as you add risk, be sure to always protect your base and remember the rule about preserving capital. Don't put essential funds into moderate or high-risk situations. Otherwise, you could lose everything and end up back at square one.

Where should you start? The first step is to accumulate some funds. Easy for him to say, you may be muttering. I can barely make ends meet, and he's telling me to put some money aside.

Well, come on—I didn't say this was going to be a piece of cake. But if you don't make a start, you're never going to get there. Here are some ideas to consider:

Tax refund cheques: Almost every salaried person gets one because Revenue Canada structures its tax tables to make sure your employer withholds a bit too much each year. Instead of blowing that money, put it towards your wealth-building program.

CSB Payroll Plans: Buy some Canada Savings Bonds on a payroll deduction plan when the next issue comes out. It will only cost a few dollars a month and any interest charges will be tax deductible.

Family allowance cheques: Set up a special account for your child and deposit the cheques into it. More on this in Chapter Five.

Child tax credit: Save it, don't spend it.

Pay raises: Decide now to put aside 10% of every pay raise you and your spouse receive in the future for wealth-building purposes. You'll be amazed at how quickly your fund grows. Of course, at 15% or 20% it will grow even faster.

Moonlighting: If you find some way to make a little extra money in your spare time, put a hefty chunk of it away for wealth building—say half. Have fun with the rest.

Windfalls: Sometimes money can appear from totally unexpected sources—a small lottery win, an insurance claim, an inheritance, a gift from a relative. If you do get lucky, at least half should go into the wealth-building program.

Remember, you don't have to start big. Small amounts will grow faster than you think. But you have to make the effort—even if it involves some small degree of personal sacrifice.

When you get some money, what then? Start by holding it in CSBs, Treasury bills, or something similar. Establish a conservative RRSP program. When you have enough money available, consider buying a family home if the market seems right. Then adopt an accelerated mortgage paydown plan. I'll provide details of how to go about all this in subsequent chapters.

When you reach the point where all these things are in place, then you can start looking at some higher-risk ventures. And they can be a lot of fun, especially when you score. But sometimes you really have to have good nerves.

As an example, let me go back to a situation I touched on in the last chapter—the fall and rise of oil. As I told you, when oil prices collapsed in early 1986, the value of stocks in Canadian petroleum companies followed suit. Even blue ribbon firms like

Imperial Oil saw their share values sink to their lowest levels in years.

The doomsayers were in full cry. Oil prices were going to fall to $5 a barrel, or even worse. OPEC was dead. They were going to hang a "closed" sign on Alberta. Shares of Imperial Oil sagged to below $35 on the Toronto Stock Exchange.

In the midst of all this, a few investors paused to think about the underlying realities. Yes, there was an international oil glut. Yes, OPEC countries were busily undercutting one another's prices in a desperate bid to maintain market share. Yes, the result was a steep fall in oil prices.

But the world was still consuming a hell of a lot of the stuff, and would continue to do so for the foreseeable future. And they weren't making any more of it. So surely, these investors reasoned, the price fall had to be temporary. Prices would recover, and so would share values.

So they took a calculated risk. They bought Imperial Oil. Within a year they had more than doubled their money.

It doesn't always work out that way, of course. Oil prices might have fallen further. Or they could have taken much longer to recover. But the potential reward looked to be worth the risk— and, as it turned out, it was.

Here's another example. When the news of the Chernobyl nuclear accident flashed around the world, one of the first reactions of U.S. investors was to sell stocks in utilities which were strongly committed to atomic power. Prices of some of those shares dropped over 20% in two days.

A few people looked beyond the immediate panic and felt the dumping of those stocks was a classic case of overreaction. They moved in and bought. Within a week most of the share prices had rebounded to the range they had traded in before anyone in the West ever heard of Chernobyl. The risk-takers scored big!

So intelligent risk can dramatically accelerate the wealth-building process. But you must know what you are doing, what the downside is, and what the potential rewards are. If you don't know, don't go. And don't even consider higher-risk wealth-building techniques, tempting as they may be, until you have a solid base firmly in place.

This book will give you what you need to build that base. The risks can come later, at your choosing.

Banks and Wealth: Oil and Water

I BLAME IT ON Monopoly. From the time we were kids, that insidious game conditioned us to believe that the Bank was the source of all wealth. It was the Banker who dispensed the cash, handed out the property cards, held our mortgages, and seized our assets when we couldn't pay the street repairs assessment. No wonder we grew up believing that the words "bank" and "wealth" were synonyms.

Well, I hate to disillusion you, but it's not true. In fact, if those two words have any relationship at all, it's as antonyms. "Banks" and "wealth" are like oil and water. The two simply don't mix.

That doesn't mean banks aren't useful. They are, in much the same way your neighborhood convenience store is useful. But as with the convenience store, you'll pay a premium price to use a bank's services.

Banks do two things for you. They facilitate the flow of money, allowing you to carry out financial transactions with a minimum of fuss. And they are a source of capital (although not the only one, by any means) if you need to borrow to finance your home, your investments, or your business (which are the only reasons why most people should borrow).

Although they would like you to believe otherwise, their traditional role has not been to help you build wealth—at least not in the most effective way. One caveat to that comment, though. I'm talking here about our tradition-bound megabanks— the behemoths we've developed in this country as a result of long years of very restrictive banking policies. Some of the smaller banks—particularly the super-aggressive overseas banks which have set up operations here in recent years—do offer genuine wealth-building services. The problem is that most of them are not easily accessible to the average person, either for reasons of geography (they have very few offices, only one in many cases) or because of restrictions on the size of account they'll handle (many of them will show you the door unless you have $100,000 to put down.)

So for most of us, the only bank that really counts is the branch of one of the Big Five down at the corner. And wealth builders they're not.

Oh, they're trying. Some of them will now handle your stock transactions—an unheard-of idea a decade ago. But this is a new field for banks, one in which they don't have much background or expertise.

Some are attempting to remedy that by buying established brokerage firms; others are building their own brokerage services from scratch. It remains to be seen just how beneficial for the wealth builder this strange new partnership between the ultra-conservative money lenders and the super-aggressive stock sellers will be.

And, yes, the banks offer various financial products which they claim will help you build wealth: premium savings accounts, term deposits, guaranteed investment certificates. If you take a close look at what they're selling, however, you'll find that their products are almost always the least competitive in the marketplace. Why put your money in a bank term deposit paying 7% when the trust company down the street is offering 8%? Would you buy a Pontiac for $15,000 when you could get it for $14,000? Of course not.

Nor have the banks bent over backwards to offer more wealth-building choices for the ordinary customer. Take the example of Government of Canada Treasury bills. These are short-term notes (terms of less than a year) issued by Ottawa as part of its financing program. Treasury bills are safe, pay a good rate of interest, and can be sold any time you need quick cash, often with no penalty. Although they're not quite the same, think of them as short-term Canada Savings Bonds.

Institutions and well-heeled investors have been making use of Treasury bills for years. The chartered banks were happy to do the deal for them—as long as the minimum order was $50,000 or $100,000. But if you were an ordinary investor with, say, $5,000 to invest, the banks didn't want anything to do with you. You could buy their term deposits instead. Too bad if the interest they pay is substantially lower than what Treasury bills are offering!

It took an aggressive brokerage community to make Treasury bills available to the average investor by bringing the minimum purchase limit way down. Now anyone who knows anything at all about investing uses them at one time or another, buying them through a stockbroker. The banks, meanwhile, continue to maintain their aloof position. That's fine, if that's the way they prefer to do business. The serious wealth builder will simply go elsewhere.

We still need the banks, of course. The key for the wealth builder is to think of them as cost centres rather than profit centres, and to use them in the most efficient way possible.

Start from the assumption that, for the most part, the financial products and services offered by our major chartered banks are overpriced. Why? Because they're big and dominate the marketplace. And because failures of a couple of small banks and some trust companies in recent years have made people nervous about dealing with any but the bluest of the blue ribbon financial institutions.

But the reality is you will almost always do better dealing with trust companies and credit unions when it comes to buying financial products. They tend to pay higher rates of interest on your deposits and to charge you somewhat less when you borrow. There are circumstances in which this may not always hold true, of course. But the serious wealth builder should bear this in mind in making financial decisions. As long as the money you entrust to any financial institution is protected by the Canada Deposit Insurance Corporation (and I'll talk more about this in Chapter Sixteen), you should not hesitate to seek out the best available deal.

The banks categorically deny it, of course, but many people believe that the heavy loan losses incurred in recent years with Third World countries have influenced bank policies regarding retail customers. One woman put it this way: "I'm getting fed up with paying for the Brazilian debt every time I use my bank."

Any time I've raised the issue on a radio broadcast, I've received telephone calls from bank public relations people protesting it just isn't so. The presence of other financial institutions, such as trust companies and credit unions, means they have to remain competitive if they're to survive.

Perhaps. My feeling is the big banks have such a dominant position in the financial marketplace that they can get away with a lot more than anyone else could. And they take advantage of that.

Anyway, whatever the reason, the banks have been putting the screws to their customers in recent years by jacking up service charges at an unreasonable rate.

I've now gotten into the habit of asking my bank for a statement of their service charges every few months and comparing it with the previous one. Try it sometime if you're in the mood for a little teeth gnashing.

You won't find all the charges have increased. The banks did that for a while, but gave it up when the publicity became embarrassing. Now they're more selective, but the effect is the same. You're paying a lot more for those little services you once took for granted.

The problem is the amounts can often seem so trivial you don't pay much attention. You have to look at them in percentage terms to understand the extent to which the banks are hitting you.

Recently, for example, I got a note from the Bank of Commerce saying that the charge for returning my cancelled cheques was increasing by 50¢ a month. Nothing, right? Except that the previous charge was $1 a month. That made it a 50% increase! How many businesses do you know of that have been able to hit their customers with those kinds of price hikes in recent years?

At about the same time, I received another notice from the same bank that my safety deposit box charge was going up by $5, to $35 a year. That represented a more modest 16.7% price increase—but that was still high by the standards of that time.

Another money-raising technique our impoverished banks are using is to add service charges where none existed before. There once was a time (ah, for the good old days!) when you could phone this bank and ask them to switch funds from one account to another. No one ever dreamed of asking us to pay for that. Well, no more. Now you have to pay. One more free service down the tubes.

So what does the wealth builder do? Minimize the costs wherever possible. Ask your bank for a list of their service charges. See what you're paying and add up the total over a year. Then figure out if there's a less expensive way to do it, either by switching your business to a trust company or credit union or by cancelling some of the services you don't really need.

If you're borrowing, make sure you get the best possible interest rate—and that means checking out other options. More on this later.

And finally, if you have some junior wealth builders in the family, don't make the mistake of teaching them the virtues of thrift at an early age by opening up a small bank account for them. Banks used to encourage this kind of activity, seeing it as a good way to develop future customers. Now they're acting as if it's just a nuisance—to the point where they'll actually confiscate your child's money at the first opportunity!

You think I'm kidding? It happened to my youngest daughter.

If you read carefully through your list of bank service charges, you'll probably find a section dealing with inactive accounts. It will read something like this: "Charge for maintaining an inactive account for six months with a balance of $5 or less: account balance."

What that means in real life is that if your seven-year-old received a $5 cheque from Aunt Nell for his birthday and you took him down to the bank to open up an account with it, he (and you) could be in trouble. If no more money is put into the account for six months, the bank will simply take it away! Try explaining to your seven-year-old where his money went. Good luck.

If the cheque was for $10, they'll give your kid two years before confiscating it. If Aunt Nell sprung for $25, he'll have five years to do something with the money before the account is declared inactive.

Oh, but the interest on the money will keep the account active, you say. Think so? Read further into your list of bank service charges. Try this line: "If the balance remaining after such charge is $5 or less or consists solely of interest accrued since the last transaction . . . then there will be an additional service charge equal to the account balance."

In other words, they'll snatch back your kid's interest too. Not a great way to start wealth building early in life. But, sadly, typical of the way the big banks treat their retail customers these days.

So use the banks, because you have to. But use them with discretion and minimize your costs in the process. And never, never think of them as wealth builders. Life is not a Monopoly game.

Your Family Can Make You Rich

I F YOU HAVE KIDS, you know what it's like. You love them dearly, but boy, are they expensive. From the moment they're born, they cost. Cribs, baby toys, diapers, clothes, shoes, school supplies, bicycles, bedroom furniture, groceries, sports equipment, allowances, driving lessons, university fees. There's always money going out, and the older they get, the more expensive they are. And it seems like a one-way street—it all goes out and nothing comes back.

There was a time when children were looked upon as an investment—the Victorian equivalent of a retirement annuity. Grow a bunch of them and then let them support you in your old age. But it doesn't work that way any more (except maybe in the Third World). I don't know many people who want to be dependent on their children when they retire—nor many children who want to be saddled with that kind of financial burden. Child dependence is out. Independence is in.

So kids have become what a hard-nosed business person would describe as a cost-centre. They dissipate family wealth, in the process making it particularly hard for younger couples to start accumulating funds for investing. We accept this cheerfully, of course, because children bring a different kind of wealth to our lives: the wealth of family relationships, of nurturing and bonding, of a sense of parental accomplishment in watching them evolve into useful and interesting adults.

But this is a book about money, not the joys of child raising. Still, wouldn't it be nice if you could somehow combine the two? Have all the pleasure (and anguish) of bringing up a family and turn some profit from that as well?

Well, there are ways to gain some financial benefits from your children—and I'm *not* talking here about bringing back child labour. You're unlikely to recover all the costs involved in raising them, of course—although, over the years, you may be surprised at how close you come. But you can certainly make the financial burden of child raising less painful and accelerate your whole wealth-building process.

The key is in understanding our constantly changing tax system and knowing how to use it to best advantage as it relates to your kids.

Let me start with something very basic to illustrate what I mean. As soon as your first child is born, the federal government celebrates the occasion by sending you money. Every month for the next 18 years, a Family Allowance cheque will roll in. The amount will increase from year to year depending on inflation, and will vary somewhat from province to province (some provinces supplement Ottawa's payments with cheques of their own). But whatever the amount is when you read this, it will seem negligible in the context of your total family income and expenses. For most people, it gets lost in the financial shuffle—deposited into the general family bank account and spent.

Well, if you're a young family and you're doing that, you're missing a terrific opportunity to start a wealth-building program and save taxes at the same time. You should be taking those cheques and depositing them in a special account in the child's name, right from the moment the first one arrives. The reason is that family allowance cheques, when invested on the child's behalf, are considered to be the child's property—not the property of the parents. If you think this is simply a technicality, you're right. But it just so happens that our tax system thrives on such technicalities. If you play by the rules, they can work to your advantage in ways you may never have thought possible.

Let me give you an example of how this particular technicality can be used in the early stages of your wealth-building process. Suppose you have a new baby this year. And let's say that your family allowance cheque is around $33 a month, or $396 a year. Instead of spending that $33 on groceries or whatever, you set up an account for the baby at your local bank or trust company and deposit those cheques into it as they arrive.

As the money builds in the account, you put it into guaranteed investment certificates in order to maximize the interest it earns. To keep things simple, let's assume you average a return of 10% a year until your child turns 18, and that there is no increase in the $33-a-month payment. How much money do you think you'd have at that point?

Would you believe over $18,000? At that stage, your child would be earning almost $2,000 a year in interest, which would be tax-free if he or she had no other income.

That tax-free status is what makes this mini-wealth-building technique work so effectively. Because the money is the child's, at least as far as Revenue Canada is concerned, it won't attract any tax—unless, of course, your youngster becomes a child movie or TV star earning more money than you. That tax-free status means the money can grow at a much faster rate than if you, the parent, invested it yourself and had to pay tax on the earned interest. Since tax-free wealth building is one of the basic strategies described in this book, this technique offers those readers who are parents an opportunity to get a head start.

Now, banking family allowance cheques for your child may seem pretty fundamental. But the plain fact is that most people don't do it, even those who are familiar with the concept. If you're in a situation where you can apply this approach, for heaven's sake do so! It's a way to establish a tax-sheltered wealth-building program that won't hamstring you financially. And the self-discipline you muster in the process will pay off as you gradually adopt more complex and demanding wealth-building techniques.

YOUR FAMILY CAN MAKE YOU RICH

Obviously, the older your children are when you read this advice, the less effective the family allowance technique is going to be. There are fewer years to make deposits, and less time for the magic of compound interest to work.

But if your kids are older, there are other things you can do. And you can also bring your spouse into the act.

The point to remember always is that our tax system treats us as individuals. Revenue Canada does not consider the combined income of married couples or family units in making its assessments. That provides some opportunities for wealth building through tax saving by splitting income within the family. You're far better off putting $5,000 in additional revenue into the hands of a child with no other income than in having it end up in the taxable income of the highest earning family member.

Unfortunately, there used to be many more ways to achieve that end than there are now. Tax reform and a general tightening up in Ottawa have taken their toll on income-splitting techniques among family members. Still, there are some things you can do if your family situation is right.

If you have children over 18
You can make interest-free loans to them. The kids can then invest the money. The return on that investment is considered income in their hands. If they have little or no other income, that money will end up being tax-free.

If you have a family business
Hire your spouse and your kids. They have to perform a legitimate function and be paid a fair wage. As long as you're careful about that, you'll have no problem. But what can my kids do, you may ask? Lots of things—use your imagination. One of my daughters handles my filing. It saves me a lot of time, and the small amount I pay her is more than worth it. My son, who's a computer nut, handles all the work in that area. My wife looks after all the company finances. There's a lot they can do if you give it some thought.

IF YOU'RE A TWO-INCOME FAMILY

You have to be very careful in planning your wealth-building program, especially since tax reform has created both new pitfalls and new opportunities. Start by taking a close look at your combined income and decide where and how you can begin accumulating some funds. Your current lifestyle and financial obligations are obviously going to figure prominently in this exercise, but unless you're flirting with personal bankruptcy you should be able to find cash to put aside. If you need some ideas, check Chapter Three again.

When you've worked out a program you can live with, your strategy should be to implement it in such a way that the lower-income spouse receives any investment income. That's because he or she will be taxed on that money at a lower rate, leaving more in your pocket.

How do you do that? By having the lower-income spouse provide all the money to invest.

Suppose, for example, that the husband is earning $40,000 a year as an office manager while the wife earns $15,000 a year as a free-lance writer. And let's say their provincial tax rate is 50% of the federal tax payable. Under tax reform, any interest income received by the husband will be taxed at a rate of 39%. But if that same income goes to the wife, it's only taxed at 25½%. By putting the interest income into the wife's hands, the couple gets to keep an additional 13½¢ of every dollar.

So if this particular couple decided that, between them, they could put aside $100 a month for wealth building, they'd come out much farther ahead by having the wife take that money from her own earnings and invest it in her own name. That's because Revenue Canada would regard any interest earned on those funds as hers—and assess tax accordingly.

How much difference would it make? Well, let's say this went on for five years, with the invested money compounding at 10% a year. At the end of the fifth year, the couple would have over $8,000 put aside. That would be generating $800 a year in interest income. If it were in the husband's name, the tax bill would be $312. In the wife's name, the bill comes to $204. It's worth some advance planning.

Finally, before we leave the subject of family, I'm often asked how to teach children about money. It's not easy. You don't want to put so much emphasis on the subject that your children become obsessed with it—something that is very easy to do. On the other hand, you want your children to develop a sensitivity to the value of money and a basic understanding of the purpose it can serve beyond being just a medium of exchange. It's a fine line but one that's worthwhile trying to draw. Wealth building is a long-term process, one that should involve all members of the family unit. If your children learn the right techniques and attitudes at home, they'll benefit from them when it comes time for them to establish their own families.

But be careful. Avoid trying to do too much too soon. That's a mistake I made in the case of my own family. My lack of financial training undoubtedly contributed to it: I didn't want my children to waste the most efficient wealth-building period of their lives because of a failure on my part to give them the grounding they needed.

But like everything else in life, timing is critical in imparting this kind of information. Pre-teens simply aren't ready for it. In fact, most of them can't handle anything more complicated than allowances, a bank account, and some simple explanations of the relationship between value and money.

It's around the time children hit their mid-teens that they become more sensitive to the subtleties of money management. This often coincides with a first job or a highly-prized but expensive objective they want to achieve, such as paying the additional insurance costs so they can drive the family car. That's the point at which you can start going beyond the basics in laying the groundwork for a more sophisticated approach to money and wealth.

You're going to have to commit some of your time and imagination to the process, though. You can't just hand them a copy of this book and tell them to read it—it will sit unopened on the shelf. The time will come when they'll seek out more information on their own. But not at the outset.

So how then? By exposing your children to some of the building blocks of wealth in a way they'll find exciting and stimulating.

One of the most successful things I ever did in this regard was to give my children stocks as a Christmas gift. Now if that sounds unusual, consider this: lots of people give their children or grandchildren cash or Canada Savings Bonds as Christmas, birthday, or Hanukkah gifts and don't think it unusual. All I'm suggesting is that you be a little more imaginative in the type of financial asset you choose to give. If you approach it right, you may open up a whole new world for your kids.

Even though we live in a capitalist society, most children have no understanding of what the stock market is or how it functions. That's because they are never exposed to it: very few schools offer courses in investing, and most parents don't have a clear idea of what the stock market is about or how to make money in it.

Giving your children stocks as a gift is a way to spark their interest and encourage them to learn more on their own. It's not as easy as buying a plain old Canada Savings Bond, of course. But CSBs are tucked away in a safety deposit box and forgotten. They don't exist as far as the kids are concerned, except in an abstract way.

Stocks, on the other hand, are a real financial adventure. It doesn't end with the certificate they get in their Christmas stocking; in fact, that's just the beginning.

If the stocks are registered in their names, all sorts of things will start to happen. The mail will start bringing quarterly and annual reports about the company's activities and performance. There will be invitations to shareholders' meetings, proxy solicitations, and dividend cheques. If your kids are lucky, they may benefit from stock splits, or rights issues, or special dividend declarations. Each of those occasions is a chance for them—and perhaps you—to learn something more about the stock market, how companies operate, and the way in which a capitalistic society works. And it will all happen in a painless and interesting way.

You'll find your children getting fired up by the idea that they actually own a piece of a major company. The key is to give them stocks in a firm that interests them. It would be nice if it had great growth potential as well, but it's more important that the idea of the company and the things it does turns them on.

When I first bought stocks for my kids, I thought this part through pretty carefully.

My youngest daughter was just entering her teens at the time. She was still in the cuddly stuffed animal stage, so I decided Irwin Toy would be a logical choice for her.

My son was not quite two years older and was into pop music. He got shares in the CHUM broadcasting empire and was especially excited when he found out that meant he owned a small piece of the MuchMusic pay-TV channel.

My oldest daughter was in her last year of high school and was taking a basic economics course. I bought her shares in what was then Goliath Gold Mines, on the theory that since she was learning about the critical role of gold in our economy it might excite her if she owned some.

I bought the shares through a brokerage house that was having a pre-Christmas special with reduced commission fees to encourage people to give stock to their kids. The shares were registered in the children's names, and I got hold of a copy of the latest annual report from each company to include with the certificates. I completed the package by taking a recent listing from the stock market pages and circling their companies so they would know what the stocks were worth and where to track them.

The reaction that Christmas morning was terrific. The kids were totally surprised and genuinely excited about becoming shareholders. The results were as I had hoped: all three became more interested in the stock market, especially my son, who started tracking the performance of his CHUM shares on a regular basis.

And though I didn't buy the stocks for their profit-making potential, it turns out they did quite well. The CHUM stock split 3 for 1 within a year. (That means he received three shares for every one he owned.) The Goliath Gold was rolled into the new

Hemlo Gold Mines company and my daughter sold it about a year later for more than twice what I'd paid for it. Irwin Toy didn't perform as spectacularly but has had a nice capital gain and a dividend cheque arrives for my youngest daughter every quarter. That's what I call a profitable education.

The success of the stock experiment inspired me to find other fun ways to teach the kids about wealth-building techniques. My next venture was into mutual funds.

Here again, the idea was to introduce them to an investing technique through the reality of actual ownership, rather than in an abstract way. The kids were starting to put some money aside for university so I suggested to them that it might be interesting to invest some of their savings in mutual funds. I explained how such funds work and picked out a no-load fund (one that charges no sales commission) that allowed minimal quarterly deposits. I proposed they put in $100 every quarter, which they felt they could handle. And I suggested they sign on for the distribution reinvestment plan, which meant that all their earnings would be used to buy additional fund units.

The results have been intriguing. The children receive regular reports from the fund and look at them carefully. They are very conscious of the fund's performance, and the current value of their investment. And they're highly critical of the fund's managers when asset values decline! It's at those times that I sit them down and give them a little more information on market forces and what moves fund values up and down.

As a result, they've developed a basic understanding of how mutual funds work and a critical faculty for assessing good, bad, and indifferent performance. The result, I hope, will be to make them more effective at wealth building at an early stage in their lives.

So how do you teach your kids about money? By bringing the subject to life for them. Involve them in real world financial situations. Teach them about different kinds of investments by encouraging them to undertake them themselves, within the limits of their financial ability. When an investment prospers, spend some time with them discussing why it went well. Even more important, spend time talking about why a particular investment turned out to be a loser.

If you don't know much about investing yourself, then learn with them. It's a terrific opportunity to spend quality time together.

One word of warning, though. Not all kids will be interested in money and wealth, just as all kids aren't interested in sports. If you've introduced the concept in an imaginative way and your child doesn't take to it, don't force the issue. Maybe the timing's wrong. Or maybe he or she just couldn't care less even though the subject fascinates you. I was an ardent stamp collector when I was young; my children just yawned when I brought out my old collection and tried to interest them in the hobby.

A surprising number of youngsters today have the potential to be seriously interested in the concept of wealth building. They just need to be exposed to it in an exciting and challenging manner. If you want them to have the best possible future, it's up to you, as a parent, to do that job. Nobody else will.

Your Home is Your Financial Castle

CHAPTER 6

W HAT YOU'VE READ up to now has been the *hors d'oeuvre*. Now comes the main course—the actual steps you need to take to put together a successful wealth-building plan.

Not surprisingly, it starts with the most basic of all assets—the family home. That's because, as far as I'm concerned, there is no better way to begin accumulating wealth than to own your home.

Oh sure, it is possible to lose money on a family home, as I explained in Chapter Three. But frankly, you have to work pretty hard at it or be very unlucky. For most people, their own home is the best investment they've ever made. That's why it's one of the cornerstones of wealth building. If you're still in the rental stage of your life, buying a house as soon as possible should be your number one priority.

The beauty of owning your own home is that it meets all of the criteria of a first-class asset. In fact, it's hard to conceive of anything better.

To begin with, it's an appreciating asset. Like anything else, residential housing is subject to short-term market swings. But over the long haul, any well-located property which is properly maintained is going to increase in value, usually substantially. Just check out the house prices in some of the better located older sections of your town or city. When fairly ordinary 60-year-old homes can be sold for $300,000 and up, as they can in places like Toronto and Vancouver, there's a message which any aspiring wealth builder would be foolish to ignore.

Second, your home is a tax shelter—probably the best one you'll ever own. The government won't tax the capital gain you realize when it's sold, no matter how large it is. And if anything happens to you, it can pass tax-free to your spouse.

Third, it's a bankable asset. Many people don't make use of the equity they build up in their homes over the years, and allow that money to sit idle. That's a classic example of inertia at work. New financial instruments such as home equity lines of credit now make it possible for you to tap into the profit you've built up in your property without actually selling the home or locking yourself into a rigid mortgage repayment schedule. That means you can use the money in your home to take advantage of other investment opportunities that may come along.

Finally, your home is a usable asset. It's not a piece of paper or a bar of metal that may represent wealth but has no function in your daily life. Your home fulfills a number of basic physical and emotional needs, which is perhaps why many people don't consider it an investment. It provides shelter, acts as the central focus for the family, offers (I hope) a tranquil refuge from the problems of the world—in short, your house is your spiritual home base.

But, besides being all those things, it is also a major investment. If you go about it intelligently, you can pyramid the equity you build in your home into a financial base larger than you may think possible right now. But if you screw up . . .

Let me describe a couple of ways in which you could screw up, so you'll be on the lookout. These are real-life, true stories and they explain why some people end up taking a terrible financial beating on their homes.

The first involves the friend of mine I referred to briefly in Chapter Two—the one who got whipsawed by speculating in housing just when prices were at their peak. I'd like to tell you the whole story because it clearly illustrates how buying a family home for the wrong reasons can hurt you.

This friend bought a small house in a good section of north Toronto in the late 1970s. It was a nice little place, nothing spectacular, but very comfortable for him and his wife. A good starter home.

Then came the great housing craze of the early 1980s. It started in Vancouver and rapidly spread east. House prices went sky-high. Bidding wars became the order the day: you put your house on the market at a wildly inflated price and then stood back and watched as frantic buyers bid it up yet another ten or twenty percent. The speculators had a field day as people who feared prices were going out of sight scrambled to buy while they could still afford a home. It was our own version of Germany's famous 1920s inflation, when people rushed to buy everything they could before the prices went up again.

My friend got caught up in all this. He sold his small home for a very good profit and decided to get in on the housing action himself. After all, everyone else was making big money, why shouldn't he? So he went out into the market, found a much larger place which he figured was undervalued and could be turned over quickly, and bought it.

It was a disaster—total and unmitigated. To begin with, the house he bought was in deplorable condition. In his haste to close the deal, he hadn't checked it out as thoroughly as he should have. When he and his wife went in after signing the papers, they were appalled at what they found. I won't sicken you with the details; let's just describe it as filthy. They had to work day and night for weeks to put the place into habitable condition. By the time they were finished, they were both exhausted.

Even worse, that was just about the time the housing market collapsed. Mortgage interest rates had shot up to ridiculous levels. Buyers were vanishing from the scene like flies in a frost. The speculators had fled the market. And people like my friend were left holding the bag.

And what a bag! He put the house up for sale at close to what he had paid for it. No takers. He dropped the price. Still no takers. He dropped it again. Still none, and now residential housing was a glut on the market.

In the end, he took a $70,000 beating on the property, a horrendous loss by his (or anyone's) standards. He learned a lesson, as he ruefully admitted later. But it cost him a small fortune in the process, plus months of frustration and aggravation. And it was several years before he was able to accumulate enough capital to buy another house.

You can learn the same lesson free. It's very simple: don't speculate with the family home. Choose a property that is well located, that suits your needs and is priced fairly. Pay down your mortgage quickly (more on that in the next chapter). If there's a sudden run-up in prices in your area, don't be tempted to sell and get into the speculation game. Remember, your home is your key wealth-building tool. Use it wisely.

How else can you lose money on a home? By a sudden, often unpredictable shift in economic conditions. And this is a tougher situation to cope with, because it's not of your own making.

As I mentioned in Chapter Three, the most recent example of this turnabout occurred in Alberta in the early to mid 1980s. As in most other Canadian cities, house prices in places like Calgary and Edmonton had shot up during the boom. When the boom ended, they fell, just as they did everywhere else. But the situation in Alberta was somewhat different.

For years, the province had been enjoying good times. The petroleum industry was strong and expanding. Agricultural products were bringing in high prices. Industry and governments were teaming up to create visions of multibillion dollar megaprojects which would reshape the face of the West and create thousands of new employment opportunities.

It was the time to be an Albertan. Unemployment was down, taxes were the lowest in the country, consumer spending was high, the provincial government operated with a budget surplus, and new millionaires were being created almost daily. Companies like Dome Petroleum enjoyed unlimited access to banking capital — debt counted for little alongside the tremendous growth opportunities. The future belonged to Alberta.

In the midst of all that euphoria, a lot of people went out and bought houses. In many cases, they stretched themselves to the limit financially to do so. But why not? The economy was good, jobs were plentiful, and it was time to make a commitment.

And then, as I described earlier, it all went sour. Not only did the housing boom go bust; so did Alberta. The good times collapsed under the weight of the Trudeau government's ill-conceived National Energy Policy, an international recession, and a slump in commodities prices. The sharp drop in oil prices, which came later, further exacerbated the whole unhappy situation.

And the proud new homeowners? They saw the value of their properties tumble with the Alberta economy, to the point where many homes were actually worth less on the open market than the value of the mortgages that were being used to finance them. To make matters worse, the slowdown in economic activity had thrown many of those homeowners out of work. They found themselves facing the prospect of keeping up mortgage payments on a devalued property with income that consisted mainly of unemployment insurance cheques.

The predictable happened. People in record numbers simply walked away from their homes, leaving the financial institutions to pick up the pieces. There hadn't been anything like it since the Great Depression. In 1984-85, more than 5,000 people defaulted on their mortgages in Alberta, according to Canada Mortgage and Housing Corporation. That was five times as many as in Ontario, which has a much greater population. For those folks, owning a home was not a great wealth-building experience.

I'm not telling you all this to frighten you away from home ownership, far from it. My contention is that owning your own home is a basic step in the wealth-building process—something which Canadians seems to be losing sight of, given statistics which indicate that the long-term trends in home owning in this country are down.

No, I'm giving you these horror stories to illustrate that things can sometimes go wrong and to emphasize the importance of treating the purchase of a home as an investment decision. It's often too easy to get caught up in the emotion of home buying and to lose sight of the investment implications as a result. And that problem isn't the exclusive preserve of first-time buyers; many supposedly seasoned home purchasers allow themselves to fall into the same trap. Don't be one of them.

Now before you panic, let me describe the other side of the housing coin. A very good friend of mine moved to Toronto in the late 1970s. He and his wife bought an older home on a pleasant street in the city's northern district. The area was nice enough, but certainly wouldn't rank as one of the most expensive in the city.

They paid just over $100,000 for the property. Over the next few years they put a lot of work into the place, fixing it up. But the additional amount they invested was peanuts compared to what was happening to the house's value.

By 1987—a decade after they had bought it—their old house was valued at over $400,000! Just by living in their home and fixing it up, they had added hundreds of thousands of dollars to their net worth. That's what I call effective wealth building.

How do you look at a house as an investment? In the same way you consider any other investment decision.

Start with examining the profit potential. The last thing most people think about when they buy a home is what will happen when the time comes to sell it. That's something to worry about years from now; right now that little two-bedroom, vine-covered cottage is too adorable to pass up.

But the fact is, you will sell that home some day—whether to move to a better neighborhood or another city, or to trade up to a larger house, or because the kids have gone off on their own, or.... When that day comes, the price you get—and therefore the profit you make—will be determined mostly by the wisdom you showed in making that initial purchase. And in the meantime, if you've chosen a property with better-than-average growth potential, you'll have more equity in your home to use to finance other investments.

Let me tell you my own unhappy story in this regard. When we moved to Toronto in the mid-1970s, we had already bought and sold two houses. But despite that experience, I was not as aware of the importance of assessing the investment potential of a home as I might have been. Like most people, we did our shopping on the basis of our perceived needs and our financial situation. Other considerations didn't really enter into it.

In the end, our choice was narrowed down to two properties, both in the same area of the city. One was priced at $128,000. It was a large, pleasant, comfortable home on a good street, backing on a ravine. Nothing spectacular, but okay.

The other choice was a classic two-storey executive home in a prestige neighborhood about a mile away. It was on a quiet cul-de-sac, close to schools and shopping and had every amenity, from a swimming pool to a screening room. It also carried a higher price tag—$175,000.

We could have afforded it, but it would have really stretched us to the limit. So we opted for the less expensive home. If I had looked at the decision from an investment viewpoint, we would have made a different choice.

As I write this, the home we did buy has a market value of around $300,000. That's a respectable appreciation, of course. But the house we passed up would sell right now for around $500,000. What was a value difference of less than $50,000 in 1975 has soared to $200,000 in the years since.

That's what I mean when I stress looking at a property's investment potential before you buy. Sometimes paying a little more at the outset for the right home can end up producing big financial dividends down the road.

What sorts of things will make a home attractive to future buyers and thereby maximize its profit potential? Start with the classic real estate cliché: location, location, and location. The fact is that *where* you want to live is going to have the greatest influence on what you pay today, and what your house will be worth tomorrow. If you're in a major metropolitan centre, that means the farther out you go, the more house you'll get for your money. Try it yourself. Take one of the main highways out of town. Once you get beyond the city limits, check the prices of comparable homes at each successive exit. The downward pattern will become apparent pretty quickly: the farther away you are, the lower the price.

The converse is equally true: the closer to the city centre, the higher the price, all other things being equal. If you're looking for the best value appreciation potential, that tells you to buy as close to the centre as you can afford.

What else should you consider? Well, you should pick a quality neighborhood, preferably one that's well-established. Look for good access to schools, shopping, and transportation—but ensure none of them is right in your backyard. Houses bordering on school property, for instance, suffer from a higher incidence of vandalism and break-ins than other homes in the same area. Avoid corner lots—for some reason, Canadians don't like them.

In choosing an architectural design, stick with the traditional. The more off-beat you get, the smaller your potential resale market—and therefore, the lower the appreciation potential. Most people want a detached, two-storey single family home. If you appreciate modern design and glass walls, fine—but don't expect the market to share your tastes.

You should check out the local planning act and zoning regulations before you make any offer. That pretty land right behind you may already be earmarked for an apartment building or, even worse, a major commercial complex. I can't think of a faster way to ensure a rapid drop in the value of your new home than to have a gas station open up right behind you.

Once you've found a place you think fits the bill, spend a little money to have it properly inspected before you submit an offer. Don't be stampeded by an agent's warnings that the house may be picked off by another buyer; his or her interest is to close the deal and get a commission, not to be sure that you're making the best possible choice. A thorough building inspection shouldn't cost more than a couple of hundred dollars and it could save you thousands in repair bills. I didn't do it when we bought our Toronto house and it was only after we moved in that we discovered the place was poorly insulated, had a shower stall that leaked, and that the heating system was improperly balanced. It cost a lot of money to put all that right—something I would have insisted the previous owner do if I'd had the foresight to use an inspector.

Obviously, you should also examine your own financial condition when deciding whether to buy a home. It's not much fun being "house poor"—spending a disproportionate amount of your income on mortgage payments, property taxes, utilities and maintenance. In that sense, homes are like children—both can absorb a lot of money.

I've been house poor, unable even to go out to a restaurant occasionally because the budget was so tight. It's not a condition I want to experience again. But there are times when the sacrifice is worthwhile. If we had been willing to spend a few years being house-poor back in the mid-1970s, for instance, our family net worth would be $200,000 more than it is today.

Deciding how big a financial sacrifice you're prepared to make to acquire a home is a tough personal decision. But if you treat it as an investment opportunity, it becomes more manageable. The greater the prospect for capital gain, the more acceptable short-term financial pain should be.

But a word of caution. You don't want that short-term pain to turn into long-term disaster. Remember those Albertans who ended up walking away from their homes. That's not a sensation you want to experience!

It's one thing to be house poor. It's quite another to stretch yourself so thin financially that one bad break—a sudden upturn in mortgage rates, for instance—might mean you could no longer afford the house. That's why financial prudence is essential in making a home purchase decision. Before you plunge in, take some time to analyze carefully *all* the costs involved. What does the house cost to heat each year? How much are the water taxes? How fast have the property taxes been going up? How much would the monthly mortgage payments go up if interest rates increased by one point? Two points? When will the house likely need a new roof? A new furnace?

It may be tiresome but you have to look at those numbers before going ahead. You need to be sure you can handle all the existing costs—and that you have at least a little flexibility in the event something unexpected hits you later.

The general rule of thumb is that not more than 30% of your gross family income should be eaten up by principal, interest, taxes, and energy costs. If you want to be conservative and give yourself something of a cushion in the event mortgage interest rates move up, reduce that percentage by a couple of points.

You can exceed the 30% ratio slightly if you exercise discipline in your other financial commitments. But if you pass the 35% mark, you're entering high-risk territory. An unexpected development—anything from a sharp increase in mortgage interest rates to the loss of a job—could leave you no alternative but to sell. If you're in that situation now, the best advice I can offer is to set up a mortgage reduction plan and get your payments down to a more manageable level as soon as possible. More on that in the next chapter.

If you work out all these numbers beforehand, give your real estate agent firm instructions accordingly. Tell him or her what you're prepared to pay. Stay a little on the high side in your estimate—you don't want to miss out on a good buy that may be priced a few thousand dollars higher than the limit you've calculated. But make it clear to your agent that you don't want to look at anything beyond the price point you've established. The country is full of people who fell in love with a house that was beyond their means and lived to regret it. Don't join the group.

The timing of your housing purchase will be a major factor in these calculations. There are periods when you can pick up homes at good prices—and times when the chances are you'll pay too much. Clearly, you want to choose the best time to buy so as to minimize your financial risk.

When is that time? When the marketplace is deserted. The other buyers have fled to the sidelines. Sellers are desperate. Prices are being slashed, but even that doesn't move more houses. Uncertainty and fear predominate.

That's what happened when the early '80s housing boom collapsed. For a long time, the housing market in this country was depressed. Mortgage interest rates were moving down from their peaks, but everyone was still nervous. No one wanted to make a commitment.

That was the time to buy. There were lots of houses on the market and very little action. Lots of people who bought then found themselves sitting on very large profits within just a few years.

Psychologically, it's not easy to be a buyer in down times. It's always easier to run with the herd, to buy when the world is bullish. But be assured it will cost you a lot more if you try it that way.

A couple of other tips on the psychology of house buying.

First, keep your cool. Don't go wandering through a house, raving about how wonderful it is and publicly falling in love with it. The vendor will notice. The real estate agent will notice. And it's in both their interests that you pay as high a price as possible. Keep your enthusiasm to yourself. If both the agent and the seller think the sale may be shaky, they'll be a lot more flexible in meeting your terms.

Second, don't buy too quickly. It may be tough, but waiting a few weeks, or even a few months, could save you thousands. Don't go into the market in the spring or early summer, for instance. That's when the big rush is on, because people want to have their plans settled and their moves completed before the start of the next school year. Bide your time. By late summer, those sellers who have committed themselves to a move and haven't been able to unload their old home yet will be getting desperate. That's the time when there are real bargains to be found.

One last thought: one of the best ways to judge the value of a particular type of investment is to talk to people who have already tried it. If they've done well, chances are you may also.

If you don't already own a home, try it. Talk to people that do. Ask them if they think it was a good idea and if they're satisfied with their home as an investment. I'll bet you at least 90% of them say yes.

I'll also bet that if you follow the guidelines in this chapter, you'll end up making a lot of money on your home. And you'll have established the first cornerstone of a successful wealth-building program.

Of course, you have to pay for the house. So that's what we'll look at next.

Living Mortgage-Free

T HE GOOD THING about mortgages is that they enable you to buy that all-important family home years before you might otherwise be able to afford it. The bad thing is that the mortgage issuers charge you an arm and a leg for the privilege.

You think I exaggerate? Consider this:

You're about to buy your first home, a pleasant little townhouse, well located. You've scrimped and saved to pull together $15,000 for the downpayment. The balance will be financed by a $60,000 first mortgage, amortized (a fancy term that simply means spread) over 25 years, at an initial rate of 10½%. Assuming the interest rate were to remain unchanged (it won't, of course, but this is just a simple example), and that you were to take the full 25 years to pay off the mortgage, how much do you think it would have cost you by the time you finished?

Hold your breath for this one! Would you believe $167,100? No, that's not a misprint. That $60,000 mortgage would end up costing you over $107,000 in interest payments by the time you managed to pay off the original principal. No wonder financial institutions are in heavy competition for your mortgage business!

The aspiring wealth builder doesn't have to read any further to understand the message. Pay off the mortgage as fast as you possibly can! The more quickly you do so, the faster funds will be freed up for use in other aspects of your wealth-building program.

It's especially crucial to start the pay-down program (extra mortgage-reducing payments) early in the life of the mortgage. That's when it will have the greatest money-saving impact.

As one mortgage expert put it to me: "The interest rate you're paying on your mortgage is in essence the tax-free rate of return you'd have if you didn't have to pay it."

To understand why paying off a mortgage quickly is so important, you need to know something about how mortgage payments are structured. Essentially, they are a mixture of principal and interest, calculated in such a way as to reduce the outstanding balance you owe to zero at the end of the amortization period.

In practical terms, this means that the early payments on a mortgage will be almost entirely interest. You don't start to make a real dent in the principal for several years. On the other hand, the earlier you start reducing the principal, the more interest you'll save over the life of the mortgage.

Let's go back to that dream townhouse with its $60,000 mortgage. The monthly payments will amount to $557. At the end of five years, therefore, you will have turned over $33,420 of your hard earned money to the financial institution holding the mortgage. And how much will you still owe them at that point? A total of $56,640. You've only managed to reduce the principal by $3,360 during that long, five-year period. The rest of the money you paid—just over $30,000—went to cover interest charges. Sorry, folks.

The mortgage bind is especially acute here in Canada because there's no tax relief from the government on those payments. Even after their sweeping tax reforms, our American neighbours retain that particular tax plum. We can only look on with envy.

All of this dictates a strategy of mortgage reduction early in the game. Even a small amount can have wondrous effects.

Suppose, for example, that at the end of the first year you made an extra payment of $1,000 to reduce the outstanding principal. Nothing else changed. Any idea how much interest you would save over the life of the mortgage? Again, you may not believe this, but it works out to $9,669.21!

What happens is this: that single payment at the end of the first year reduces the total time it will take you to pay off the mortgage by 19 months. Instead of taking a total of 300 months (25 years x 12 = 300) it will take 281 months. The interest you save as a result is almost 10 times your $1,000 payment. Not a bad return on that modest investment!

Now suppose you kept doing that for the next four years. Remember that by making only your regular payments, you managed to reduce your principal owing to $56,640. By making five extra $1,000 payments, though, you'll reduce the total amount of interest you'll spend on paying off the mortgage to $75,991.62. That's a saving of $31,105.22 over what you would have paid in interest had you not made those annual $1,000 payments. I know those numbers seem amazing—most people can't believe that $5,000 in prepayments made in the early years of a mortgage can save that much money. But it's true—they can. That should be more than enough incentive to get you started on this particular wealth-building strategy.

Those numbers emphasize the importance of ensuring your mortgage has a generous prepayment clause. That means doing some careful shopping around when you select a lender, especially if you plan to sign up for a longer term. (The "term" of the mortgage is the period for which you agree to pay the lender at current interest rates. Typically, it will be for a minimum of six months to a maximum of five years, although there are some seven-and ten-year terms now available. Don't confuse "term" with "amortization"; they're two different things. You'd have to sign up for five consecutive five-year terms to pay off a mortgage with a 25-year amortization.)

When you're out mortgage shopping, it's also important to understand the distinction between a "closed" and an "open" mortgage. A closed mortgage usually does not allow you to make any extra payments against the principal without incurring a substantial penalty. However, some lenders will allow for limited penalty-free prepayments within a closed mortgage, usually on the anniversary date. Open mortgages allow you to pay off the full balance at any time, without penalty. But you're usually charged a higher interest rate for that added flexibility.

Generally, it's not worthwhile to pay extra for an open mortgage. But you should be sure that if you get a closed mortgage, the prepayment provisions are good. Typically, you'll be allowed to pay up to 10% or 15% of the original principal on each anniversary date. So on a $60,000 mortgage, you should be permitted to pay down the principal by $6,000 to $9,000 each year, without penalty. You should also be allowed to make extra payments over and above that, with a maximum penalty of three months' interest.

The longer the term you select, the more important those prepayment provisions become. At the end of each term, you're allowed to reduce the principal as much as you like. So if you're planning on consistently choosing six-month or one-year terms, prepayment clauses aren't a big issue. But if you plan to lock in for several years in order to protect yourself from the impact of whipsawing interest rates, be sure you get a mortgage with generous prepayment provisions. There's nothing worse than having a five- or ten-year mortgage with no flexibility to pay it down.

Some people tend to shrug off this advice, saying they won't have enough money to make prepayments in any event. That's being short-sighted. You don't know what may be coming a year or two down the road: a big raise, a new job, an unexpected inheritance, maybe even a winning lottery ticket. If some extra money does show up, the first place the wealth builder will direct it is towards the mortgage. But if there are no prepayment provisions, you're stuck. Make sure you get a mortgage that has them.

Another technique for reducing the onerous interest costs of carrying a mortgage is to choose a shorter amortization period at the outset. It will cost you more in the short run. But it will save a heck of a lot of money in the long term.

Once again, let's go back to the townhouse with its $60,000 mortgage. Suppose that, in this case, you opted for a 20-year amortization period instead of 25 years. What would happen?

To begin with, your payments would go up. Instead of $557, you'd be writing a cheque for $590.09 every month. But that extra $33 and change would mean big savings down the road. If you took the full 20 years to pay off the mortgage, the total cost would be $141,622. That's over $25,000 you've saved by choosing the 20-year amortization; cash you can put into your pocket. And it's after-tax money, too!

If you selected a 15-year amortization, your monthly payments would go up to $654.99. But your total cost of paying off the mortgage would drop to $117,898. That's almost $50,000 less than the 25-year term would cost.

Clearly, it's to your advantage to select the shortest amortization period you can afford. The sooner you get that mortgage paid off, the less it will cost you—and the faster you'll have funds available to do more interesting things with your wealth-building program.

As long as you have a mortgage, you should have two overriding objectives in mind: minimize the amount of interest you pay the financial institution that holds it, and reduce the principal as quickly as possible. Prepayments and shorter amortizations are two techniques for achieving those goals. Another one involves the term you select for your mortgage.

And that may be the one single decision that gives homeowners the most sleepless nights. There are many factors involved in making it—your best guess as to the future course of interest rates, your financial position, your risk tolerance level, and your basic psychological make-up. No wonder making a choice drives many people up the wall—and then leaves them second-guessing themselves for months afterwards.

Unfortunately, I can't solve all the problems for you. But maybe I can make things a bit easier.

First, let me go back a few years. In the summer of 1984, the *Financial Times of Canada* interviewed five experts, asking them what strategy should be used by people who had mortgages coming up for renewal. At the time, one-year mortgages were going for 12¾% and five-year terms were 14½%, with the rates for intermediate terms somewhere in between. The experts were asked what term they would advise people to select. Two suggested a five-year term, two opted for three years. Only one counselled a one-year term.

That advice really made me angry, and I said so on a CBC radio program a week or so later. Interest rates were clearly in the process of coming down from their 1981-82 highs. They had taken a temporary upward blip at the time, but few people expected that to continue. The disinflation psychology had set in, and the cost of living trendline was heading still lower. Yet here were the so-called experts, telling people to lock in their mortgages at those high rates for another three to five years. The banks and trust companies just love that kind of advice!

Just a year later, in mid-1985, five-year mortgage rates had dropped to 11¾%. Anyone who had followed the "expert" advice and selected a five-year term the previous summer would have been paying over $1,600 more in interest each year on a $60,000 mortgage at that point. And rates continued to decline still more after that.

There are two morals to this story. The first is: put not your faith in experts. The second is: don't go "long" when rates are high.

In fact, I might even say don't go long, ever. In most circumstances, I feel the best mortgage strategy is a short-term one. There are exceptions, of course, but here's why I favour short over long when it comes to choosing a mortgage term.

Let's go back to my two basic tactics in dealing with mortgages: pay as little interest as possible and reduce the principal as fast as you can. A short-term mortgage strategy permits you to do both, although you have to exercise some self-discipline. It also helps if you have good nerves.

To begin with, you have to understand exactly what you're doing when you choose a longer term for your mortgage. You're really purchasing an insurance policy—in this case, you're covering yourself against the possibility of higher interest rates in the future.

Now some people like lots of insurance. They pay big premiums to protect themselves against everything from flash floods to plane crashes. If you're one of those, then perhaps the longer-term mortgages are best for you—they'll give you the peace of mind you crave.

But you'll pay for those restful nights. In fact, when you discover how much it actually costs you, you may decide the price is way too high. You may even start tossing and turning with worry about how much money you're throwing away!

Let's go back to 1984 and those five-year mortgages. Suppose you had bought your townhouse then and you'd signed up for a $60,000 mortgage for five years at 14½%. What would have happened?

By the summer of 1988, the fourth anniversary of your unfortunate decision, you would have paid the mortgage company $34,846.08. Of that, only $1,380 would have been applied against the principal. The balance would all be interest.

Now let's suppose that you had chosen a one-year term in 1984—the approach I recommended at the time. What would have happened?

Your interest rate would have been 12¾%. By mid-1985, when it came time to renew, you would have made payments totalling about $7,810. Of that, $376.32 was applied to principal; the balance was interest.

By mid-1985, one-year rates were down to 10½%. At that point, you decided to renew for one year. Over the next 12 months, your payments totalled $6,703. Of that, $602.80 went towards reducing your principal; the rest was interest.

Now it's summer, 1986. You're up for renewal again. Now your one-year mortgage is going for around 9¾%. The next year costs you just over $6,352 in payments—$743.18 applied against your principal, the balance in interest.

By mid-1987, most one-year rates are sitting at 10¼% for a closed mortgage, 10¾% for an open one. Because you've adopted a short-term strategy, you continue to opt for the closed mortgage at the lower rate. Your payments for the next year come to $6,579, with $764.25 applied to the principal, the rest to interest.

So what's the scorecard by mid-1988?

The homeowner who listened to the experts and chose a five-year term back in 1984 has made total payments of over $34,800 and reduced his or her principal by $1,380.

The person who adopted a one-year strategy has made total payments of $27,444. His or her principal has been reduced by $2,487; the balance has gone to interest. He or she has also had to pay renewal fees of, say, $75 each year—an additional outlay of $300.

So the five-year "insurance policy" has so far cost over $8,160 more, calculating the increased interest paid and the difference in the principal still owing. That's the "premium," if you like. And the "policy" still has a year to run. If that's the sort of thing that makes you sleep better at night, be my guest. I'd rather have the money.

Obviously, if interest rates had been moving up instead of down, the story would have been quite different. So if you're in a period when a long, steady rise in interest rates looks like a real possibility, locking in for a longer term might be a good idea.

Frankly, though, I think the odds are against coming out ahead by choosing longer mortgage terms. High interest rates are bad for the economy; they can only be tolerated for relatively short periods. The natural tendency for business people, bankers, and politicians is to want to see interest rates stable or lower, rather than heading up. If you stick with a short-term strategy, you may end up getting burned occasionally. But those high interest rate periods shouldn't last long.

One warning, though. If you're on such financial thin ice that even a slight upward nudge in mortgage interest rates would put your home at risk, lock in for a longer term. In any financial decision, you have to look at the downside—and if that risk is losing your home, it isn't worth it.

I made the point earlier that there's a certain amount of self-discipline involved in the short-term strategy. Here's why. Even though staying short can mean hundreds or even thousands of extra dollars in your pocket, I don't want you to spend that money. I want you to use it to reduce the outstanding principal on your home at each renewal. It's a second, essential part of the short-term strategy—and one which will help cushion the shock if interest rates do move up sharply at some stage.

Basically, your goal is *to pay down principal instead of making interest payments*.

Here's how it works. Let's say that back in 1984 you decided to choose a one-year mortgage term. But you decided at that time that the money you saved by going that route, instead of signing up for five years, would be used to reduce your outstanding loan balance. Using the same interest rate structure as before, let's look at the results.

Year one (1984-85): Your 14½% mortgage will cost you $8,711.52 in annual payments. The 12¾% mortgage costs $7,809.84. Your saving is $901.86. Renewal charges are $75, leaving you a net $826.68 ahead. You apply that to reducing the principal at renewal time. You now owe the bank $58,797.

Year two (1985-86): The annual cost for the 14½% mortgage hasn't changed. But your one-year mortgage is now at 10½% and so costs you only $6,684. Your savings this year are $2,027. Again, you use that balance to reduce the principal. Now you owe the financial institution $56,176.

Year three (1986-87): Rates are down again, so your cost for carrying the one-year term is down to $6,046. After deducting your renewal fee, you're left with $2,590 to put against the principal. Now you're into the bank for $52,878.

Year four (1987-88): The interest rate moved up slightly over the previous year, but you still saved another $2,667 to pay against your principal. Now your mortgage loan is down to $49,518.

By way of comparison, keep in mind that the poor fellow who took the five-year mortgage has paid out exactly the same amount of money to this point as you have. But he still owes the bank $58,620, while you've now reduced your loan to just over $49,500.

That's how this short-term strategy cushions you from the impact of interest rate hikes. Your loan is being retired at a much faster rate, which means that if interest rates do go up at some stage, you'll be paying those higher rates on a lower balance.

Now I know there are going to be some people who read all this and groan. They're locked into long-term mortgages and only now, for the first time, do they truly understand the implications of what they've done. Now they want to get out and switch strategies. But it's too late. Or is it?

I have a friend who bought a new house in July of 1983. To finance it he took out a $100,000 mortgage with a 25-year amortization. The term was five years at 13¼%.

In mid-1986 he suddenly realized this wasn't such a great deal. Other people were signing new mortgages at around 10%, while he was still saddled with one at 13¼% that had two more years to run. On $100,000, that meant he was paying more than $3,000 a year in additional interest costs.

So he pulled out his mortgage agreement, which was with a large trust company, and read it over. He discovered the arrangements were quite interesting.

The mortgage was so tightly closed for the first three years that he wasn't even allowed modest prepayment privileges. But for the last two years, the terms changed. He was allowed to pay off as much of the principal as he liked, subject to a three-month interest penalty.

So he did some calculations. He found he was paying about $1,000 a month interest on his existing mortgage. His penalty for getting out of the contract would therefore be about $3,000 plus fees of around $85. Let's call it $3,100.

He then worked out how much interest he would save if he replaced his old mortgage with a new two-year term at 10¼%. It came out to just over $5,700. In other words, by paying the penalty and getting out of his five-year mortgage, he would save himself a net $2,600 in interest costs over the two years.

He decided to go for it and called the trust company. They weren't thrilled, to say the least. In fact, they did everything they could to discourage him from going ahead. First, they told him flatly he couldn't do it. When he insisted the clause was in the mortgage agreement, the tone switched. Well, yes, the trust company acknowledged, the agreement says that. But that clause was really intended to be used only if he sold the house. And he wasn't doing *that*, was he? The implication was that they had tried to do their customers a favour and they were being taken advantage of by some unscrupulous wretch.

My friend insisted. After all, the clause was there. And it didn't say anything at all about resale of the house. He was told grudgingly that he would have to take it up with the manager. All of this, remember, for a privilege that was clearly spelled out in the original contract.

In the end, he got his way—because when it came right down to it there was nothing the trust company could do to stop him. After all, *they* had drafted the contract in the first place.

Now all good stories should have a moral—at least in this book. This particular one has two.

The first is that you should never assume you're irrevocably locked in to an unattractive mortgage deal. If after reading this chapter you decide you want to change your strategy, get out your contract and go over it line by line. Look especially for prepayment and penalty clauses. If you do find a loophole, then do the same sort of calculations my friend did to see if you can save money by refinancing.

The second moral is, don't be intimidated by the blustering of financial institutions. Remember, they don't want people paying off high-interest mortgages prematurely—it costs them money. So they may go out of their way to make the process difficult. Don't let them bluff you! If you have a legal right to discharge the loan, insist on it. They'll back off.

Before I end this chapter, I want to restate one more time the two basic principles that should guide your mortgage strategy, because they are central to using your home to build wealth.

First: Pay as little interest as possible.

Second: Reduce the outstanding principal as quickly as you can.

Follow those two simple guidelines and you will be astounded at how quickly the equity in your home will grow.

The Interest Rate Rollercoaster

T HESE ARE NOT normal times for interest rates. Far from it. It's not usual for prime rates to rise to over 20% and then fall to less than half that within a few years.

It isn't normal for rates to gyrate up and down on the basis of how international currency traders view the outlook for the yen or the deutschemark from one week to the next.

It certainly isn't routine to see mortgage rates make significant moves in response to factors which have nothing at all to do with the housing market or even with our financial institutions.

Yet all these things are happening in this topsy-turvy economic world. The result is a wild, often unnerving interest rate rollercoaster ride that offers both great opportunity and tremendous risk to the wealth builder.

In more settled periods, interest rates tend to be relatively stable, moving only slowly up or down over an extended period. During such times—the 1950s and '60s were recent examples— planning is easy. Mortgages are available for long terms at fixed, modest rates (some readers may even remember the days of 25-year terms for mortgages). Investments in interest-bearing vehicles pay low, guaranteed returns over several years. Borrowing costs can be budgeted with confidence, knowing that unexpected events aren't going to suddenly create a major cash flow problem.

Safe, solid, and stable—all good words to describe those conditions.

You can also add "dull" to the list.

If nothing else, today's conditions create an exciting, ever-changing interest rate environment. If you know how to take advantage of that to minimize your costs and maximize your investment returns, you can use interest rate volatility to build your wealth more quickly.

In order to do that successfully, however, you need a basic understanding of exactly what forces drive interest rates. Unless you understand those dynamics, you won't be able to work out any coherent strategies because you'll have no idea what's likely to happen in the future. Neither do most economists, you may mutter. True. But you may have a better chance than they do because you'll be applying an extra dimension most of them don't seem to have: common sense. If that seems unfair, sorry—but I constantly see projections from top economic forecasters which look more like outrageous guesses than reasonable predictions with some grounding in reality.

So much for that mini-tirade. Back to business.

There are a number of factors which drive interest rates. They do not, perhaps surprisingly, include bank profiteering. In fact, our financial institutions prefer low interest rates to high ones. Lower rates encourage more people to borrow, reduce the risk of loan defaults, and carry a built-in disincentive to pay off a loan quickly.

So what does influence the rates? Here are the main forces:

General economic conditions: When times are bad and the economy is threatening to slide into recession or is already there, the natural tendency is for interest rates to fall. That's because lower interest rates encourage business investment and consumer spending, two forces which act to stimulate the economy and help to get things moving again. Conversely, when the economy is strong and tending to overheat, interest rates will tend to move up in an effort to put a brake on growth before it reaches an unsustainable level.

Inflation: As a general rule, the higher the inflation rate, the higher the interest rates. There are a couple of reasons for this.

First, investors demand a reasonable "real" return on their money—that's the difference between the rate of interest they receive and the inflation rate. For example, if the inflation rate is 5% and the interest rate on a one-year Guaranteed Investment Certificate is 11%, the real rate of return before taxes is 6%. Second, higher interest rates will tend to slow down the economy, which in turn should slow the growth in the inflation rate. The 1981 experience is an excellent example: a government fearful of runaway inflation kept jacking up interest rates until the economy almost collapsed. The long-term result was a period which has come to be known as disinflation—a time of declining inflation rates.

The Canadian dollar: Interest rates will sometimes spike up for no other reason than that international currency traders are driving the value of our dollar lower than the government and the Bank of Canada would like it. That happened in the winter of 1986, when our dollar hit a then all-time low of less than 70¢ U.S. The government responded with a major jump in interest rates, the idea being to attract more foreign capital into the country. That, in turn, means foreigners are buying rather than selling Canadian currency, which increases its value. Such currency driven gyrations are usually temporary in nature and thus create some excellent opportunities for wealth builders who know how to profit from them.

The U.S. dollar: Simply a variant on the Canadian dollar scenario, except in this case it's the U.S. buck that's under seige. U.S. interest rates move up to defend it and ours dutifully follow suit. This is exactly what was happening in the spring of 1987.

U.S. financial policy: Canada has very little independence when it comes to interest rate policies. And, despite NDP clamouring, it's unrealistic to expect we'll ever see a genuine made-in-Canada interest rate policy in our lifetime. We are too closely integrated into the North American economic structure (read U.S.) and we are too small to exert much influence on its policy direction. So no matter how much we fume about it, the reality is that the general direction of our interest rate structure is going to be governed to a large extent by decisions made in Washington. Another reality: our interest rates will almost always be somewhat higher than those in the U.S. That differential is needed to attract foreign investment—the sad truth is that international capital needs substantial inducements to put money into Canada rather than into the U.S.

There are other factors which can affect rates, but those are the main ones to be aware of. Now let's develop some strategies for using this information to build wealth.

Let's start with borrowing costs. As I pointed out in the last chapter, your main objective during times of interest rate turmoil is to avoid locking yourself in for a long term when rates are high. As basic as that advice sounds, there are many people who don't understand that simple principle. The result is financial disaster— long term commitments at inflated rates. Remember the folks who locked in 17% mortgages for five years!

If you're borrowing during periods of fluctuating rates, the message is simple: stay short. Don't lock in to long-term commitments unless you're absolutely convinced rates are heading up for an extended period. Some signs to watch for if you think that's the case: general economic conditions should be strong and heating up still more, labour unions should be obtaining outrageously high settlements, the cost-of-living index should be moving up, and interest rates should be in a clear upward trend. If those signs are present, then lock in your borrowing rates. If they're not, stay short term. It all goes back to one of the basic rules of mortgage management: keep your interest costs as low as possible.

Another consequence of interest rate volatility can be significant differences in the rates charged by financial institutions. A personal line of credit offering about the same privileges can cost two to three percentage points more at Bank A than at Trust Company B. That makes it essential to shop around before signing anything. And if you think two or three percentage points isn't a big deal, consider this: two extra points on a 10% loan adds 20% a year to your borrowing costs. If the loan is for $10,000, that's an additional $200, after tax, you'll be paying out unnecessarily. Surely you have some better use for that money!

Now for the investing opportunities in a volatile interest rate market—and here's where things get fun, because the chances to make money are terrific. There are some downside risks too, of course. But you should be able to keep these within tolerable limits.

Let's start with what for most of us is the first investment we ever make: Canada Savings Bonds. (If you're wondering, I don't regard bank accounts as an investment; they're simply a place to store money temporarily).

Canada Savings Bonds (or CSBs as they're usually called) are the most widely used investment vehicle in the country. They're also the most misused, because most people who own them don't take advantage of the opportunities they present.

There are two things that make CSBs unique. One is the redemption feature—you can cash them in at any time and receive the full face value of the bond plus accrued interest. The other is the guaranteed minimum return. When you buy a CSB, the government sets a floor rate at which interest will be paid after the first year. For example, the issue that came out in October 1986 carried a 7¾% interest rate in the first year, with a 5¾% minimum thereafter. (That was the case until the 1987 issue came out. It had no floor rate. Whether this precedent will be retained in future years remains to be seen.)

These two CSBs features can be used to increase your interest income—but only if you know the right strategies and are willing to move when conditions dictate.

Unfortunately, as I pointed out in Chapter Three, most Canadians don't do anything more imaginative with their CSBs than store them in a safety deposit box, collect the annual interest and wait for the bonds to mature. That's their loss. You can do better.

Let's look at a couple of examples.

The first one I call the Trading Up Tactic. I referred to it indirectly in Chapter Three. Now it's time to look at it in greater detail and offer a classic illustration of how to use it.

The 1983 issue of Canada Savings Bonds carried a first-year interest rate of 9¼%, with a guaranteed minimum after that of 7%. At the time, many people felt the first-year rate was low but the government got away with it and the bonds sold reasonably well.

Withing a few months, however, economic conditions changed dramatically. Interest rates moved up sharply, both for borrowers and savers. As thousands of people began cashing in their bonds, the government responded by increasing the rate to 10¼% on June 1, 1984. That was stingy by interest rate standards at the time. But Ottawa felt it was enough to slow down the redemption rate, and they turned out to be right. CSB holders rolled over and went back to sleep. That contented the federal government. After all, if most people don't mind collecting low interest on their bonds, why should the mandarins worry?

Interest rates continued to move higher, however, and for every notch the rates moved up, CSB holders were increasing their subsidy of the uncompetitive bond interest rates.

By July, things had deteriorated so badly that Government of Canada Treasury bills—short-term notes which are every bit as safe as CSBs—were yielding well over 11%. It was clearly time for people with more than a few hundred dollars in CSBs to employ the Trading Up Tactic. (Except those who had bought bonds in 1981. I'll explain why later.)

Implementing the Trading Up Tactic was simple. CSB holders went to their financial institution on August 1 (always cash in your bond on the first day of the month to maximize interest payments) and redeemed them. They then took the money to a broker and invested it in 91-day Treasury bills, maturing at the end of October. That strategy meant the money would be available to purchase the new CSB issue if it looked attractive.

The result? Anyone who used the tactic received an additional one percentage point of interest for the three-month period. On a $10,000 investment, that amounted to $33.33 extra money. On $50,000, the switch produced $166.67. Don't turn up your nose at amounts like that, especially when it is, in effect, free money. As any good wealth builder knows, you have to take advantage of every opportunity that comes along. Even if the additional profit is small, it all counts—and in the process you'll get used to recognizing opportunities and taking advantage of them. Then, as the amounts you're dealing with increase, so will the extra dollars you earn.

By the way, the government confirmed the CSB rates were too low that October. When the 1984 issue came out, the rate was set at 11¼%—which is where it should have been at months before.

Opportunities to use this tactic arise quite often. But there are a few guidelines you should use before undertaking it.

First, be sure the yield you can actually receive on Treasury bills is at least half a point higher than on the CSBs. A full point would be even better.

Second, don't rush to cash in CSBs that have a high guaranteed minimum. This is a short-term tactic; don't sacrifice longer-term financial benefits to use it.

Third, be sure you have a source for purchasing Treasury bills before you proceed. A stockbroker is best—some offer T-bills in minimum amounts of $1,000. If you don't have a broker, this tactic becomes difficult. You can try it using term deposits at banks or, perferably, because of their higher rates, small trust companies. But you'll need at least $5,000 in CSBs to go this route, the minimum amount most financial institutions accept for deposits of less than one year.

Fourth, this obviously isn't something to try if your CSB holdings are minimal. In fact, you simply can't do it if you only have a few hundred dollars.

If you do have enough money in CSBs but you've never bought Treasury bills before and aren't sure what they're all about, a brief explanation might be in order at this point.

Until recently, trading in T-bills was strictly a rich person's game. If you didn't have at least $50,000 to put up, you couldn't play. Now that's all changed—you can get in on the action for as little as $1,000—thanks to the aggressiveness of the brokerage industry.

T-bills are short-term borrowings by the federal and provincial governments, with maturities of less than a year. The 91-day bills are the most common, but they also come in maturities of 182 and 364 days. You buy them at a discounted price and redeem them at maturity for their face value. The difference is your interest on the transaction. For example, you might pay $970 for a $1,000 T-bill that's due in 91 days. When it matures you collect the face value of $1,000; the difference is your interest on that transaction. (In this case, you're collecting interest at an annual rate of about 12%.) Since the bills are government guaranteed, they're as solid an investment as you're going to find.

As a short-term place to park your money, T-bills are excellent. But there are some things you should be aware of if you want to use them.

For starters, you may have to do a bit of searching to find someone who will actually sell you the bills. The brokerage industry has led the way in making them available to the smaller investor (the chartered banks still only want your T-bill business if you have big bucks to invest). But different brokerage firms have different policies in selling them.

Minimum purchase requirements, for example, can vary all over the lot. Some firms will take $1,000 if you're a regular customer. Others will require $5,000 or even $10,000 minimums. You have to do some checking.

And while you're at it, find out what interest rate they're paying. The retail T-bill market is highly competitive and interest rates can vary from one brokerage firm to another. You want to get the best rate you can.

As you're checking the market, be aware that for many brokers, Treasury bills are almost a loss-leader—they make relatively little profit from them. Instead, they're frequently used to attract other business. I once had to listen to a long sob story from a broker I'd contacted about how little money he made from T-bills. He'd be happy to sell me some, of course—but only if I sent some other business his way. I took my purchase elsewhere.

This approach to selling T-bills means you often won't get the same kind of service you would if you were buying stocks and bonds. For example, I like to use them as short-term investments in a self-directed RRSP. But the trust company administering the plan requires that the actual certificates be delivered to them for safekeeping. Many brokerage firms won't do that, claiming that even something as minor as delivery costs can make the whole deal uneconomic.

When you do find a source for your T-bills, don't be surprised to discover that they're available in maturities other than the standard 91, 182, and 364 days. That's because brokerage houses stockpile them—you buy from their holdings. They'll quote you an interest rate slightly below what they're receiving on the bills—that's where they make their profit. A typical spread is half a point—if the brokerage firm is holding 9% T-bills, they'll sell them to you at 8½% and pocket the difference. So the interest rate quoted daily in the financial pages of the paper is not what you'll actually receive when you purchase the bills from a broker. That's why it's so important to check out the retail rates before taking any action.

Now let's get back to some more interest rate tactics, using Canada Savings Bonds. The second one you should be aware of is something I call the High Floor Ploy. It works when interest rates are high. Here's how:

As we've already seen, CSBs carry two interest rates. One is the rate you'll receive during the first year. The other is the minimum the government guarantees to pay you in subsequent years—the "floor" rate. The obvious conclusion is that the best bonds to hold are those with a high minimum interest guarantee—a "high floor."

The 1981 CSBs offered the classic opportunity to use the High Floor Ploy. These bonds paid an incredible 19% interest rate in the first year. That was enough to have people falling over themselves to buy them. But even more important, although most buyers didn't recognize it at the time, was the floor rate. The lucky purchasers of that issue bought themselves a guaranteed minimum interest rate of 10½% until the bond matured in 1988. As interest rates declined during the mid-1980s, that guaranteed return became the most outstanding feature of the bonds. The High Floor Ploy paid off handsomely! And people who cashed in those bonds early ended up kicking themselves.

There wasn't much opportunity to use the High Floor Ploy for several years after that 1981 bonanza. But high interest rates will inevitably come again at some point. When they do, be ready to cash in—if the government goes back to a floor-rate policy.

Canada Savings Bonds certainly aren't the most exciting investment around. But, properly used, they have a place in every wealth builder's investment portfolio. Their redemption feature makes them as good as cash. And the interest rate they pay is usually (but not always) competitive. Just remember to keep a close eye on them when the interest rate rollercoaster really kicks into high gear.

Building Wealth With GICs

CHAPTER 9

C ANADA SAVINGS BONDS aren't the only way to build wealth using your new understanding of interest rates. Term deposits (TDs) and Guaranteed Investment Certificates (GICs) offer excellent opportunities to increase investment income safely. But you have to know how to use them correctly.

Let's assume you've started a modest wealth-building program. Maybe you have some Canada Savings Bonds, perhaps you've purchased a home. But that's about it. Any other funds you have are accumulating in a savings account at your bank or trust company. That's where you should be looking first for ways to increase your wealth-building capacity.

The interest being paid on ordinary savings accounts is, to put it bluntly, lousy. You'll never become wealthy by leaving your money there; all you're doing is allowing the financial institution to borrow that money from you for its own use at very low cost. If you think subsidizing banks and trust companies is a good idea, fine. I have better uses for my money.

You should never hold more than $1,000 in an ordinary savings account. There are other things you can do with that cash which are every bit as safe, and which will give you a far better return. One option is premium savings accounts. They pay above-normal interest rates if you maintain a high balance. Check with your financial institution to see what they offer and the conditions attached to them. Another is TDs and GICs. They're available at all banks, trust companies, and credit unions and if you haven't yet looked into them, you should do so.

The first thing you need to understand is how they differ from each other. Many people are fuzzy on this point—including some so-called experts. A recently published dictionary of financial planning terms suggested that the only essential difference between them was that term deposits were issued by banks and GICs by trust companies. Otherwise, the dictionary said, the two are the same.

Well, don't believe it. Nor is there much validity to another widely held belief—that term deposits are short-term investments while GICs are longer-term.

So what's the real difference? Let's start with GICs. These are medium-term investments, usually of one to five years, that are firmly locked in. Once the financial institution has your money in one of these, you can't get it out before maturity no matter how much you beg, whine, or plead. You get compensated for this inflexibility by the higher interest rate you receive. But you'd better be darn sure you won't need the money in the meantime before you invest in one of these.

Term deposits, by contrast, are not locked in. If you need your money you can get it out at any time. But you'll pay an interest penalty for early withdrawal. And you'll receive a lower rate of interest over the life of a term deposit then you would from a comparable GIC.

Many financial institutions offer both choices, for both short and long terms. If you're investing for less than a year, you'll usually need a minimum of $5,000 for a term deposit and substantially more for a GIC (Short-term GICs are rarely used by individual investors.) Investments for one year or longer usually have a $1,000 minimum. The return on a GIC will typically be one to two percentage points higher than on a TD, depending on the term you choose. For example, in the fall of 1986 the Toronto Dominion Bank was offering to pay 7¾% for a five-year term deposit. But if you were willing to tie up your money for five years in a GIC, you'd receive 9¾%.

Usually (but not always), the longer the term you select, the higher the interest rate you'll receive. At the time TD Bank was paying 9¾% for five-year GICs, it was offering 8¼% for one-year deposits. A 30-day GIC was paying only 6½%.

Those differences can add up over a period of time. Suppose, for example, that you had invested $1,000 in a one-year TD Bank GIC in the fall of 1986. At maturity, you'd have $1,082.50—your original deposit plus $82.50 interest. If rates stayed the same and you repeated that process each year for the next four years, reinvesting the principal and accumulated interest each time, you'd end up with $1,486.41. Not bad, considering you started with $1,000.

But now let's suppose you'd locked in for five years from the outset, at 9¾%. When the GIC matures, the bank will pay you $1,592.30. That's $105.89 in additional interest—22% more than you would have received by opting for annual renewals.

Either way, you'd be much better off than if you'd left the money in a savings account. TD's daily interest savings accounts were paying just 4¾% at that time.

That's a key point to remember. The interest rate you earn by putting your money into instruments like this will always be higher than what you'd receive in an ordinary savings account.

That's how you can make your savings work harder for you, and build wealth more quickly.

So much for the basic groundrules. Now for some ideas on when you should consider using TDs or GICs.

TERM DEPOSITS (short)

Look at these when you want to park your money for a short period of time while receiving a better rate of interest than your bank account offers. For example, suppose it's November and $10,000 worth of Canada Savings Bonds have matured. You plan to buy a house in the spring and use the money as part of the downpayment. You could always hold the funds in your daily interest account until May, when you plan to make the purchase. But you'd be further ahead opting for a 180-day term deposit, which offers an interest rate 1¾% higher. By the time the TD matures and you're ready to make the downpayment, you'll have an extra $86.22 in your pocket—enough for a set of kitchen dishes.

Term Deposits (long)

This is an option to consider if you want to improve your rate of interest but retain the flexibility to withdraw the money if you need it. Go back to that $10,000 you received in the fall of 1986 when your CSBs matured. This time, let's assume you still plan to use the money to purchase a home, but you're not sure when. It might be two or three years down the road, but it could be sooner if a big raise comes through. You don't want to lock your money into a GIC. But you'd like a better rate of return than the new CSB issue is offering, which is 7¾% the first year, with a 5¾% minimum guaranteed after that. It's the future that really worries you—interest rates have been falling for several years and they might drop still more. A 5¾% return isn't really what you had in mind. But you don't want your money locked away.

Here's where a term deposit can help. Toronto Dominion Bank was offering 7¼% on two- or three-year TDs in the fall of 1986. You'd be giving up a little in the first year compared to the CSB offering. But you'd be sure of collecting that 7¼% two or three years down the road, when the CSBs might be paying only 5¾%. And you could get your money out earlier if you decided to buy the house, although you'd have to pay a penalty in the form of reduced interest if you did that.

Net result: you've sacrificed some interest income, but you've preserved your flexibility. And you've protected yourself against the possibility of lower interest rates over the next two or three years.

(By the way, a five-year term deposit at that time was paying 7¾%, the same as the CSBs. If you'd gone that route, you wouldn't have lost any interest at all in the first year.)

Before we move on, a word about the penalties for cashing in early. These will vary, depending on the circumstances and the financial institution you're dealing with, but they can be substantial.

Suppose you put your money into a 30-day term deposit. Two weeks later an emergency arises and you *must* have the funds. In most cases, you'll receive no interest at all. In effect, your penalty is 100% of the interest that would have been due you.

Now let's assume you have a two-year TD paying 8¼%. At the end of the first year you want the money. In this case what you'll receive depends on whom you do business with. For instance, most of the big banks would pay you only about 4% in this situation. That means your penalty for cashing in early is about half the interest you would have otherwise collected. But this policy isn't universal. Some banks and credit unions will do much better. So if you think there's a strong chance you might want to cash in the term deposit before maturity, check out the policies of various financial institutions and go with the one that will hit you the least hard.

GUARANTEED INVESTMENT CERTIFICATES

When you purchase a GIC, you're tying up your money for a fixed period of time. In return, you receive a highly competitive interest rate—usually about the best that's available to the average investor. Before you make that kind of commitment, you have to ask yourself two questions:

1. Am I reasonably certain I won't need that money before the GIC matures?

2. Do the signs indicate that interest rates are going to remain stable or in a downward trend during the period I'll be holding the certificate?

Clearly, the second question is tougher to answer than the first. But if you review the interest rate indicators I described in the last chapter, you'll at least be in a position to make an informed judgment before going ahead.

I stress this point because one of the most frustrating experiences in building wealth with interest rates is locking yourself into a five-year GIC and then seeing the rates take off. You don't want to be one of the many people who tie up their funds at 10% and then fume as rates rise to 12%. You want to be part of the other, smaller group—the people who invest at 13½% and then sit smiling as rates fall to 9%.

As you might expect, GICs significantly outperform such investments as CSBs when interest rates are declining. Let me give you a personal example.

In the fall of 1982, the new issue of CSBs came out. They offered 12% in the first year with a guaranteed minimum of 8½% after that. At the same time, five-year GICs were available from large trust companies at 13%. I had nearly $9,000 that I wanted to put into some form of interest-bearing vehicle. My decision came down to CSBs or a GIC. Looking at all the signs, my feeling was that interest rates were on the way down. I chose the GIC.

When it matured in the fall of 1987, that GIC was worth $16,283.89. If I'd invested the same amount in compound interest CSBs, it would have been worth about $14,200. That's a difference of $2,000 over the five-year term. Considering the size of the original investment, that's a lot!

That's how to use GICs to your advantage—lock in your returns when interest rates are high so that you can keep building wealth at a better-than-average pace when they're low.

Where you buy TDs and GICs depends on what you want. Banks and many credit unions offer all these options. Trust companies are more limited: they offer term deposits for up to 364 days only. If you want to deposit your money for a longer period with a trust company, it has to be in a GIC. Normally, trust companies will offer better rates than the major banks—and the smaller the trust company the more attractive the interest rate is likely to be.

Why that rate difference? Because smaller trust companies need to offer it to attract business. After the spate of failures of banks and trust companies in the early 1980s, many people were reluctant to deposit their money in smaller, less well-known financial institutions. To get business they had to offer more—just as Canada has to offer higher interest rates than the U.S. to attract international investment.

That situation can produce some terrific investment opportunities. Frequently, some of the more aggressive of the smaller trusts have special promotions, designed to generate new business. For example, in the autumn of 1987 Financial Trust was offering a special term deposit which guaranteed 9¼% interest for up to 364 days, but allowed you to withdraw your money at any time without penalty after 60 days. At the time, the major banks were offering only 5½% interest on 60-day term deposits. The Financial Trust offer represented a great opportunity for the average investor to get top interest rates for a full year while retaining the flexibility to get out without penalty any time after the first two months.

If you've never heard of Financial Trust, or some of the other small firms that offer higher rates, your natural inclination may be to stick with the big banks for security. After all, they don't pay a lot. But your money is safe there. Isn't it?

Yes, it probably is. But if the interest spread between the banks and the small trust companies is as large as the one I've described above, you might want to consider the options carefully before passing up an opportunity to earn more.

One major factor in your decision should be that TDs and GICs of not longer than five years are protected by deposit insurance, up to the $60,000 maximum. So as long as you don't invest more than that with any single financial institution, you're protected by the Canada Deposit Insurance Corporation in the event of a bankruptcy. Credit unions are protected by similar provincial plans; ask for details if you're considering a credit union deposit.

You should also do some homework before investing in a TD or GIC. The financial papers (*Report on Business*, *Financial Post*, *Financial Times*) regularly publish a list of current interest rates. So do most major daily papers. If it's too much trouble to look up the best rates there, call a stockbroker. Most of them monitor the fluctuation of GIC and TD rates on a daily basis. Since rates change frequently, you'll want the most up-to-date information.

Now, let's suppose you've done all your homework and have satisfied yourself a GIC is the way to go. You've locked in for five years at what you think is a great interest rate. Then disaster strikes. Your company is taken over by a larger firm. As part of the rationalization process, you lose your job. Nothing to do with your performance, they assure you. We just don't need two people doing the same thing and old Fred over there has been around for 25 years.

Suddenly you really need to get at that GIC money. But you're locked in. Or are you?

If you had the foresight to purchase a GIC that's transferable, you may not be.

Not many people know it, but stockbrokers run a secondary market in GICs. That means they're in the business of buying and selling GICs issued by regular financial institutions. So if you're locked in for several years and suddenly need the money, you have an alternative. The bank or trust company that issued the certificate won't redeem it. But you can take it to a broker and sell the certificate there—*as long as it is transferable*.

You're not going to get rich doing things this way. The broker will pay you a discounted price for your piece of paper. For example, suppose you have a $1,000 five-year certificate at 11% with four years left to run. You've already earned $110 interest, so the GIC right now is worth $1,110. The broker will pay you something less that that to take it off your hands—how much less depends to a large extent on where interest rates are when you go to sell it and how much time there is left before maturity. If interest rates have gone down since you bought the certificate and it still has four years to run, you'll get a better price for it. That's because it will be offering a better return than someone could get buying a new GIC. Conversely, if interest rates have gone up, the amount you'll receive will be less—you may even sacrifice part of your principal just to get it off your hands. But at least it's a way to get most of your money out. If you're ever in this situation don't go to just one broker for an offer; you may get a better price somewhere else.

The broker who buys your certificate will then turn around and offer it for sale to his or her clients. That means you can buy a "used" GIC from a broker if you wish. Usually the return you'll receive will be slightly higher than if you deal with a bank or trust company, perhaps by a quarter of a percent or so. This could happen in one of two ways: either the interest rate on the GIC is higher than current rates, or the broker will sell it to you at a discount from face value to make the real interest yield more attractive.

If you want to compare returns on "used" and "new" GICs, contact a broker and ask for the current list of GICs they're offering. These will be certificates issued by banks and trust companies; the only difference is that they've gone through the buying and selling process I've just described.

Compare the rates being offered by the broker with what you could get if you went directly to a financial institution. Remember, you'll be taking over the GIC for the balance of time remaining until it matures. If the term and the interest rate is right for your purposes, take advantage of it.

One reminder before I end this chapter. If interest rates appear to be moving up, don't lock away your funds for a long period. The time to do that is when interest rates are high. Those opportunities don't come along often but when they do, grab them.

Bonds: The Easiest Investment

L ET ME BEGIN this chapter with a sad story. Once upon a time, many years ago (it was back in the early 1960s, as I recall) my mother-in-law asked me for some investment advice.

She wasn't a wealthy woman, far from it. But she managed to put some money aside, about $2,000. That may not sound like much now but in those days, when $10,000 a year was a big salary, it was quite a bit.

She didn't want to keep it in her bank savings account, which paid virtually no interest. She didn't trust the stock market. What could she do with it?

Bonds, I said.

You mean Canada Savings Bonds?

No. *Real* bonds. The kind that people trade. I'd never invested in a bond in my life at that stage. But I'd read an article.

Bonds. I repeated. A rock-safe investment that will pay you a good return.

Well, okay, she said dubiously. She should have known better. *I* should have known better.

She put her hard earned $2,000 in Manitoba Telephone bonds paying 7% interest and maturing in 1993. They seemed safe and sure—bonds issued by a public utility and guaranteed by a provincial government.

For a couple of years, all seemed well. She received a $70 interest cheque twice a year and never gave the bonds another thought. The fact that interest rates were starting to creep up didn't bother her, and I'd forgotten at that point I'd ever put her on to the bonds. All was well.

Or at least it was until one day, several years later, she decided she'd like to sell the bonds and get her money out. She visited a broker with the certificates and was told that, yes, the bonds could be sold. She'd receive, let's see, $1,200 for them.

Naturally, she was stunned. Here was a supposedly safe investment, suggested by her son-in-law of all people, that had lost almost half its value. She couldn't figure out why—and at the time, neither could I.

Her Scottish blood refused to allow her to sell the bonds and take the loss. When she passed away a few years later, she still had them. My wife inherited them and put them into an RRSP. It was only in the mid-1980s, when interest rates dropped and the maturity date drew near, that those Manitoba Tel bonds returned to a market value that was something close to what my mother-in-law had paid way back in the early '60s. Some financial advisor I was! Fortunately, I've learned a little bit since.

One of the things I've learned is that bonds are one of the easiest ways to build wealth—*if* you understand what you're doing and you apply your observations of interest rate patterns to your investment strategies. CSBs, TDs, and GICs are all perfectly valid ways to make money via the interest rate route. But for maximum returns in relative safety, nothing beats bonds. And no, I'm not giving you the same line I gave my mother-in-law so many years ago. Or at least, I'm not giving it to you for the same reasons.

You can also lose a lot of money in bonds, as my mother-in-law did along with everyone else who held them during that long period when interest rates were steadily moving up. So be careful.

There is one simple, basic fact you have to fix firmly in your mind about bonds. When interest rates go up, bond prices fall. Conversely, when interest rates go down, bond prices increase. Once you've grasped that, all you have to do is figure out which way interest rates are moving and then sit back and cash in. Easy, huh?

Of course that's overly simplistic. If it were that easy everyone would be a millionaire. The trick, of course, is guessing right on which way interest rates are moving and then having the courage to take advantage of the situation.

Let me give you a simplified example—and I stress, it *is* simplified. Suppose you bought a $1,000 bond when interest rates were 10%. You'd get $100 interest a year. Now you want to sell it, but interest rates have gone up. Similar bonds are now paying 12%. Do you think anyone is going to buy your bond for $1,000? Not on your bip-bip. They'll want a 12% return on their money, not 10%. So to sell the bond you'll have to price it so the $100 a year it pays in interest will give the buyer a return on his investment of 12%. That means you'll have to sell him the bond for around $835. You've just lost money!

If, on the other hand, interest rates had gone *down* to 8% in the meantime, it's a different story. Your bond is still paying $100 a year interest. But now, with rates at 8%, your buyer will have to pay $1,250 to get that return. Your bond just went up 25% in value and you've got a nice capital gain.

Identifying the general interest rate trend isn't as hard as it sounds. That's because interest rates move in long cycles—usually several years. There'll be blips along the way, of course. One took place in the winter of 1986, when the Bank of Canada pushed up rates as part of its battle to defend the plunging Canadian dollar. But that upward spike was temporary and only lasted a few months. By the summer of 1986 the crisis had passed and interest rates had resumed the long decline that began in 1981-82.

The key to building wealth with bonds is to catch the trend once it's begun and ride it—rather like a surfer riding a wave. Of course, sooner or later the wave crashes and the surfer wipes out. But it's a great ride while it lasts.

You don't want to wipe out, of course. And you don't have to if you're careful and pay attention to your bond investments.

At this point, perhaps a word of explanation about bonds is in order.

As you have probably gathered by now, I'm not speaking here about Canada Savings Bonds. They aren't true bonds at all; rather they're a type of savings certificate.

The bonds I'm describing are issued by governments, crown corporations, municipalities, and private companies as a means of financing their capital expenditures or operating costs. Financial people refer to them as "debt instruments," because they represent money the issuer owes—rather like sophisticated IOUs, if you like. Stocks, by contrast, represent equity—an actual piece of the ownership of a company.

Bonds are bought and sold on the Bond Market, which is one of the mythical lands of the financial world. By that I mean it doesn't exist—at least not in any physical form. You can't walk onto the floor of the bond market and watch the traders at work, as you can on the stock exchange.

Bond trading is a telephone and, increasingly, a computer game. The "bond market" is a collection of traders across the country, sitting at their desks and networking by telecommunications. Not very glamorous, perhaps. But that's the reality.

There have been entire books written about bonds, so obviously this one chapter isn't going to point out every nuance involved in trading them successfully. But here are the four key terms you need to know for starters.

Coupon: The interest rate the bond pays, based on its face value. Bonds are normally sold to individual investors in $1,000 units. So a bond with a coupon rate of 9% would pay $90 a year in interest, usually in semi-annual payments.

Maturity: This is the date at which the bond matures and you can cash it in at face value. No interest is payable after that date.

Yield to maturity: The annual rate of return you'll receive on a bond you buy today and hold until its maturity date. That yield can be very different from the coupon rate, depending on the price of the bond, time left to maturity, and the general interest rate picture.

Rating: A measure of the safety of the investment, expressed in letters. A rating of AAA means the chances of the issuer going belly up and leaving you holding a worthless certificate are almost nil. A bond with a D rating, on the other hand, is a signal to run quickly in the opposite direction unless you're prepared to take big risks in hopes of a spectacular return.

As you learn more about bonds, you'll find you can make use of all these variables to improve your returns. But the thing I like about bonds is that you really don't have to bother with all of this stuff if you don't want to.

What you *do* have to be aware of is that the longer the time to the bond's maturity, the more volatile it will be and, therefore, the more risk is involved in the investment. Bonds with 20 years to maturity will move more sharply in price than those with, say, five years. That's why my mother-in-law's Manitoba Tel bonds did so badly; they were long-term.

The other thing you need to know is that you don't have to go through the agony of selecting exactly the right bond. This is what makes bond trading so different from the stock market. With stocks, you not only have to identify which way the market is moving, you then have to pick specific stocks that you believe will perform exceptionally well. Bonds are different. Most bonds with similar maturity dates and ratings will tend to move in the same direction in the market. You don't normally expect to find one 20-year Government of Canada bond moving up while another is going down.

That means that once you decide you want to invest in bonds, you don't have to do a lot of soul searching to decide which one to choose. If you're just starting out, stick with Government of Canada bonds. Don't even touch anything else until you have a clear understanding of what you're doing. Decide whether you prefer short-term bonds (which I define as those with maturity dates no longer than five years out), medium-term (5-10 years), or long-term (over 10 years).

Generally, the longer the term you choose, the greater the risk you're assuming—and the larger your potential gain or loss.

Short-term bonds are less risky simply because their maturity date is relatively close. At that time they can always be cashed in at face value. So if interest rates rise—causing bond prices to fall—short-term bonds won't usually suffer as great a loss as long-term bonds will.

Conversely, long-term bonds are a way you can make big money if interest rates decline. Prices of those bonds will increase more because the holders can collect the coupon interest rate, which is now substantially more than new bonds are paying, for a longer period of time.

So if you believe interest rates are in a downward trend, buy some Government of Canada bonds. The maturities will depend on your risk tolerance—you might choose a blend of short, medium, and long-term bonds.

That's what I did in the summer of 1984, during one of those periods when interest rates had taken a temporary upward spike. I was convinced they'd start moving down again within a few months, so I bought a mixture of Government of Canada bonds.

Interest rates did in fact drop during the autumn and, of course, the value of the bonds went up. When rates started to turn around again in February 1985 I sold some (not all) of the bonds and took some profits.

On one, my profit worked out to about 23% on an annual basis—this was a combination of interest and capital gain. On the other, my annualized profit was just under 25%. Given the very low risk involved in this particular investment, I consider that a respectable rate of return—certainly much more than I would have received by investing in CSBs or GICs. I only wish I'd known all this when my mother-in-law asked me for advice back in the '60s.

Now, I'm not suggesting that you should become a bond speculator by any means. Normally I hold my bonds for much longer than a few months; it was just that this particular situation seemed to present a good opportunity for quick profits and, as a good friend of mine is fond of saying, "Nobody ever went broke taking a profit."

If you're just starting out, you might want to consider buying only Government of Canada bonds with a maturity of less than 10 years. Another good rule is to buy only when the interest rate is at a level you'd be content to live with if you held the bond to maturity. And, of course, you should only be buying if you feel interest rates stand a good chance of moving lower.

Follow those basic rules and you won't wipe out—even if the wave does crash.

Finally, a few words about a new type of bond investment that's become popular in recent years. They're called stripped bonds (in the States they're known as zero-coupon bonds) and they're yet another way to profit from interest rates. Here's how they work.

Let's take a Government of Canada bond with a face value of $1,000, maturing in 15 years and paying 10% interest. If you purchased one of these, you'd receive two separate components. One would be the bond itself, guaranteeing repayment of the principal on the maturity date. The other would be 30 coupons, one of which you'd cash in every six months to collect your interest.

When you buy stripped bonds (or stripped coupons) you are buying these components separately. You can buy the bond alone, without the coupons, at a discounted price and hold it until it matures. The increase in value during that period would be, in effect the interest on your investment.

The advantage of this to the investor is that you can buy more assets because of the discounted price. For example, a 15-year stripped bond priced to yield 10% until maturity would cost about $240 to purchase—its "present value" in financial terms. That means you could hold four such bonds for every one regular bond. That, in turn, increases your profits if interest rates fall and bond prices rise—or your losses if the opposite happens.

Buying stripped coupons simply means you're purchasing the other component of the bond—the semi-annual interest coupons. Again the same principle applies: you buy the coupons at their present value and cash them in at maturity. The advantage here is that because the coupons become due every six months, you can vary the maturity dates to suit your own needs.

When interest rates ticked up in 1984, stockbrokers pushed stripped bonds and coupons aggressively. They tried to demystify the concept by giving these bonds hyped-up names like Cougars and Tigrs that made them sound more like cars than bonds. Some of the ads conveyed the impression these new investment vehicles were nothing more than fast-buck gimmicks: "How to turn $2,000 into $25,000 with no effort" was one ad claim.

That type of promotion may have turned off a lot of people. Too bad, because strips are a respectable investment—and were especially so at that time.

Stripped bonds and coupons carry the magic of compound interest to its ultimate degree. Unlike GICs or CSBs, you can lock in a guaranteed interest rate for 15, 20, even 25 years into the future. That offers some intriguing possibilities.

For example, when interest rates were sky-high in the early 1980s, think how great it would have been to guarantee yourself a 17% or 18% return on your money for as far ahead as you can see. In mid-1984, when brokerage houses were strongly promoting the strips, you could have locked in returns of 13% to 14%. I bought strips with a face value of $77,000 at that point, with various maturity dates into the 1990s. They cost me just under $26,000, and yielded 13.6% to maturity. They turned out to be one of the best bond investments I ever made—my only regret was that I didn't buy more.

When you can get strips with those kinds of yields, those seemingly preposterous advertising claims do come true. You can turn $2,000 into $25,000—if you can get a 13.5% return and you're prepared to wait 20 years. And if you wait five years longer, that original $2,000 will balloon to over $47,000.

Sounds terrific. But there are some buts.

First, if you hold the strips until maturity you have to regard them as very long-term investments. That's why they're best suited to the young; this is not the sort of thing you buy if you're approaching retirement age.

Second, strips don't pay any income. You only collect when the bond or coupon matures. If you need a steady income flow, this isn't the way to go.

Third, the interest rate that looks good today may not seem so hot five or ten years from now. Remember my mother-in-law's Manitoba Tel bonds. You'll have to decide whether the rate being offered on strips is likely to seem reasonable over the long haul.

Fourth, it's not always easy to resell a stripped bond. The secondary market is still not well developed. If you need to get your money out, you may have some difficulty.

Fifth, stripped bonds are very volatile. Their value will rise and fall much more sharply than ordinary bonds, as interest rates move. At one point the Ontario Securities Commission felt it necessary to issue a warning about the volatile nature of this type of investment. If you intend to hold the strips to maturity or you want to speculate in them, fine. But be aware that the prices can swing wildly.

Sixth, there are important tax considerations in owning strips. Revenue Canada requires you to declare the accrued interest and pay tax on it every three years—even though you haven't actually received one cent of real income! The way around this is to hold your strips within a Registered Retirement Savings Plan. In that case, no tax would be payable—you just let the money accumulate until you're ready to cash in.

Like any other bond, strips offer the best opportunity for profit when interest rates are high. So keep your eyes open for buying opportunities—periods when interest rates are up in response to some temporary condition, such as a dollar crisis. That's when the odds are in your favour. Take advantage of it.

The Credit Card Squeeze

I'LL MAKE A DEAL with you. Open your wallet or purse and count the number of credit cards you're carrying. If you have two or less, I'll pay you $5. But for each one over two, you pay me $1.

If I could persuade every reader to take up that offer, I'd have so much money I wouldn't know what to do with it. Most of us own too much plastic. The average Canadian carries three credit cards and most people in higher-income groups have more. And we're being bombarded with sales pitches for new ones all the time.

What have credit cards to do with wealth building? A lot. An essential part of any wealth-building program is the effective management of your financial resources. You must be able to handle credit well and to make intelligent choices in the credit instruments you use. Credit cards are the first experience many people have with borrowing. Unfortunately, that first experience often turns into a financial disaster which can take years to put right.

Part of the fault for this lies with our credit granting institutions themselves. Some of the gimmicks that are being used in the hot pursuit of credit card market share smack of hucksterism at its worst. Royal Bank's Premier Visa Card borrowed an idea from the successful "frequent flyer" plans by offering points for the dollars you spend—one point for every $100 charged to the card. The rewards were everything from teddy bears to an all-expense trip to France on the Concorde with a weekend in

Paris and dinner at Maxim's. Card users needed 5,000 points—
$500,000 worth of purchases—to claim that one. That would
even take a heavy credit card user like me a few years to achieve.

The big U.S. based Citibank promoted its prestige Visa card
by borrowing a merchandising device from Canadian Tire. Card
users received one Citibank dollar for every $10 charged. The
Citibank bucks could then be redeemed for partial payment on a
variety of merchandise.

Royal Trust used a much simpler device when it launched its
Gold MasterCard—a 1% rebate on everything purchased on the
card. It was another merchandising ploy to grab a respectable
share of the market. But, as I'll explain later in this chapter, it was
one the smart credit card user could turn to his or her advantage.

It's not just the premium card companies who are aggressively
pursuing your business. My youngest daughter worked briefly one
summer for an outfit which kept dozens of people busy every day
doing telephone solicitations for Bay cards. The pay was poor
but the bonus incentives for signing up customers were good. At
one point, my daughter confessed later, she pleaded with a
potential customer to sign up so she could meet her quota, telling
the surprised man on the line to cut it up and flush it down the
toilet if he didn't want to use the card after he received it.

The fact that banks, trust companies, department stores, and
oil companies are going to such lengths to persuade you to sign
up should tell you something. Credit cards are a very profitable
business for them. They are not, conversely, very profitable for
you—unless you use them correctly.

If you're a normal credit card user, you can probably save
yourself hundreds of dollars each year by applying some basic
financial management discipline. That's money that could be
channeled into productive wealth-building activities. And by
handling your cards more effectively, you'll reduce the risk and
inconvenience of having them lost or stolen.

How? Here's a guide to intelligent credit card use that may
help.

An initial suggestion: Don't carry more than two personal
cards. Unless you have some unusual credit requirements, you

don't need any more. This isn't just an exercise in keeping a neat purse or wallet. Most major credit cards now charge annual user fees, so you're paying a lot of money for the privilege of carrying around all that plastic, especially if you're not making regular use of it.

Which two cards should you keep? That depends on how you use them. Take out all your credit cards and spread them on a table in front of you. Then take out those you used less than four times over the past year. They have to go—any card used that infrequently isn't worth keeping.

I'll admit, it's not always easy. But it's a necessary exercise. Let me tell you what happened when I did it.

My first casualty was my En Route card—that's the one issued by Air Canada. I'd carried one for several years but never found myself in a situation where I wanted to use it. When they announced they were going to start charging a user fee, I cancelled it in a hurry.

Next to go was Diner's Club, for basically the same reason. I was paying for a card I rarely used. The only reason it stayed in my wallet so long was that I'd forgotten I even owned it.

After that it was Visa's turn to get the chop. I used to carry two of them—don't ask me why; I'd picked up a second one at some point and since it kept arriving automatically in the mail, I never bothered to cancel it. Then they introduced user fees. That was all the motivation I needed. I cancelled one immediately. Then, after shopping around a bit, I found a Visa issuer that still gave the cards free. I cancelled the other card I'd been carrying and switched.

Finally came American Express. I'd owned an American Express card for years, and thought Peter Ustinov's TV commercials for it were terrific. It was a real wrench to cut it up. But when I discovered I hadn't used it in 14 months, I decided the money I was spending on the annual fee might be better used somewhere else.

There are times when a card like American Express is useful, because it has no fixed spending limit. If you tend to run up large travel and entertainment bills, you don't run the risk of having a disdainful waiter hand your card back because you've exceeded your credit limit. But I wasn't in that situation. I pay off my bills as they come due and the credit limits on my cards are more than adequate for my needs. It got the chop.

Incidentally, in the months following the cancellation of my American Express account I received several form letters telling me, in polite terms of course, what a fool I was and offering me the chance to reconsider. They pointed out all the benefits I was foregoing and implied that without an American Express card my social status would fall to zero. I read all these sales pitches very carefully and looked again at the benefits they described. They only reinforced my decision—I'd never had occasion to use a single one of the benefits offered by the card, besides simply charging things, of course. And when I thought about it, I realized I wouldn't use them in the future either. After a while, the letters stopped. I guess I'd been finally relegated to AmEx Siberia.

If you go through this same exercise, you may end up with three or four cards left on the table. Of those that remain, select the two with the widest acceptance. These will most likely be Visa and MasterCard. Now look again at the others that are still there—maybe it's a gasoline card and a department store card. Ask yourself whether you couldn't just as easily use one of the bank cards when you're making the purchases you normally use those cards for. If the answer is yes, add them to the discard pile.

Once you've made your final decision, don't just cut up the cards you don't need and forget them. Cancel them with the issuer, otherwise you'll continue to receive replacement cards at the expiry date, with accompanying invoices. And, of course, pay off any outstanding balances that may remain.

When you've completed this whole process, you should be down to two basic cards. Now let's consider how to use them most intelligently.

Rule one: Reduce your user fees to an absolute minimum. Ideally, aim for zero net cost. It's still possible, but you have to work at it.

I'm strongly reluctant to pay credit card issuers for using their product. It may be because I remember when most credit cards were free. It's only in recent years that they've had all kinds of user charges and transaction fees tacked on. Add to that the fact that I know the merchants are paying the card companies a percentage of everything I charge to my cards and I figure the issuers are getting enough from me.

Finding out where to go for free credit card services isn't easy, though. And since card issuers are constantly changing their policies, a good deal one year might be a lousy one the next. Here's a couple of places to start looking, though.

Guaranty Trust. For years they offered a Visa card that had no user fees and no transaction charges. This is still their policy as this book is being written, but I can't guarantee things won't have changed by the time you read this. So check and see whether this policy is still in force. If so, it's the best Visa deal around.

Bank of Montreal/National Bank of Canada/National Trust. Many MasterCard issuers have moved to user fees but, at the time of writing, these institutions maintained a no-fees policy. If that's still the case when you read this, a MasterCard from any of them is good value.

Rule Two: As a general rule, avoid status cards. You can now get gold cards, platinum cards, emerald cards, prestige cards, premier cards, and heaven knows what else. They'll all cost you— sometimes a lot. And the merchandising can be tempting, as we've already seen. The range of extras these cards offer runs all the way from membership in an exclusive wine club to free medical insurance coverage when you travel outside Canada. If you really feel you'll make good use of these, fine. But be sure. After all, how often are you likely to want to make use of a 24-hour travel service?

The fact is that most of these cards are bought as a means of acquiring status. If you want to pay through the nose for the chance to impress a head waiter, you're welcome to it. Frankly, I can think of many better ways to use the money.

There are a few exceptions to this rule, though. Occasionally, a status card will offer a particular benefit or service that makes it worthwhile. Some, for example, charge substantially less interest on outstanding balances than regular cards. (As you'll see in a moment, I don't recommend carrying a credit card balance from month to month but if you insist on ignoring that advice, you should at least pay as little interest as possible.) Others, like the Royal Trust Gold MasterCard, offer a small discount on every purchase.

So don't completely ignore solicitations for premium cards. Read the conditions carefully. What you're trying to determine is whether the card will, all things considered, cost you money or pay you money. If you determine you'll come out ahead financially by using the card, then feel free to violate this rule with impunity.

Rule Three: Don't use your credit cards to finance purchases. If you don't pay off your balance in full every month, you're actually using them as a means to borrow money. That is an absolute no-no. If you need to borrow money, there are far less expensive ways to do it, which I'll discuss in the next chapter.

Even the banks, if pressed, will admit privately that carrying a credit card balance and paying interest on it makes no sense. They try not say it too loudly, though—after all, interest on credit card balances is one of their main revenue streams from these pieces of plastic.

Almost every financial advisor I know agrees that carrying a credit card balance is foolish. I read articles in newspapers and magazines all the time that repeatedly stress this point. And yet about half of the credit card holders in Canada do it—that's several million people. It's the single most common money management mistake people make.

Why do they do it? In part, because of the convenience factor—it's much easier to use a credit card to finance your purchases than it is to negotiate a bank loan. They may also feel the amount of interest they're paying isn't enough to get excited about. That's because they haven't done their math.

The spread between an ordinary loan and the interest rate on your credit card may be anywhere from 5% to 8%. This assumes you're using Visa or MasterCard, not one of the department store cards which charge such outrageously high interest it's a wonder they've escaped prosecution for loan-sharking.

If you carry a balance of $2,500 on your card, that means you're paying anywhere from $125 to $200 a year more in interest than you should be. That's too much money to be throwing away. If you're in that situation now, look for a way to reduce the interest charges on your credit card debt while you pay off the outstanding balance. Consolidating your outstanding balances in a bank loan or a personal line of credit (see the next chapter) is one possibility. Interest costs in either case should be much less than the card companies are charging. Another option is to switch the debt to a low-interest card. Canada Trust pioneered this field with their SuperCharge card, introduced in the fall of 1987. It's essentially a discount credit card, with interest charges substantially below those applied on an ordinary Visa or MasterCard. Whatever option you choose, make sure you don't add any more to your outstanding balance. Concentrate on paying it off as quickly as possible and take a solemn vow not to make the same mistake again. If you can't stick to it, cut up the rest of your cards. If you can't manage them properly, you shouldn't have them at all.

By the way, don't be surprised if you keep getting charged interest even after you've paid off your balance in full. Credit card issuers have some cute little tricks to keep you on the hook as long as possible. Here's a letter I received from a listener to one of my CBC radio broadcasts that explains how they manage this. This particular case involved a Bank of Montreal MasterCard.

"On November 29, I discovered I had missed making my payment, which was due on November 27," he wrote. "Realizing that I would incur interest charges, I decided to leave the payment until the next statement arrived, as previous experience had taught me that the interest was the same for two days or for thirty days.

"The following statement came with an interest charge of $16.09. Fair enough, I missed the payment, I pay the interest. I paid the outstanding balance and figured that was the end of the situation.

"Much to my surprise, on my January statement there was a further interest charge of $6.97.

"I feel that this second interest charge is excessive and unwarranted and until this amount is credited to my account I will not be using my Bank of Montreal MasterCard."

You can see this gentleman's point. He had paid off his account in full, he thought, yet he was still being charged interest. Unfortunately, those are the rules of the credit card game—not just for the Bank of Montreal's MasterCard but for most other cards as well.

When I called the Bank of Montreal about this complaint, they explained it this way: the interest charge on your statement is the amount you've incurred up to the date it was prepared. But the clock doesn't stop ticking while they wait for you to pay. They keep adding interest charges based on the average daily balance outstanding in your account until they receive full payment. That means that the faster you pay, the better off you'll be.

Let's look at another example. Suppose your last statement date was February 28 and you had interest charges on that bill. If you went to the bank of March 4th to pay off the full amount, you'd be charged interest for four extra days beyond the date showing on the statement. But if you waited until March 28, you'd find another full month's interest tacked on to your next bill—even though you thought you'd paid off the account in full.

The moral of this story is, if you're incurring credit card interest charges, pay off the bill as quickly as possible and stop the meter. Better still, don't put yourself in that spot. Pay off the entire balance every month, and make sure you don't miss a payment. That way you'll pay no interest at all, which is the key to good credit card management.

By not carrying a balance from month to month, you are, in effect, obtaining an interest-free loan from the credit card issuer each time you make a purchase. Obviously, it's a short-term loan—it lasts only from the day you make the purchase to the date it shows up on your statement and payment is required. But that can be as long as six weeks in certain circumstances. That means you have the use of the money during that time, without cost.

That interest-free period offers an opportunity to gain another small edge in your wealth-building program. If you use your credit cards frequently, as I do, it means you are constantly deferring payments on your purchases for four to six weeks. If your balances average $1,500 a month, it means you can hold that amount in a daily interest account, earning interest for you, while your credit card transactions are being processed. Assuming you spend about the same amount each month on credit card purchases, that amounts to a perpetual deferral of payment—you'll always have about $1,500 more in your bank account than you would have if you paid for everything by cash or cheque. If your financial institution is paying 5% interest, that would produce an extra $75 a year in investment income for you.

That's one reason why I use credit cards to make purchases whenever possible. My monthly credit card invoices are in the $2,000 to $2,500 range, which means I'm earning over $100 in additional interest this way. (The other reason I like cards is the ease by which I can keep track of family spending through the invoices.)

I add to my credit card related earnings by using a Royal Trust Gold MasterCard. I know, that sounds like I'm violating my own rules about status cards and user fees. But the 1% discount the Royal Trust card gives on all purchases is enough to pay for the costs associated with buying the card and provide me a very hefty profit as well. As a result, my credit cards are actually contributing to my monetary wealth, not subtracting from it. That's the objective you should be aiming for.

However, if you succeed, don't expect to be terribly popular with credit card issuers. They're in business to make money off the cards, not to subsidize aspiring wealth builders. So they're trying to come up with all sorts of devices to make it difficult, or even impossible, for us to use their cards for our own profit.

One such device is commonly known as the Debit Card. It looks like a credit card, it feels like a credit card, it even seems to act like a credit card when you buy something. But once the cashier punches in the transaction it does terrible things—like electronically whisking money out of your bank account at that very instant. So long, interest-free loan.

As I write this, the debit card is still in its experimental stages. But the financial institutions are solidly behind it and it may be just a matter of time before electronic payments take over from the credit card as the currency you use when you go shopping. At that point, you'll have to rethink your whole approach to cash management. Thankfully, we're not there yet.

While credit cards are still around, there's one other thing I should warn you about. Store owners don't particularly like people using credit cards. Since they have to pay a percentage to the card issuer, it cuts into their profit if you pay with plastic instead of cash.

Sometimes, they'll offer you a small discount to use cash or a cheque to pay. Their contracts with the card issuers say they're not supposed to do that but some do anyway. Other times, they'll use various ploys to talk you out of using your card.

My wife ran into that situation recently. After 20 years of faithful service, our clothes dryer passed away. We'd seen it coming for some time, as the service calls increased and the repair bills mounted. So my wife had already been shopping around and had a new one picked out. It was just a case of going in and placing the order.

So she went to the store and ordered the machine. It was a top-of-the-line model; with installation, the colour charge, and tax the whole thing came to $660.

When the bill had been made up, my wife offered her credit card as payment. Now this store prominently displayed signs saying it accepted all major cards. But the owner balked. He moaned and whined about the card. He complained that if my wife insisted on using it, it would cost him about $20 in fees and processing. His profit margins were so tight, that meant he'd be just about giving the dryer away. Groan. Snivel. Couldn't she write a cheque instead? It wouldn't cost us any more and he'd consider it a favour. Grovel.

So she agreed—as I'm sure a lot of you would. After all, we all hate to see a grown man cry.

When she got home that night and recounted this little episode to me, I blew my top over the store owner's behaviour. He had to know that every time he persuaded someone to go along with him on this, he was adding to his own profit at his customer's expense.

Here's how. To pay by cheque meant we had to withdraw $660 from our daily interest account six weeks earlier than we would have done had it been a credit card transaction. Given interest rates at that time, that would have worked out to about $4 in lost interest. On top of that, we lost the 1% discount from using the Royal Trust Gold MasterCard. That amounted to an additional $6.60.

Taking the two together, writing the merchant a cheque was adding over $10 to the cost of an already expensive dryer. The additional $20 he was making was more than half paid for out of my pocket!

Maybe that doesn't sound like such a big deal to you. But as I said at the outset, part of the wealth-building process is understanding how to manage money effectively. That means you don't throw away $10 bills for no reason.

I called the next morning and cancelled the deal. We went to another store which had the same dryer, ironically at a slightly cheaper price. And they didn't say a word when we offered the credit card as payment.

CHAPTER
12

Making Debt Work for You

D EBT IS THE Number One enemy of the wealth builder. It compromises your ability to save. It erodes your asset base. In extreme circumstances, it can even destroy you financially.

Debt is the Number One ally of the wealth builder. It allows you to become wealthy using other people's money. It accelerates the wealth-building process. In extreme circumstances, it can even make you a millionaire years before you ever dreamed possible.

How's that for two totally conflicting views of debt? Now I'll confuse you even more. Both of them can be true, depending on your circumstances.

I don't think there's any concept in the wealth-building process that's more misunderstood than the use of debt. Perhaps that's because most beginning wealth builders don't really understand what debt is all about. They tend to relate it to consumerism— the debts incurred by purchasing a car or new furniture, or by taking a vacation. They don't generally understand debt's relationship to building wealth.

That's what this chapter is all about—to help you distinguish between constructive and destructive debt and to understand how to use debt effectively in your wealth-building plan.

Let's start with the most destructive kind of debt. I call it Beginner Debt, because it's the kind of debt most frequently undertaken by younger people just starting out in life. It has four main characteristics:

1. It is incurred for consumption purposes. By that I mean the money has been borrowed to purchase goods or services, not for business or investing purposes.

2. It carries a high interest rate. This is because younger people usually start in lower paying jobs and have few assets, thus making them higher risks. A large proportion of this debt may be credit card related.

3. Servicing the debt requires a disproportionate share of the household income. In other words, it costs you more each month to meet the financing payments than you're comfortable with.

4. Interest on the debt is not tax deductible.

It's extremely easy to fall deeply into Beginner Debt and our society actively encourages people to do so. Financial institutions and retail outlets make credit available to almost anyone, literally for the asking. Our newspapers and television screens are cluttered with ads offering easy terms for big ticket items like appliances, electronic equipment, furniture and cars. It's all part of the Why-wait-when-you-can-have-it-now syndrome. It's easy, it's seductive. No wonder millions of people fall for it.

And what happens? The easy money debts pile up. Repaying them becomes an increasing financial drain on the household. There's no money left once the debts have been serviced and the necessities looked after. There's not even enough to go out to a movie occasionally; how in blazes are you supposed to start a savings program?

Debt like that is to be avoided at all costs. It undermines the wealth-building process and takes control of your financial destiny out of your hands. Stay away from it!

I know that's far easier said than done, especially when you're just starting to build a family household. I'm aware that I'm suggesting you make personal sacrifices—that you live with your old car or buy second-hand furniture or pass up a trip south next winter. And I know foregoing those comforts isn't pleasant.

But if you seriously want to build personal wealth—if you want to create an independent lifestyle for yourself while you're still young enough to enjoy it—then it is a sacrifice you have to make. There are no compromises on this one. If you load yourself down with Beginner Debt, you'll face years and years of struggle just to get out from under. And, as I've said before, those are the most precious years of all in the wealth-building process.

The rule is very simple: *Don't take on consumer debt under any circumstances.*

If you've already accumulated a consumer debt load by the time you read this, your number one priority should be to pay it off as quickly as possible. Above all, don't add to it.

Now, I recognize it's not always possible to avoid Beginner Debt. Hard times, such as the loss of a job, can create circumstances in which no other choice exists. Fair enough. But most Beginner Debt doesn't originate that way. It comes from societal pressures which encourage you to want too much too soon. Call it what you will: greed, ambition, aggressiveness. It all comes down to spending money you don't have in order to live better sooner. That's destructive debt, no matter how you look at it. The committed wealth builder will avoid it at all costs.

If that's destructive debt, what is constructive debt—the kind described in the second paragraph of this chapter? That's debt that is used to build wealth; debt incurred to acquire assets that are going to help you move ahead financially. I call this Investment Debt. Its main characteristics are:

1. The debt is incurred for investment or business reasons. You are borrowing money for the purpose of increasing your assets, with the objective of using the funds for personal profit. (I would consider a student loan to be Investment Debt—you are investing in yourself.)

2. The interest rate is competitive. This is because the assets you purchase with the funds from the loan can be held as collateral, thereby entitling you to a preferred interest rate.

3. The repayment program for the loan is manageable, and may be covered in part by profits from the investment.

4. Interest on the loan will often (but not always) be tax deductible.

The most common type of constructive debt is a mortgage. Very few of us can afford to pay cash for a new home. And if we saved until we could, house prices would keep moving ahead at such a pace that we could never catch up.

That's why a mortgage is a wise form of borrowing. It allows you to purchase an asset today that you couldn't otherwise afford—a family home. And that asset will increase in value as the loan you incurred to purchase it is paid off.

We've already dealt with mortgage management at some length, so I won't go into it again. Suffice to say that as long as you handle your mortgage intelligently, and pay it off as quickly as possible, it is an excellent way of using borrowed money to build wealth.

Another type of constructive debt is the loan you undertake to enable you to maximize your RRSP contribution. I'll deal with the importance of RRSPs in later chapters. The point I want to make here is that you should do everything possible to make your maximum allowable RRSP contribution each year. If that requires taking out a loan, do so. Just be sure to repay it as soon as possible, perhaps by using the income tax refund your RRSP contribution will generate.

Neither of these investment loans is tax deductible. The government used to give you a tax break on interest costs relating to RRSPs but unfortunately, that benefit was dropped several years ago.

Most other types of Investment Debt are tax deductible, though. As a general rule, the interest on money borrowed to acquire an income-producing asset, or one with a reasonable expectation of generating income within a certain time, would be considered tax deductible by Revenue Canada.

That means money borrowed to purchase such things as a rental property, Canada Savings Bonds, a stock portfolio, and mutual funds would usually be considered eligible for interest deductibility.

Funds borrowed for a summer cottage, home improvements, a new deck, and certain types of investments, such as commodities, would not qualify.

Your objective is to ensure that most or all of your debt beyond your mortgage and any short-term RRSP loans is tax deductible. If the government wants to help subsidize the cost of your wealth-building activities, why not let them?

At this point people often ask why they should borrow at all. Why go into debt if you don't have to?

Good question, and a natural one. Canadians, quite rightly, tend to be leery of debt. My mother-in-law's Scottish heritage— which many Canadians share—made her rebel at the very idea of owing money to anyone.

There's nothing wrong with that attitude, and certainly living debt-free may cause you to sleep better at night. But the reality is that well-managed debt can help immensely in the wealth-building process.

Let me illustrate. Let's say you're one of those people who refuses to get into debt for any reason, even if the risk seems low and the opportunity great. The country has just come through a period of economic turmoil, which pushed interest rates up to the mid-teens. Now conditions are stabilizing and it looks like interest rates have peaked and have started to turn down. It seems like a great opportunity to invest in Government of Canada bonds.

You've managed to put aside $10,000. You read in the paper the Government is about to go to the bond market with a new issue. The coupon rate is 14½%, the bonds have a 20-year maturity and they're priced at par. You think it's a great investment and invest your $10,000.

Sure enough, interest rates do fall. At the end of one year, the market value of your bonds has increased 15%. You sell. What's the result?

Sale price of bonds	$ 11,500
Interest for one year	1,450
Total proceeds	12,950
Profit	2,950
Return on $10,000 Investment	**29.5%**

Not bad at all. You can feel pretty proud of yourself.

Oh, by the way, I bought some of those bonds too. Like you, I only had $10,000 saved. But I borrowed another $40,000 at 16% interest, using the bonds as collateral. So my total investment was $50,000. I also sold out after one year. How did I do?

Sale price of bonds	$ 57,500
Interest for one year	7,250
Gross proceeds	64,750
Less after-tax interest on borrowed money (assumes 43.5% tax bracket)	3,616
Less repayment of loan principal	40,000
Net proceeds	21,134
Before-tax return on $10,000 investment	**111.3%**

Gosh, I guess I did a little better, even though we both started with the same amount of money. That's because I used other people's money to purchase more assets than I otherwise could have afforded. The technical term for that is *leveraging*, and it's the way you can make borrowed money work to build wealth for you.

Oh sure, you say. But suppose it hadn't worked out that way? Suppose the bonds had gone *down* 15% instead of up.

You're right. That's the danger in leveraging. You can use it to magnify your profits. But it will also increase your losses if you guess wrong. Let's see how great a risk I took.

First, let's look at what would have happened to you if bonds had gone down 15% and you'd sold after one year.

Sale price of bonds	$ 8,500
Interest for one year	1,450
Total proceeds	9,950
Loss	50
Loss on $10,000 investment	**0.5%**

You lost money on the deal, but not very much. The high coupon rate on the bonds limited your risk.

Now, what happened to me?

Sale price of bonds	$ 42,500
Interest for one year	7,250
Gross proceeds	49,750
Less after-tax interest on borrowed money	3,616
Less repayment of principal	40,000
Net proceeds	6,134
Loss	3,866
Loss on $10,000 investment	**38.7%**

I ended up losing more than a third of my investment while you virtually broke even. In effect, I put almost $4,000 at risk to make potential profit of over $11,000. You had virtually nothing at risk—but your profit was less than $3,000.

You might decide you'd be much more comfortable doing it your way—smaller profits for less risk. And there's nothing wrong with that approach, especially when the investment climate is uncertain.

But there are times when leveraging is the right move—the odds appear to be strongly in your favour, the upside potential is good, and the downside risk is manageable.

You're the one who has to decide when circumstances are right for you to take that chance. But you should certainly keep leveraging available as a possible investment option.

You should also be aware, however, that tax reform has made leveraging less attractive than it used to be. I'll explain why in Chapter Eighteen, so if you are considering borrowing to invest, be sure to read that first.

Let me stress one more thing at this point. Beginning wealth builders should be very cautious about borrowing to invest. Start with your mortgage and make it your first priority to reduce the principal substantially. Only when you have achieved that goal should you consider borrowing for other investment purposes. There are risks involved in using other people's money to invest that should not be undertaken until you've established a firm financial footing.

When the time comes that you do want to try leveraging, start small. The amount of risk you undertake by incurring Investment Debt is directly proportionate to the size of your loan. Begin with $1,000 or so, just to get the feel of leveraging and a practical understanding of how it works. There'll be plenty of time to do some high-rolling later, if that's what you want. Your first priority is to gain some experience in Investment Debt without putting yourself seriously at risk. If the first attempt works out well and you're comfortable with it, you can borrow a little more for the next project. Just remember to pay off the loans as you go along—don't allow them to accumulate to the point where you wake up some morning and discover you've created a debt mountain you can't handle.

That leads us to the question of where and how to borrow.

There are plenty of people who want to loan you money and there are many types of loans. The place to start is with your bank. They know you and the interest rates they charge will be competitive. Have a talk with the manager, explain your needs, and ask him or her to explain the options available.

When you go for the appointment, be sure to bring some basic financial information with you. The manager is going to want to know about such matters as your household income and your current debts. He or she will want a list of your current assets. Don't be concerned if your list isn't impressive; as long as you have a steady job, a decent salary, and a good credit record, you shouldn't have much difficulty. There will be questions about what you plan to do with the borrowed money and what collateral, if any, you intend to put up. You'll be asked for an estimate of how long it will take you to repay the loan.

What your banker is trying to find out is whether or not you're a good risk. Banks are especially careful about this these days— they've been hard hit by Third World loan defaults and they can't afford very many bad loans here at home. So expect a friendly grilling and don't be offended by it.

When the banker is done, it's your turn. Ask hard questions about the loan options available to you. Find out whether the interest rate is fixed or variable. Ask whether the bank has programs that offer better rates (sometimes they do but don't mention them until pressed). The banker's objective is to make sure you're a good risk; yours is to pay the bank the least amount possible in return for the use of their money.

Do not, under any circumstances, finalize any deal at the first meeting. Get all the details, then visit a few other financial institutions to see what they're offering. Don't overlook credit unions in your market survey; they sometimes have the most attractive deals around.

You may be surprised at the variations in loan plans between financial institutions. You can frequently save a lot of money in interest costs by taking the time to investigate.

Although there are numerous variations on the theme, you'll probably find yourself considering three borrowing alternatives once you've looked around.

1. *Some type of installment loan.* This will involve a fixed term and an agreed repayment schedule of blended principal and interest. The interest rate may be fixed for the duration of the loan, or it could be subject to review periodically. Interest charges on loans of this type are usually higher than on the other options you'll have.

2. *A demand loan.* It's exactly what it sounds like. There is no fixed repayment schedule but the financial institution can demand payment in full at any time. That rarely happens, but it's always a possibility you must be alert to. Demand loans are somewhat harder to obtain—you have to have collateral or be perceived as an excellent credit risk. The interest rate will be somewhat lower than on an installment loan, but will be variable and may change as frequently as every month.

3. *A personal line of credit (PLC).* These have become the hot way to borrow because of the convenience and flexibility they offer. You should look closely at this option before making a final decision.

PLCs have been around for a long time, but they used to be the preserve of the wealthy. Financial institutions only began to aggressively promote them to ordinary consumers in the mid-1980s. Since they're relatively new to most people, I'll devote some space to explaining them.

First, you must understand that not everyone can get a PLC. One banking official told me that only about one third of the people who qualify for a credit card would be eligible for a line of credit. You have to undergo a fairly intensive screening, but if you're credit worthy and have a steady job, chances are you'll qualify.

Why should you want one? Because they are just about the cheapest way, other than a mortgage, for the ordinary person to borrow money. And, as I've said repeatedly, when you borrow money your objective is to pay as little interest as possible.

A PLC is simply an authorization by a bank, trust company or credit union that allows you to borrow money from them in any amount, up to a predetermined limit. You don't have to make use of that borrowing power until you need it, and you're only charged interest on the amount you actually use.

For example, your bank may give you the authority to borrow up to $10,000 on a PLC. You pay nothing until you actually draw funds against the account. If you decide to borrow $2,000, you'll be charged interest on that amount and the credit balance available for your use will drop to $8,000.

Once you're approved for a PLC and your limit is established, a special cheque book will be issued to you. If you want to borrow, you simply use one of these cheques and it's done. No further authorizations are needed. Some financial institutions also allow you to access a PLC through a special credit card.

Once you've drawn on the PLC, you'll receive a monthly statement. This will show your outstanding balance, the amount of credit you have left, and the current interest rate being charged.

That interest rate can vary from month to month; be sure you stay aware of what you're paying and satisfy yourself that it's competitive.

The statement will also show you the minimum payment due that month—typically, it's 3% of the outstanding balance but that can vary from one financial institution to another. You can pay that amount, or more if you like. There's no penalty for paying off all or part of the outstanding balance at any time, which means you have a high degree of flexibility with this type of borrowing.

The interest rates on PLCs can vary widely among financial institutions, so you really need to spend a little time checking out alternatives before you commit to anything. Usually, however, you'll find the interest rates are low compared to other types of consumer loans. In fact, in some cases they won't be far off prime, which is the rate banks charge their best corporate borrowers. If you can get almost as good an interest rate as the folks with million-dollar loans, you aren't doing too badly.

Some financial institutions offer a choice between secured and unsecured PLCs. The secured loan offers the best rate, but you have to put up top quality collateral—CSBs, a good stock portfolio, GICs or something similar. The unsecured PLC won't offer as good a break on interest rates, but you should still find it better than other types of consumer loans.

One variation on the PLC which started attracting a lot of attention in 1986-87 was the home equity line of credit. This offshoot of the PLC allows people with substantial equity in their home—those who followed my earlier advice about paying down the mortgage—to tap into those funds for investment purposes.

The home equity line of credit is really a cross between a regular PLC and a mortgage. It permits you to turn the equity in your home into usable cash as you need it, without tying yourself to a rigid repayment schedule.

If you're not quite sure just what equity you have in your home, call in a real estate agent and ask what price it would be listed for if you decided to sell. From that estimate, subtract the outstanding balance due on your mortgage. The difference gives you a good idea of your equity.

If you've owned a house for some time and/or live in a real estate market that's been hot in recent years, you may be surprised to find just how much idle cash is sitting in your house. That doesn't mean you should rush right out and spend it. I repeat, debt of any kind is not something you undertake lightly. Furthermore, home equity lines of credit have some hefty costs attached to them. But if you're at a stage when incurring some Investment Debt seems like a smart move, this is certainly an option to consider.

The main drawback to these loans is the upfront cost. You are actually putting another mortgage on your property, which means you'll end up several hundred dollars out of pocket once all the appraisal and legal fees are paid. The only consolation is that's a one-time charge. Once the home equity line of credit is established, it's in place for as long as you want it.

The borrowing power available to you through one of these loans is immense—probably far more than you'll ever want or need. Typically, a lender will grant you a home equity line of credit of two-thirds the appraised value of your property, less any outstanding mortgage. So let's assume you have a home that's worth $125,000, with a first mortgage that still has $45,000 owing. The equity in the home is therefore $80,000. The lender will give you a line of credit for two-thirds of that amount— which means you have over $53,000 in borrowing power to make use of.

The danger, of course, is that you'll get carried away and use that money unwisely. Here's where self-discipline is important. Use that money for wealth-building purposes and it can help make you rich. Use it to travel around the world and you'll end up with a big chunk of consumer debt that will take a long time to pay off.

Home equity lines of credit are about as inexpensive a way to borrow as you're going to find. In most cases, the interest rate is tied to prime—it may actually be the prime rate, or slightly above. However, as with PLCs, the interest rate can vary from month to month. If there's a sudden run-up in rates, you could find yourself paying much higher interest charges than you had anticipated.

As far as repayments go, these are the ultimate in flexibility. Most of them allow you to pay interest only if you wish—no reduction in the principal is required. That means you can carry an outstanding balance for as long as you want, and pay it off at any time. That's especially useful if you're using the money to invest in something that doesn't pay regular income—perhaps a stock. You don't have to pay off the principal on your loan until such time as you sell the asset and (you hope) take a profit. At that stage you can pay off the loan and pocket the rest. Of course, your home equity line of credit remains open, ready for the next time you want to use it.

Let me say it one final time. Borrowing to buy consumer items is something you *never* do. Borrowing to invest is something you undertake at the right time *with caution*. Use debt to build your wealth, not to destroy it, and you'll have mastered one of the key techniques of financial success.

RRSPs – The Second Key to Wealth

W HILE I WAS supervising the revision of Hume Publishing's "Successful Investing & Money Management" course, the question of a new title for the lesson on Registered Retirement Savings Plans came up. Many people tend to think of RRSPs as boring; we wanted a title that would grab attention and motivate students to study the lesson carefully. In short, we wanted a single phrase that would capsulize the incredible wealth-building power of this investment form.

The title we finally chose was "The Million Dollar Money Machine." I liked it then and I still do. It may sound like hyperbole, but let me assure you it isn't. A Registered Retirement Savings Plan can in fact make you a millionaire, if you start contributing early enough and make regular payments.

Let me hasten to clarify one point. By the time your RRSP has a million dollars in it, a million won't buy as much as it will today. Inflation will take its toll on purchasing power and that can add up over the years. But your RRSP million will still be worth plenty—and you'll accumulate it much more quickly than you're likely to do any other way.

I'm so sold on the wealth-building potential of RRSPs that I regard them as one of the two cornerstones of personal financial success—the other being the family home. In fact, I believe you should pay off your mortgage and maximize your RRSP contributions before you consider any other form of investment.

According to a recent survey, about one-third of Canadians have an RRSP. The percentage among people I talk to in seminars and workshops seems to be even higher than that. Clearly, many of us are aware of the existence of RRSPs and have taken steps to set up one or more.

Too many Canadians still haven't discovered how valuable these plans can be, however. The head of a major tax preparation firm told me recently that they see hundreds of people each year who don't even know what a Registered Retirement Savings Plan is. I'm sure few readers of this book would fall into that group but just in case, a Registered Retirement Savings Plan is a government-approved program which permits you to deduct your contributions from taxable income (up to certain limits) and allows investment income within the plan to accumulate tax-free. Funds withdrawn from an RRSP are treated as ordinary income in the year you take them out.

The problem I often find with many RRSP holders is that they don't understand the potential of these plans. They tend to regard them purely as retirement insurance—something that will generate a little extra income for the sunset years to supplement a company pension and the Old Age Security and Canada Pension Plan payments. This attitude leads to sloppy use of RRSPs, especially when you're younger and retirement seems many years off. Contributions are made on a haphazard basis, depending on whether or not spare funds are available. Management of the money already in an RRSP is frequently non-existent. Those funds are treated almost as if they were Monopoly money. It's a sort of "The money's locked away so it isn't real" approach.

If you're one of those people, then it's time to wake up. Not only is that RRSP money real; it can be used in dozens of imaginative ways to build your wealth quickly. And the money is *not* locked in until you retire. You can draw it out any time you want—just be certain you take the tax consequences into account when you do so.

Let me give you an example of just how much wealth potential exists in your RRSP. One night after a curling game, I was having drinks with some friends and the subject of RRSPs came up. I'd been doing some research on the subject at the time, so I tossed out a Trivial Pursuit type question for discussion.

I asked my friends to assume they had a relative who was 24 years old. This person was not a member of a company pension plan and his earned income allowed for a maximum RRSP contribution of $4,800. I told them to assume this relative contributed the same amount every year until age 71—the last year you can contribute to an RRSP. That would mean 47 years of contributions, which would mean he'd put $225,600 into the plan over his lifetime. I also told them to assume he was a good money manager and was able to average a 15% annual return on his investments over that time. How much, I asked, would the RRSP contain when he was 71?

I could hear the mental wheels clicking all around the table. Finally, one woman suggested the RRSP might contain as much as one million dollars. Someone else guessed $1.5 million. Then another lady went way, way out on limb and offered a guess of $5 million. She was quickly pooh-poohed by the rest of group.

As it turned out, she was closest to the mark—although her guess was way off. At age 71, the amount in the RRSP I described would be—if you're reading this book standing up, you'd better sit down. The total would work out to $26,184,018.94. I know it's unbelievable—over $26 million in an RRSP. That's more than 100 times the value of his contributions to the plan. I couldn't accept it when I first saw the number, and even after I worked through the whole calculation I still thought it was a mistake. I had to get a financial expert to confirm it for me.

As you can imagine, that caused quite a sensation around the table. People don't realize how dollars can multiply in an RRSP until they're confronted with numbers like that.

To be fair, you have to be an excellent money manager—and very lucky—to average a 15% return on investments over 47 years. But even at a more realistic 12%, you'd still build up $9 million in assets during that time. And keep in mind the maximum contribution allowed is substantially more than $4,800 a year.

Of course, as I've already pointed out, $26 million won't have anything like the buying power half-a-century from now that it does today. The higher the average inflation rate during that time, the more the value of your money will be eroded. But even if inflation were to average 10% a year—an unacceptably high rate over a sustained period—that RRSP money would purchase an annuity worth about $4,000 a month in today's dollars.

So why aren't we all going to be millionaires somewhere down the road? To start with, some of us just don't have enough years left until retirement—although even if you're in your fifties when you start, you can still build a comfortable nest egg. As for younger people, many don't have the extra cash to sock away in an RRSP—just maintaining a household is all they can manage. And, finally, too many people with RRSPs don't pay proper attention to them.

Why do RRSPs build wealth so effectively? Two reasons.

First, the tax deduction created by RRSP contributions allows you to put more money to work sooner than you might otherwise be able to. It's a form of leveraging if you like, except in this case you're not borrowing the money—the government is *giving* it to you.

Suppose you're in the middle tax bracket, with a marginal federal tax rate of 26%. If your provincial tax rate is 50% of the federal rate, you pay a combined rate of 39% on your last dollar earned.

Let's say you're allowed a maximum RRSP contribution of $4,000 this year. That generates a tax refund of $1,560—which means that your out-of-pocket cost for contributing to the RRSP is only $2,440. But you have the full $4,000 working for you inside the plan. The government has put up the difference.

That's why it pays to borrow to make up any shortfall in your RRSP contribution. Suppose you don't have enough money put aside in a given year to make the full contribution to which you're entitled. Borrow the balance for a few months, and pay off the loan with the tax refund. That way you've got more money working on your behalf—and a larger government subsidy than you would have received had you only contributed the amount you'd saved.

The second reason RRSPs work so effectively is that all the investment income earned inside the plan is tax sheltered. The government doesn't get a nickel of it until you draw it out.

It's those tax-free earnings that allow the RRSP to grow so rapidly. All the interest and dividends you earn outside a plan are heavily taxed, as are any capital gains over the $100,000 lifetime exemption. But inside a plan, the money that would otherwise go to the government in taxes instead works on your behalf.

Let me give you an example of how important that is. Again, we'll assume you're in the 39% tax bracket. Let's see how the same investment—a five-year $10,000 GIC at 10% compound interest—would fare inside and outside an RRSP. I've assumed here that the tax owed on the GIC outside the RRSP would be paid separately each year and would not be deducted from the combined principal and interest on which the compounding would be calculated.

	Tax rate	Total tax paid	Value after 5 years	After-tax return (Net of tax)
Inside RRSP	0	0	$16,105.10	$ 6,105.10
Outside RRSP	39%	$ 2,380.95	$13,724.15	$ 3,724.15

As you can see, the after-tax return is over 60% higher inside the RRSP. It doesn't take much imagination to see how those numbers will magnify over many years, especially when increasingly larger amounts of money are involved.

RRSPs are really the last great tax shelter in Canada—and the only one that can be easily used by everyone. With the advent of tax credits, RRSPs are also one of the few ways higher income people can obtain a full tax benefit. Your contributions continue to be deducted from taxable income, not converted into credits at a lower percentage than your marginal tax rate. (Canada Pension Plan contributions, for instance, are converted to tax credits at a

17% rate. This means taxpayers in the 26% and 29% brackets don't receive full tax relief for their contributions.)

By now, I hope you're convinced of the value of using RRSPs to build wealth. The next step is to take a careful look at how much you're allowed to contribute so that you can start a savings program that will enable you to put in the full amount allowable each year.

There's been a great deal of confusion about RRSP contribution limits in recent years. The federal government, while remaining fully committed to the concept of RRSPs, has changed courses several times on the contribution limits that will be allowed to taxpayers. The program discussed here is the one that emerged from the tax reform proposals of June 1987. Although I hope this is the final version, there's no guarantee the government won't change its mind again, so you should be aware of any new developments in this area.

Your RRSP contribution limits will be significantly affected by whether or not you belong to a pension plan. If you don't, your life is relatively uncomplicated. For the 1988 tax year *only* you will be allowed to contribute 20% of your earned income to an RRSP, up to a maximum of $7,500. (Earned income includes salary, income from your own business, and certain special payments, such as retiring allowances and alimony and maintenance. It does not include investment income.)

After 1988, the rules change. Starting January 1, 1989, the maximum percentage contribution will drop to 18% of earned income. However, the maximum dollar contribution levels will increase on the following timetable:

Year	RRSP Limit
1989	$ 8,500
1990	10,500
1991	11,500
1992	12,500
1993	13,500
1994	14,500
1995	15,500

After 1995, the maximum contribution limits will be indexed to average wage increases.

If you belong to a pension plan and make regular contributions, things won't be as simple. For 1988, you'll be allowed to put 20% of your earnings into an RRSP, *less* whatever you've contributed to your pension plan. Total for the two cannot exceed $3,500.

For example, suppose your salary is $30,000 and you contribute 5% of that to a company pension plan. That works out to $1,500 a year. That leaves you $2,000 you can tuck away in an RRSP in 1988.

In 1989 that relatively simple calculation disappears, as pensions and RRSPs are more tightly integrated. The new system will be so complex that it will no longer be possible for pension plan members to calculate their own RRSP contribution limits. Revenue Canada is going to have to do it. You'll get a notice from them each fall, telling you what you can contribute. That number is going to be calculated by taking the total of all pension contributions made the previous year by you and your employer and then applying what's called a pension adjustment (PA for short). I won't even attempt to explain how that's arrived at except to say that the better your pension plan benefits, the less you'll be allowed to contribute to an RRSP once the PA is factored in. It's hard to believe the federal government would create a system so totally beyond the comprehension of most Canadians, but that is what's going to happen unless someone wises up before it's too late.

The 1989 tax year will also see the introduction of the long-awaited carry-forward provisions for RRSP contributions. After that, you won't be penalized if you cannot make your maximum allowable RRSP contribution in any given year. You'll be able to carry forward the unused contribution for up to seven years— which should certainly allow you adequate time to raise the money.

Those carry-forward provisions will allow for a great many new financial strategies after 1989. For instance, a young couple who has just taken on a mortgage can devote a higher proportion of income to reducing the debt in the early years, when it's most important, while still retaining their RRSP contribution entitlements for later use. A freelancer or a commission salesperson, with an up and down income can decide not to contribute to an RRSP in lean years but save the entitlement until her income— and therefore her tax bracket—is higher. That way, she gets more tax savings for her contributions.

Now that you know all the advantages and the rules governing RRSPs, the next step is to decide what kind of plan to choose. Your watchword here is caution. The RRSP market has become highly competitive; everyone out there wants your business. Don't be distracted by all the shrill claims that you'll see in the ads. They may well be true—some RRSP programs have produced amazing returns. But, generally speaking, the larger the potential return, the higher the degree of risk. If you're just starting out, you're better to adopt a more conservative approach. Choose a plan that offers a solid, guaranteed return on your money and let the magic of compound interest go to work for you. You can diversify into other types of investments later, but begin with a solid cornerstone.

There are so many types of RRSPs available that it's almost impossible to keep track. The main ones are:

Savings-type plans: These function very much like savings accounts. They're safe, but the interest rates are extremely low. You should never put your money into this type of RRSP; it would take forever for the million-dollar money machine to work.

Mutual fund plans: These invest your money in stocks, bonds, real estate, precious metals, etc., depending on the type of plan. I'll discuss them in greater depth in a later chapter.

Self-directed plans: These allow you to do your own managing and choose your own investments. I think everyone should have one; I'll explain why in the next chapter.

Guaranteed investment plans: These would typically invest your funds in Guaranteed Investment Certificates of varying maturities. This is a good alternative for the beginning RRSP wealth builder, combining safety with a reasonable return. The higher interest rates are when you open a plan, the more attractive it is. Just be careful not to lock in for too long if it appears interest rates are on the rise.

Just about every type of financial institution you can think of offers one or more of these plans—banks, trust companies, credit unions, stockbrokers, life insurance companies. Just walk in and tell the first person you see you want RRSP information. They'll quickly point you in the right direction.

Finally, I want to end this chapter by discussing one of the questions I'm asked most frequently by beginning wealth builders—is it better to put money into an RRSP or to pay down the mortgage, if you can only do one?

It's not an easy question to answer. Both are excellent ways to use your money. Both are essential to the wealth-building process. Which is the better route at any given time is going to depend to a large degree on your personal situation: your age, tax bracket, the interest rate on your mortgage.

However, here are some things to consider in making the decision:

1. The longer your mortgage has to run, the more the scales tip towards reducing the principal. As we've already seen, any reduction in principal in the early years has a tremendous impact on the total amount of interest you pay over the life of a mortgage.

If you have a $50,000 mortgage at 11% that you've just incurred and you make a $5,000 payment against it while keeping the monthly payments the same, you'll clip eight years off the original 25-year amortization period. That will save you over $41,000 in interest costs over the life of the mortgage—tax-free money in your pocket.

2. The higher your tax bracket, the more the balance shifts in favour of the RRSP. That's because the government is subsidizing your contribution to a greater degree. If you're in the 29% federal tax bracket and your provincial rate is 50% of the federal tax, the government will pick up the tab for 43.5¢ of every RRSP dollar you contribute.

Let's say you have $5,000 available and you're not sure what to do with it. If you put it into your RRSP, and you're in the top tax bracket, you'll get a tax refund of $2,175. Let's say you toss that back into the RRSP as well, so you've got $7,175 working for you. If you could average 10% a year on that money, you'd have just over $36,000 in the plan after 17 years.

In this situation, paying down the mortgage in the way I described in the previous example looks like the better choice. But you'll have to do your own calculations to see if your circumstances would produce a different result.

Very often you'll find that the older you are, the more frequently the RRSP is the logical choice. That's because older people are usually better established in their jobs and occupy more senior, better paying positions which put them into higher tax brackets. They've also tended to own their home for a longer period, which means the mortgage has fewer years to run, so the impact on interest saved isn't as great.

If you're like me and would prefer not to put all your eggs in one basket, consider this option: contribute the maximum allowable amount to your RRSP and then use the tax refund that's generated as a result to pay down the mortgage. Try that for several years and you'll find yourself with a mortgage-free home *and* a nice retirement fund.

If you went that route using the examples we've just discussed, you'd contribute $2,175 towards reducing the mortgage principal. That way you'd pay off the house in about 21 years instead of 25, and save over $21,000 in interest. Over that time, the $5,000 in your RRSP would have grown to about $37,000. So, all told, you'd be $58,000 ahead of where you would have been if you'd blown the $5,000 on a trip to Florida. Not a bad return — and certainly worth the initial sacrifice.

Personalizing Your RRSP

W HEN I FIRST began putting money into RRSPs, I fell into a trap—one which, it turns out, is fairly common. Since the government allows you to have as many RRSP accounts as you want, I deposited money in a variety of institutions and invest-ment vehicles. I was looking for diversification. What I got was confusion.

After a few years I had so many different RRSPs that I couldn't keep track of them, much less monitor their perform-ance intelligently. Furthermore, I didn't seem to be gaining any financial ground—the combined value of the plans wasn't in-creasing at the rate I thought it should. Looking back, I realize I had no clear investment objectives at that stage. I was simply choosing whatever plans seemed most convenient or had the strongest advertising appeal.

At that point, it occurred to me that maybe having multiple RRSP accounts wasn't such a hot idea. It took a heck of a lot of paperwork, and some incredible frustration, but I finally man-aged to reduce my RRSPs to two plans (I'll explain later why I have two instead of just one). Both those plans are self-directed. As far as I'm concerned, that's the *only* type of RRSP a truly dedicated wealth builder should have.

That's true even if you're just starting out. You'll frequent-ly read articles suggesting that self-directed plans (or self-administered, as they're sometimes called) are for sophisticated investors only. If you don't have at least $25,000 in your RRSP and a thorough knowledge of investing techniques, you shouldn't be in them.

Hogwash! A self-directed RRSP is as complex or as simple as you choose to make it. It can hold investments as easy to understand as Canada Savings Bonds or as complicated as covered call options. You can spend as much as a couple of hours a week looking after it or as little as an hour a month.

In short, self-directed plans give you the ultimate flexibility in the management of your RRSP money. They enable you to move quickly to take advantage of opportunities. And they allow you to diversify your RRSP holdings to a degree that is simply not possible with off-the-shelf plans. One other important consideration: running your own self-directed plan will give you hands-on experience in managing your own investments. You won't be giving your funds to other people and asking them to make decisions on your behalf; you'll be making those decisions yourself. They won't always be the right ones, of course, and you'll undoubtedly lose some money along the way because of bad calls. When that happens, learn from the experience. Spend some time analyzing what went wrong and deciding whether the loss could have been prevented. And remember—the pros don't get it right every time either.

That kind of investment management is an essential apprenticeship to the art of wealth building and the earlier in life you can experience it, the better. The problem is that most people starting out don't have the money to set up an investment portfolio. Anything extra goes towards payments on a house or into an RRSP.

That's why it's important to use the RRSP funds to gain money management experience. It may be the only opportunity you'll have to hone your investing skills for many years.

Now, some people might say this advice is stupid—that it will encourage inexperienced people to gamble with their retirement savings, something which is an absolute no-no. I disagree. I think the experience gained will be far more important to you in the long run than any small losses you may incur. Investing is like anything else in life—there is nothing, absolutely nothing, that can teach you more quickly than doing it yourself.

There are some cautions, though. First, don't put your RRSP money into any investment you don't completely understand. Go back and review what I said in Chapter Two about the importance of knowing exactly what you're putting your money into, and why you're doing it. Second, keep your RRSP investments diversified. Never put yourself in a position where one particular investment is exposing a large percentage of your RRSP assets to potential loss. Third, finish reading this book before you start — and be sure you thoroughly understand the investing guidelines you find in it.

If you follow those instructions, you should be able to manage a self-directed RRSP with no difficulty. And, if you're truly interested in wealth building, you'll have a lot of fun in the process.

How do you go about setting up a self-directed plan? With great care. Many financial institutions now offer plans of this type. Some are excellent, some are mediocre, some are downright poor. Here are some of the things to look for when you're shopping for a self-directed plan.

Cost

The fees involved in having your own self-directed RRSP can vary considerably. Some financial institutions charge rates that are so high as to be prohibitive. These are usually based on a percentage of the market value of all the securities in your plan. That percentage may appear small — perhaps only three-quarters of a percent. But it can add up to outrageous costs as the value of your plan builds. On a $30,000 plan, a fee structured that way would cost you $225 a year. By the time you've hit $50,000 — and, as you've seen, you can get there surprisingly quickly — the fee is up to $375. That's far too much to pay. Avoid these plans at all costs!

Also beware of self-directed plans that charge transaction fees, opening fees, closing fees, or similar add-on costs. What you want is a plan that charges one low basic fee which covers everything. There are lots of them around so you shouldn't have any difficulty finding one.

It was the brokerage industry that took the lead in making self-directed plans available at low cost. Many brokers set up their own programs by making special arrangements with trust companies, which actually hold the securities and administer the plan. This bulk buying enabled stockbrokers to introduce their own brand name self-directed RRSPs and market them to clients for $100 a year or less. The broker's profit doesn't come from that low fee, of course. It comes from the commissions generated every time you do a transaction in the account.

The problem with setting up an account through a broker is that you become a captive client. Every transaction you make in the plan has to be through that brokerage house. That's a bind. It means you may not get the best deal on Treasury bills, or that you might miss out on a new bond or stock issue because your brokerage firm isn't involved in the distribution. That can mean lost profit opportunities.

You're better off setting up a completely independent plan. You can still designate a broker to trade for you in such a plan—but you're not limited to that particular firm. Many trust companies have introduced low-cost self-directed plans of their own; a few phone calls should turn up at least one or two that charge a straight annual fee of $125 or less.

One important tax point here. Administration charges for your RRSP are tax-deductible—but only if they're paid for outside the plan. Every year you'll receive an invoice from your plan's trustee, stating that the fee must be paid by a certain date or the money will be deducted from the cash balance in your RRSP. Be sure you send in your cheque by the deadline! If you don't, the money will come out of your RRSP and you'll lose the benefit of the tax write-off.

REPORTING
One of the elements most frequently overlooked by people setting up their first self-directed RRSP is the frequency and quality of the reports you receive. If you're going to manage your RRSP funds effectively, then accurate, up-to-date information is absolutely essential. If you don't have it, you can run into real trouble.

Once you've identified a few financial institutions that offer low-cost self-directed plans, ask about their reporting policies. If you won't receive updates at least quarterly, look elsewhere. Monthly reports are best, although it may be difficult to find a low-cost plan (apart from a broker's plan) that offers them.

It's worth the effort, though. Both my plans provide me with an itemized statement every month, showing a complete inventory of my holdings. They also provide a summary of all the transactions made during the month as well as any dividend and interest payments received. And of course, there's an updated cash balance which shows me what funds I have available for new purchases. In short, I have all the information I need to make decisions.

In your search, you may find some companies that issue reports only twice a year but will do so more frequently for an additional fee. At the time of writing, Royal Trust had this policy; any reports beyond two cost $15 each. It may be worthwhile choosing a plan with a low basic fee and this additional report privilege; that way you can select a reporting schedule that meets both your monitoring needs and your pocket book.

Before you sign the papers, ask to see a sample report. Check that it covers all the points I mentioned above. Satisfy yourself that it's easy to read and that you understand all the entries.

While we're on the subject of reports, there's a point I must make—and it's so important I'm spelling it out in capital letters. ALWAYS REVIEW YOUR STATEMENTS AND MAKE SURE THEY'RE CORRECT. You wouldn't believe how often RRSP reports are fouled up, or how serious that can be.

A few years ago, I was reviewing one of my statements and discovered 200 shares of Gulf Oil stock had vanished since the previous month. The stock hadn't been sold, transferred, or anything else. It was just gone.

I called the trust company and drew their attention to it. The following month, the stock was still missing. At this point I got mad and spoke to one of the firm's vice-presidents. He looked into it and called me back the next day. Yes, I was correct. It was a clerical error—a junior clerk had inadvertently deleted the shares from my account. They would be back next month.

Of course, the error would have been discovered sooner or later, I asked. Wouldn't it? In the annual audit perhaps. Well, maybe not, he admitted. It turned out that this particular financial institution did only spot audits of self-directed RRSP accounts. If my account wasn't on the list, this particular error might not have turned up if I hadn't called it to their attention.

That really frightened me. The Gulf stock represented an investment of about $5,000 at that time. Can you imagine losing that amount of money because of a computing error? Some trainee presses the wrong key and your shares vanish! And yet, that's what might have happened if I hadn't carefully checked my account.

The securities in your self-directed RRSP are held in what's known as street form. That allows you to trade them quickly and easily, without the bother of having to sign them over when you want to sell. But holding them in street form means they are not registered in your name. There is no record, other than your confirmation slips and your monthly report, that you own them. So if they disappear from the computer screen, they could disappear totally. Scary, isn't it?

I'm devoting a lot of space to this because the Gulf incident was not an isolated one. I've had other people's dividends incorrectly credited to my RRSP. I've also not been properly credited with dividends I should have received. There has been at least one other occasion when some assets have vanished into computer limbo.

The message should, by now, be very clear. Make absolutely certain the reports you receive are accurate. And raise hell immediately if they're not.

DISCOUNT SERVICES

If you're a beginning investor, you shouldn't be using a discount broker for your RRSP account. Although discount brokerage houses are much cheaper, they're simply order takers. You have to make all the decisions; they simply execute them. You're better off paying a higher commission and obtaining advice and recommendations from a full-service broker—assuming you have a good one, of course. I'll deal with the whole question of brokers in more detail in a later chapter.

There are situations, however, when you know exactly what you want to do and why. You don't need the help of a full-service broker and you'd like to save some money on commissions.

Some financial institutions with self-directed RRSPs now offer special discount brokerage services to clients in this situation. Sometimes there is a nominal annual charge for the service, but it will be more than paid for by your commission savings. When you're shopping for a self-directed plan, ask whether this type of service is offered. You may not make much use of it at the outset, but it could be an important option as your plan grows and you trade securities more frequently.

Once you've found the right self-directed plan, the next question you face is what to put in it. You may be surprised at the number of choices you have. The financial institution you're dealing with should be able to provide you with a complete list of RRSP eligible investments. But the most important ones are shares in Canadian companies (including private firms), bonds, mutual funds, GICs, TDs, cash, and mortgages (including your own). While most of the securities must be Canadian, you are permitted to hold foreign securities worth up to 10% of the plan's value. You are not permitted to hold gold and precious metals directly, although gold shares and units in a precious metals mutual fund are okay. Also not permitted are commodity futures and collectibles such as art and antiques.

What you put in depends on how aggressive you are and the extent of your investment knowledge. You may decide to hold nothing more than Canada Savings Bonds and GICs at the outset. Or you may want to take on greater risk by purchasing strip bonds or mutual funds.

There is some debate over whether stocks are appropriate for RRSPs. One school of thought is firmly against including them, for two reasons. First, they're too risky for a retirement plan. This is the money you're putting aside for your old age, the argument runs; it shouldn't be in anything as volatile as stocks. Think what would have happened if all your RRSP holdings had been in stocks when the world markets crashed on October 19, 1987. Second, you lose the tax breaks inherent in stocks by putting them into a retirement plan. The dividend tax credit can't be claimed when the dividends are paid into an RRSP. And capital gains aren't subject to the $100,000 lifetime exemption or to the favourable tax treatment that applies when you exceed that limit.

But wait a minute, you may say. If they're inside an RRSP, dividends and capital gains aren't taxed at all. What's the issue here?

The argument is that those profits will be taxed when the funds are drawn out—and at your marginal rate (which is simply the tax bracket you're in). That means you'll end up paying more tax than you would have had the stocks been held outside the RRSP.

I don't buy that thinking. To begin with, I come at RRSPs from a different perspective. I don't regard them simply as a means to save for old age. I see them as a wonderful tax sheltered opportunity to create personal wealth. On that basis, I believe in maximizing the investment potential of my RRSPs—and that means buying stocks when the conditions are right. People who held all their assets in interest-bearing vehicles during the great bull market of the mid 1980s realized a modest return on their money. But that was nothing compared to the gains enjoyed by those of us who invested at least part of the RRSP portfolio in the stock market. Even the October 19 collapse didn't wipe out all those gains, bad as it was.

Understand me well. I am not suggesting you should be reckless with your money, quite the contrary. As I said at the outset of this book, I'm a conservative by nature. I don't believe in taking undue risk or in throwing my money away on bad securities. I *do*, however, believe in using the wealth-building power of the RRSP to its fullest.

As for the tax argument, I suggest there's another side to it. Yes, you might have to pay tax at a higher rate down the road on your dividends and capital gains. But in the meantime you have the use of that deferred tax money to reinvest and add to your wealth.

Let's suppose you purchased 100 shares of a stock for $30 each. Ignoring the commissions, your investment was $3,000. You held the stock for a year, during which you received $120 in dividends. At the end of that time, you sold the stock for $4,500. Your total profit would be $1,620, of which $1,500 is capital gain.

Inside the RRSP, there's no tax collectable on that. The profit can be reinvested and continue to grow.

Outside the RRSP, both the dividends and the capital gain are subject to tax. Let's assume you're in the top tax bracket and that you've used your capital gains exemption. The tax payable on the dividends will be about $37, depending on which province you live in. The tax payable on the capital gains will depend on the year in which all this happens. Let's say it's 1990, because that's the year the federal government's plan to require you to declare 75% of capital gains as ordinary income takes effect. Your tax liability on the capital gains will be about $515. All told, that means you'll have to hand over about $552 to the government. That money is no longer available for you to reinvest.

Suppose you planned to keep building your RRSP assets for another 15 years. If you were able to invest that $552 so that it grew at the rate of 10% a year, what do you think it would be worth at the end of that time? Just over $2,300—money you wouldn't have if that $552 had gone to the tax department years before. If you're paying tax at a rate of 43.5%, when you withdraw the $2,300 from the plan, you'll be hit for about $1,000. But you'll be left with $1,300 you would not otherwise have possessed—bonus money if you like. That's why I don't buy the tax argument.

One other point. The experts who tell you not to put stocks into an RRSP aren't saying stay out of the market entirely. They just want you to build an equity portfolio outside your plan, not in it. That's all well and good—if you can afford a second major investment portfolio. Most beginning wealth builders can't. It's a case of stocks in the RRSP or no stocks at all. You know which course I suggest.

What are the dangers in a self-directed plan? You're the main one. Don't get carried away and be tempted to venture beyond your depth. If you stick with what you know, you'll be all right.

Failure of the financial institution operating the plan is another concern, especially if you've opted for one of the smaller trust companies. But the Canada Deposit Insurance Corporation protects you for up to $60,000 for investments that would be covered if they were outside an RRSP. That includes such things as cash deposits and GICs. Other assets, such as stocks and bonds, are held for you in trust. They shouldn't be in any danger in the event of a financial collapse, unless criminal misappropriation has taken place.

So now you've got your self-directed plan and, I hope, some ideas of what you're going to put in it. In the next chapter, I'll discuss techniques you can use to make that money grow in a hurry.

Oh yes, I almost forgot. I said at the beginning of this chapter I'd explain why I kept two self-directed plans instead of one. It's to test investing strategies. One plan is very conservative in its investment approach. The other one takes more risk. I then compare results and see which approach seems to work better. So far the higher-risk portfolio has a slight edge.

Building Wealth in Your RRSP

O NE DAY A FRIEND came to me with a real dilemma. His wife had some money in an RRSP which had originally been put into a Guaranteed Investment Certificate. The certificate was about to mature and the trust company was asking for instructions on how to reinvest the funds.

Along with this notification, my friend received a list of RRSP investment options offered by that particular trust firm. There were 13 of them! This couple knew a little something about money but my friend frankly admitted they were at a loss. They didn't have any idea which of those 13 options was the right one for them—or, indeed, if any of them was.

A lot of people are in exactly that situation—maybe you're one of them. There are so many RRSP alternatives available today that trying to choose between them can induce mental paralysis. Everyone claims they have the best vehicle. How do you know whom to believe?

The answer is, you don't. If you're going to invest your RRSP money wisely, and maximize its wealth-building potential, you have to take the time to look beyond the advertising claims. You have to determine what investment alternatives really have the best track record. And you have to look to the future because, as mutual fund salespeople are obliged to constantly point out, past performance is no guarantee of future results. You have to take stock of what's happening in the world around you and what it's likely to mean for certain types of investments. And you have to give careful consideration to your own needs and objectives.

If that sounds like work, I'm afraid it is. But it's work with a big potential pay-off. Because of its tax-sheltered status, there is no way the ordinary person can build a substantial investment portfolio faster than within an RRSP. And, as I pointed out in the two previous chapters, substantial means just that—you could end up with several hundred thousand dollars, or even more, by the time you're through, if you play your cards right. But to make that happen, you must make the right investment decisions. You must pick the opportunities that combine solid growth potential with limited risk and reject those that carry high loss potential. You won't always be right—no one is. But if you can make the correct choice more often than not, you'll come out ahead.

The problem is that many people give very little thought to what happens in their RRSPs. Their main concern is the immediate tax benefit. So they sock their money in the most convenient place, get the receipt, claim the tax refund, and forget it. I'll bet you know people who do exactly that. Maybe you're one of them.

In all fairness, the maze of choices may be partly responsible for this RRSP inertia. Many people freeze when called upon to make decisions in areas they don't fully understand; they'd prefer to do nothing than risk being wrong. Perhaps if we had only three or four alternatives to choose from we'd manage our money better. But the reality is that all those options are available. If you want to use your RRSP to build wealth, you have to understand them, and be prepared to choose among them.

I cannot stress the importance of this strongly enough. Next to the family home, a solid RRSP investment program is the most important component in the early stages of wealth building. If you ignore it, you might as well forget about ever acquiring real wealth. That may seem like a strong statement, but I firmly believe it to be true. Managing your RRSP provides you with the discipline, knowledge, and experience you'll need to move on to

other types of wealth-building activities later. If you're not prepared to devote the time and effort to doing it right, you have
very little chance of succeeding in other types of wealth-building
pursuits.

I'm not just talking here about making the right decisions at
the time you make your initial RRSP contributions, although that
is, of course, very important. You have to actively manage that
money at all times. You must know where it is, how much it's
earning, and what other investment opportunities are available
for it. You must be prepared to get out of one investment and into
something else when the occasion arises—and you must have a
clear understanding of why you're doing it.

That may sound a little scary, especially if you're not used to
making investment decisions. But it really isn't all that hard. It
requires some knowledge, some common sense, some time, and
some decisiveness on your part. Once you're into it, I expect
you'll find, as I did, that it's not frightening at all. On the
contrary, it's challenging, stimulating, and, yes, fun.

In this chapter, I'll show you how to start. We'll look at the
most common RRSP investments and I'll explain how and when
they should be used to maximize your return. I'll show you how
to start a plan, and how to manage it successfully yourself.

Let's begin by assuming you've just set up a self-directed plan,
as I suggested in the last chapter. You don't have a great deal of
money in it, perhaps $5,000, and you're a little nervous about the
whole process. Perhaps you're thinking: "I'm doing this because
this guy said to. But what the hell do I do now?"

Okay, let's discuss that question. When you're just starting
out, the number one priority is to protect your capital base.
You're probably not making a large salary, and finding the money
to put into an RRSP isn't easy. The last thing you want to happen
is to lose that small nest egg. You need that money to build
on—in two ways. You want to add to your capital through
investment income. And you need to build confidence in your
investing ability. If you get wiped out the first time around, it
will probably be a long, long time before you stick your toe in the
investment pond again.

With that in mind, your first RRSP investments should be conservative in nature. You should diversify them, to give yourself experience with different types of investment choices and to reduce whatever limited risk you have even further. But you shouldn't be taking any major chances at this stage. Save that stuff for later. Right now, you're just getting your feet wet.

So where do you start? Look first at some basic interest-bearing investments—those that are easiest to understand. Investments like this should be the foundation of your RRSP at any time, even when you move into much more sophisticated areas. So start using them right from the beginning.

Plain old Canada Savings Bonds may well be your first choice. The compound interest bonds offer a good way to let your money grow painlessly; I've always held some CSBs in my plans. Perhaps $2,000 of your $5,000 stake might go there. CSBs probably won't offer as good a return as some other alternatives. But they make up for that in their very low risk and high flexibility—you can redeem them at any time and reinvest the cash elsewhere.

Next, go shopping for a Guaranteed Investment Certificate that offers a high rate of return. You don't have to trudge from bank to trust company to credit union to do that, or even make a lot of phone calls. Just check out the financial pages of your local newspaper or the *Globe and Mail*'s *Report on Business*. At least once a week many major newspapers carry a comprehensive listing of current interest rates being offered by financial institutions for term deposits and GICs. Check them over carefully. You'll usually find the major chartered banks will pay you the least for your money. The larger trust companies will fall into the middle range. The small trusts and credit unions will give you the biggest bang for your dollar.

The difference between the best and worst rates can be substantial. For instance, if you'd picked up the paper on a hot July day in 1987 and scanned the interest rate section, you'd have discovered that a one-year GIC would have paid interest of as low as 7¾% or as high as 9½%, depending on where you put your money. If you'd been investing $2,000 of your RRSP money at that point, the lowest rate GIC would have returned you $155 in interest. The GIC with the highest rate would have added $190 to your RRSP. If you think that $35 difference isn't significant in the great scheme of things, look at it this way: you would earn 22.6% more interest with the highest rate GIC than with the one with the lowest rate.

As the amount of money in your RRSP grows and you have more to invest, the dollar numbers become magnified. If you'd had $20,000 to invest in a GIC instead of just $2,000, the interest difference between the lowest and the highest would have been $350. Does that seem more impressive?

Training yourself to spot those distinctions early on will be invaluable later as you develop a larger financial base with which to work. The good wealth builder will be constantly on the lookout for every edge he or she can get. Extra dollars can add up surprisingly quickly if reinvested over a period of time. Even that modest $35 in extra interest you received by choosing the highest yielding GIC can yield fascinating results. Reinvested over the next 25 years at an average return of 10% a year, that original $35 interest bonus will grow to almost $380! Multiply that by all the other small amounts you'll gain along the way by constantly seeking out the interest rate edge, and the total impact on your RRSP investment portfolio can be significant.

One other point here. There is nothing wrong with placing your money in a small financial institution—as long as it is a member of the Canada Deposit Insurance Corporation (the CDIC). That's an absolute must. There have been too many bank, trust company, and investment firm failures in recent years to take any chances on this score. As long as the firm you deal with is a CDIC member and you're buying a GIC or term deposit directly from them, your money will be protected up to a maximum of $60,000 if anything should go wrong. Just make sure the company isn't selling investment receipts issued by someone else. There have been situations where investors thought they were dealing with a CDIC insured company only to discover that the GICs they received were actually issued by an associated firm that wasn't covered. If you have any doubts at all, take your money somewhere else.

How long a term should you choose for your GIC investment? You'll have to decide that yourself; it depends on the interest rate climate at the time you make the investment. If rates are high, you should consider locking in your investment for three to five years to take advantage of them. If rates are relatively low, stick with a one-year GIC. You can review the situation at the end of that time and decide where to go next.

You've now invested 80% of your $5,000 RRSP stake—$2,000 in Canada Savings Bonds, $2,000 in a high-yielding GIC. Those investments may not seem terribly exciting, but they're safe and solid, and provide a fair return on your investment. Now, what do you do with the last $1,000?

Since you've placed most of your money in two very secure investments, you might consider something that carries just slightly—and I mean slightly—more risk but offers a potentially higher return. Also, since you're seeking to develop investing experience, you should learn about something new. I suggest you take a look at a no-load mortgage fund.

These are among the most conservative of mutual funds (if you're not sure what a mutual fund is, I'll explain in more detail in a later chapter). Typically, they invest in residential first mortgages and the emphasis is on safety with a modest return to investors. Many banks and trust companies offer them and the initial investment required is usually very low. Your $1,000 will get you into most of the available mortgage funds without any problem.

Don't expect to make a lot of money from this type of fund. But the chances are your return will be higher than from your GIC or CSB investments. There's a risk it won't be, though—in fact it could even happen that you actually lose a bit of money with this investment. That's rare with mortgage funds, however. And if you do suffer a loss, it's likely to be very small.

For instance, the Bank of Montreal First Canadian Mortgage Fund, which has consistently been among the top performers in this group, increased in value every year from 1976 to 1987 according to data compiled by *Financial Times of Canada*. The annual return on your investment during that period would have ranged from a low of 0.9% in 1980 to a high of 24% in 1983. In most years the return on your money would have been in the 9½% to 11½% range.

The General Trust Mortgage Fund, another strong performer during that period, shows a similar pattern but with somewhat greater swings. In 1980, the fund actually lost 2% in value — the only time it went down during that 12-year span. It's biggest gain was also in 1983, when it went up 25.3% in value. Those years were aberrations, though; the rest of the time annual returns ranged from 7.7% to 15.9%.

In selecting your mortgage fund, use the same process as you did when choosing a GIC. Shop around. In this case, you're looking for two things. First, you want a no-load fund — one which doesn't charge any commission fees when you sign up. Second, you want a fund with a strong and consistent track record. That's where papers like *Financial Times* and *Financial Post* can help. Both publish monthly reports on the performance of mutual funds; buy a copy or spend some time at your local library checking out the information. Pick a mortgage fund that has a consistent record of solid returns over the years and go with it.

So here's where your RRSP portfolio stands after all this:

Canada Savings Bonds	$2,000	40%
Guaranteed Investment Certificate	2,000	40%
Mortgage Fund	1,000	20%
Total Investment	$5,000	100%

It may not be exciting, but it's an excellent start. Your investments are safe, you've achieved a modest degree of diversification, and you'll get a decent return. Now what?

Let's assume you don't make any changes in your RRSP portfolio for the first year, and that the combined yield from all your investments is 9%. You've earned $450 in tax-free money over the year, and you contribute another $2,000 to the plan. You now have $7,450 in assets, of which $2,450 is cash. What should you do now?

First, review your original investments. See if they're still solid, or if you should make some changes. Perhaps you chose a one-year GIC and, based on your experience, you feel you'd rather take $1,000 of that money and move it into your mortgage fund. Do it! Never make the mistake of allowing your money to remain in relatively unproductive investments. At the same time, don't go to the other extreme and put all your eggs in one basket. Maybe the mortgage fund had a terrific year and you're tempted to put all the GIC money into it and cash in the CSBs as well. Don't! If the next year should be a downer for mortgage funds, your RRSP would have no other revenue source and you'd end up a loser.

Let's assume that after reviewing your holdings, you decide you like the mortgage fund enough to move another $500 into it. The other $1,500 from your GIC is reinvested for another year. Now look at your free cash and think about it.

You still don't want to take any major risks. Your RRSP is growing, but you still aren't at the point where you could afford any serious reverses. Yet you'd like to add to your investment experience.

This could be the time to look at another type of mutual fund—a bond fund. There's slightly more risk here than with a mortgage fund, but the potential returns are also somewhat greater.

You've already learned the basic facts about bonds from reading Chapter Ten. You know that bonds perform best when interest rates are falling and do worst when they're on the rise. So before you make any commitment to a bond fund, you do some research to inform yourself on what interest rates are doing at the present time.

Let's assume that your conclusion is that interest rates are stable or in a downward trend. A bond fund appears to be a good alternative at this point, so you now go to the financial newspapers and check past performance. Again, you're looking for a no-load fund, which will be designated by the initials NL.

One that showed a good track record during the period from 1974 to 1987 was the Canada Trust Investment Fund—Income

Part. It only lost money in one of those years, 1980, when the value of fund units dropped 4.3%. The best performances came in 1983 and 1986, when investors realized returns of 26.7% and 23.6%. But there was little consistency in the returns—for the other years, profits varied from a measly 2.4% to a healthy 17.6%.

A fund with wide swings like that is said to have a high degree of volatility. That may make you somewhat uncomfortable, but the records show this particular fund has been among the top 10 performing bond funds in every year but one since 1974. On that basis, you decide to go with it, and invest $2,000.

The new issue of Canada Savings Bonds looks pretty good, so you use the other $450 to add more CSBs. Your RRSP portfolio now looks like this:

Canada Savings Bonds	$2,450	33%
Guaranteed Investment Certificate	1,500	20%
Mortgage Fund	1,500	20%
Bond Fund	2,000	27%
Total Investment	**$7,450**	**100%**

As a result of these moves, you've achieved a greater diversification in your RRSP, with no more than 33% of your assets in any one holding. Your investments are still quite safe—but you have added to your risk (and your potential return) by increasing your mortgage fund holdings and adding the bond fund.

I'm sure you're getting the idea of how to proceed, but let's look at one more year.

Let's assume that by increasing your risk and growth potential by adding the bond fund and switching money into the mortgage fund, you improve your average return in the second year to 10%. That's $745 your RRSP earns for you. And let's say you make another $2,000 contribution. Going into the third year, your total RRSP assets are now $10,195 (see how quickly they grow?) and you have $2,745 in new cash to invest.

Now it may be time to consider some real diversification. So far, you've put all your money into interest-bearing assets. You should now consider adding some equity to your RRSP.

You don't know very much about stocks, and you certainly don't want to get involved at this stage in individual stock selections. But there are a number of mutual funds around that invest in the stock market. This may be the time to look at one of them.

Again, you start by doing your homework. The first thing you need to determine is which funds are RRSP-eligible—not all of them are. The tables in the *Financial Post* and *Financial Times* will provide that information.

Next, check for the no-load funds. I don't mean to suggest that you should never buy a load fund. It's just that when you have only a modest amount of money to invest, I don't believe it's wise to lay out a relatively large proportion of it in commissions.

Finally, look at the performance records. What funds have consistently done well over the years, and are still going strong?

One which may catch your eye is the MONY Equity Fund, run by the MONY Life Insurance Company of Canada and available through insurance agents. It has been a steady performer and only lost money in one year between 1976 and 1987. That was in 1982, when its units dropped 10.1% in value. But it more than made up for that the following year, when it jumped an incredible 59.9% in value.

Let's say you decide you like the idea of adding an equity fund to your portfolio. You recognize that you're getting into higher-risk territory, though, so you only commit $1,500 to it. The balance of your cash you distribute as follows: $500 into your GIC, $500 into your mortgage fund, and $245 into your bond fund. Now your RRSP holdings look like this:

Canada Savings Bonds	$2,450	24%
Guaranteed Investment Certificate	2,000	20%
Mortgage Fund	2,000	20%
Bond Fund	2,245	22%
Equity Fund	1,500	14%
Total Investment	**$10,195**	**100%**

In just two full years of RRSP investing, you've established a solid position. You've given your plan an excellent base of interest earning investments. You've started to add some higher growth potential, while still keeping your risk relatively low. You've diversified your holdings among five different types of investments. And you've learned a lot about new investment alternatives in the process. A pretty good start!

As your RRSP grows, continue to follow the same pattern that I've outlined above. Here are some guidelines:

1. Review your investments regularly. If any are not performing well, search out alternatives and replace them.

2. Add new types of investments gradually, and only when you fully understand them.

3. Make sure that only a small proportion of your RRSP money is in medium to higher-risk investments. These should never exceed 30% of your total RRSP value.

4. Maintain good diversification in your RRSP. The larger your fund becomes, the lower should be the maximum percentage that's devoted to any one investment. In the example we just looked at, two assets each made up 40% of the plan at the start. But by the beginning of the third year the largest single holding was the CSBs, which represented only 24% of the total.

If you stick to those basic guidelines, you'll find yourself with a solid and growing RRSP in a relatively short time. And, equally important, you will have accumulated a lot of knowledge and experience that will help you as you move into other aspects of wealth building.

Protecting Your Assets

I N OCTOBER 1986, a young Dalhousie University law student named Adrienne Scott walked into the Halifax office of Principal Savings and Trust. She'd been attracted by a newspaper ad offering investment certificates at 10% interest, an unusually high rate at that time.

Her story, as she told it later on CBC radio in Ottawa, is relevant to every wealth builder.

She was directed to the back of the office by a woman who said the 10% certificates weren't actually being issued by the trust company itself. There she met with a man who explained that the certificates were issued by a company called First Investors, a member of the Principal Group. Because First Investors was a separate company, the certificates weren't covered by deposit insurance. But they were fully backed by deposits in major chartered banks and were as solid an investment as she could wish for. The only money that might conceivably be at risk was that portion of the interest payment over 5%, and that risk was very small.

Still, Ms. Scott was cautious. She had $64,000 she wanted to invest, $20,000 of her own money and rest borrowed from her mother. She didn't want to take any chances with it; it was money that would be needed to help finance her university education. So after asking more questions, she obtained a copy of the investment contract and took it away with her. She read it over and showed it to some members of her family and a friend.

Everyone thought it looked okay. She also talked to people who had put money into certificates issued by First Investors. They reported no problems. So she went ahead, investing her funds in several certificates with varying maturities.

Several months later she read in the paper that two companies associated with the Principal Group had effectively gone into receivership when their licenses were revoked by the Alberta government after an audit revealed their assets weren't adequate to cover the commitments they'd made on investment contracts. It appeared the firms, one of which was First Investors, had invested heavily in Alberta real estate in the early 1980s and had been hit hard by the subsequent drop in property values in the province.

At about the same time, Adrienne Scott received a letter informing her that she would be receiving a 30% refund on her deposit with First Investors within a few weeks. No mention was made of the balance of the money.

Needless to say, she was shocked. She thought she had made a safe investment, and suddenly she found herself faced with the loss of a large portion of her funds. She'd been careful, but still ended up in trouble.

Ms. Scott was the victim of a bait and switch technique that is all too common in this country. She'd gone to a trust company, a member of the Canada Deposit Insurance Corporation (CDIC), believing that any funds she placed on deposit with them would be protected. That would have been the case—but instead, she was sold an investment contract issued by an associated firm that was not covered by the CDIC—as she found out a few months later. The guarantees she was given were worthless—but they had diverted her attention from the fact her money would not be protected by deposit insurance by providing what seemed like a plausible alternative.

Ms. Scott's case is by no means unique. Some 67,000 investors were affected by the debacle within the Principal Group. Tens of thousands of others have lost large amounts of money in the collapse of other financial institutions and investment companies in recent years.

The carrot in these situations is always above-average interest rates. People are always looking for a better deal; an additional point or two on a GIC is enough to persuade a lot of folks to take a chance—especially since we all think bank failures, like car accidents, are things that happen to other people.

That doesn't mean that just because one financial institution is offering a higher interest rate there will automatically be a problem. Many smaller trust companies have to pay a premium just to get business—especially during a time when there's concern about the stability of small financial firms. As long as the investment you make is fully covered by deposit insurance, you're fine. Just make sure it is.

The importance of that coverage became even more apparent a few weeks later when Principal Trust itself was forced to close its doors. Many more depositors were affected when that happened. But most of their funds were protected by the CDIC.

As it turned out, Metropolitan Life took over the firm and created a new company, Metropolitan Trust, out of the ashes, so the CDIC coverage wasn't required. But Principal Trust depositors were secure in the knowledge that it would have been there if needed. Adrienne Scott would have been delighted to change places with them.

No aspiring wealth builder can afford to sustain the kind of loss confronted by those who put money in First Investors and Associated Investors, the second company involved. And yet it can happen so easily, and so unexpectedly it's scary. Let me tell you my story.

On November 1, 1982, I put $30,000 of my RRSP money into a one-year Guaranteed Investment Certificate with a small trust company. The funds came in part from a pension refund and partly from a retiring allowance received when the company for which I was working folded at the height of the 1981-82 recession.

I didn't pick the trust company with which the money was deposited. In fact, I'd never heard of it before. I acted on the advice of a well-known Toronto firm of personal financial consultants who'd been hired to help senior executives of the company that was closing put their financial affairs in order.

The rate being offered for this particular GIC was 14%. That was about a point higher than the rate being offered by other trust companies and chartered banks at that time.

The name of the company where I put my money? Greymac Trust.

On December 31, 1982, on the advice of the same consultants, I deposited additional pension funds worth about $13,000 in a three-year certificate with another small trust company. It was paying 13¼%—again, a higher rate than was available elsewhere at that time.

This company's name was Seaway Trust.

On January 7, 1983, only a week after that second deposit, the government of Ontario approved a controversial takeover plan involving Greymac, Seaway, and Crown Trusts. This was as a result of a complicated flip involving thousands of apartment units, a deal which eventually resulted in criminal charges against some of the people involved. The takeover of the three trust companies—which eventually put all of them out of business—took place after it became clear they had all been involved in the transactions in one way or another.

When I heard the news, I was sick. I was faced with the prospect of having years of savings wiped out by a series of unpredictable events totally beyond my control. And, of course, it wasn't just me. Thousands of other people with deposits in those companies were facing exactly the same situation.

Two things saved me. One was the Canada Deposit Insurance Corporation. Unlike Adrienne Scott's funds, my investment certificates were indeed held by trust companies which had deposit insurance.

But maximum protection at that time was only $20,000. I stood to lose $10,000 of my deposit with Greymac.

That's where the other fortuitous event occurred. Parliament rushed through legislation which retroactively increased the deposit insurance limit to $60,000, thus protecting all the Crown, Greymac, and Seaway depositors up to that amount.

I got my money out—although not with all the interest I should have received, which I'll explain later. But at that point I wasn't complaining. I was just relieved to have escaped what could have been a serious financial setback relatively unscathed.

There are two morals to this story. First, don't take advice from financial planners on blind faith, even if they have an excellent reputation. Do some thinking of your own as well. Second, make absolutely sure your money is fully protected by deposit insurance.

Never think it can't happen to you. Consider these names: Astra Trust, Pioneer Trust, Commonwealth Trust, Security Trust, London Loan, District Trust, Fidelity Trust, Western Capital Trust, Northguard Mortgage Corporation, Northland Bank, Canadian Commercial Bank. What do they have in common? In every case, the CDIC had to bail out depositors after the companies got into financial difficulties.

The reality is that North America's financial structure has been less than rock-solid in recent years. The problems haven't been confined to Canada by any means; the 1980s have seen the biggest rash of bank failures in the United States since the Great Depression. Even the big boys have had serious problems, due in part to debt defaults by Third World countries.

All this highlights the shakiness of the structure and the need for you to protect yourself. Which brings me back to deposit insurance and the importance of understanding just what it does—and does not—cover.

If you think you've got a pretty clear idea of what it's all about, try the little test that follows.

Question one: You're planning a trip to Florida next winter. You want to convert some money to U.S. dollars now because the exchange rate is favourable. You deal with a major chartered bank, a CDIC member, and one day while you're in you notice a sign promoting U.S. dollar accounts. You decide to open one so your Florida money can earn a little interest before you go. Is your money protected by deposit insurance?

Question two: You've had great success in building the value of your RRSP by using the techniques I've described. Now you decide you want to invest $40,000 in a five-year Guaranteed

Investment Certificate with a small trust company which attracted you with an offer of 10½% interest, compounded semi-annually. (Forget for the moment that this isn't such a hot idea because you'd be tying up too much of your money in a single asset. I'm just trying to illustrate a point.) A couple of weeks before the certificate is to mature, the trust company declares bankruptcy. But you know it's a member of the CDIC so you're not worried. Is your relaxed attitude justified?

Question three: You had $50,000 in a Guaranteed Investment Certificate with Victoria and Grey Trust when it was announced the company would merge with National Trust. You also had a $25,000 GIC with National. How much of your money is protected following the merger?

Here are the answers:

Question one: You have no protection at all. The odds are greatly against your chartered bank failing, of course. But if the unlikely happened and it did go belly-up, you'd have to kiss your Florida vacation good-bye. The Canada Deposit Insurance Corporation doesn't insure any deposits held in U.S. dollars, or any other foreign currency for that matter. So if you really do need a U.S. dollar account, make sure the financial institution you use is rock solid.

Question two: This may come as a surprise, but you stand to lose several thousand dollars. Your $40,000 GIC at 10½% interest compounded semi-annually will be worth about $66,700 at maturity. Since the maximum CDIC protection for any single account is $60,000, you face a potential loss of $6,700. Don't be so relaxed!

Question three: You're protected for the full $75,000 even though the amount exceeds the CDIC cap for deposits in any one financial institution. The reason is that when banks or trust companies amalgamate, deposits held in each institution at the time of the merger are considered separately for CDIC purposes. This applies until the funds are withdrawn or until the maturity date, if the deposit has a fixed term. But be careful. Additional deposits made after the merger are not protected because you're already over the normal limit.

If you scored 100% on those questions, you don't need to read any more of this chapter. It's clear you know the CDIC rules inside-out. But if you missed any of the answers, you may find the information that follows to be of help.

First, what is covered? The CDIC will protect your savings and chequing accounts in any member institution up to a maximum of $60,000 per person. (The word "person" is interpreted very broadly; companies and even governments are protected as well. So if you run a small business, your firm's account is safe up to $60,000.) CDIC also covers such things as money orders, deposit receipts, GICs, and debentures issued by its members. One caution here, though: term deposits and GICs are only covered if they're cashable on demand or have a fixed term of five years or less. So if someone offers you a GIC for longer than five years, think twice before you accept.

Some other important rules to keep in mind:

■ Any funds over the $60,000 maximum in one financial institution are not protected. But if you open an account at another bank or trust company, you start all over again. That means you could hold four accounts of $60,000 each in different banks and trust companies and have $240,000 worth of CDIC protection. Remember, though, the money must be in separate institutions. Using different branches of the same bank doesn't work.

■ If you and your spouse have a joint deposit, it's considered to be a separate "person" for deposit insurance purposes. That means you could have a joint account with $60,000 along with individual accounts for each of you at the same financial institution and all the money would be protected.

■ CDIC membership is restricted to banks, trust companies, and mortgage loan companies. If the company is federally incorporated, it must be a member. But provincially incorporated companies may or may not have coverage. That's where you have to be especially careful.

■ Credit unions are not covered by the CDIC. But provincial governments have their own insurance programs to protect depositors. If you deal with a credit union and you're not sure what protection you have, ask.

Now for the investments CDIC does *not* cover. Stocks, bonds, mortgages, and mutual funds are excluded—I'll explain the significance of that shortly.

The contents of your safety deposit box aren't protected. Foreign currency deposits are also out, as we've already seen.

These restrictions are of special importance in terms of your self-directed RRSP. The investments in your plan are only covered if the funds are in the same kind of investment instruments that would be protected if they were outside an RRSP.

For instance, in the previous chapter I constructed a self-directed RRSP that held the following assets at the beginning of the third year:

Canada Savings Bonds	$ 2,450
GICs	2,000
Mortgage Fund	2,000
Bond Fund	2,245
Equity Fund	1,500

What's insured and what isn't?

The CSBs aren't covered. But since they're backed by the Government of Canada, you aren't going to be very worried about that.

The GICs are protected, as long as they aren't for any longer than five years. So no problem there.

The three funds have no insurance coverage—mutual funds are specifically excluded from CDIC protection, even if the fund is created and operated by a bank or trust company that's a member institution. So that's where you could conceivably run into trouble. If anything should happen to the firm which operates your funds, you could have a problem. That's unlikely, unless gross mismanagement takes place because fund assets are supposed to be held in trust on behalf of the investors. Still, you need to be aware of every possibility.

So out of the more than $10,000 in assets in the RRSP you set up at your local bank, only $2,000—less than 20%—is actually protected by deposit insurance. That shows you how important it is to select RRSP investments that are as secure as possible.

One final point: if you are unfortunate enough to be caught in the failure of a financial institution, you may not get away scott-free even with full CDIC coverage. I mentioned earlier in this chapter that when Seaway Trust was closed I lost some interest I would otherwise have been entitled to. Here's how it happened.

In June 1984 the Supreme Court of Ontario issued an order formally winding up Seaway. The action was initiated by the CDIC, and in fact marked the first time the CDIC had ever petitioned a company into bankruptcy. By having the company wound up, the CDIC was able to immediately pay off all outstanding GICs. That meant that people like myself who were holding long-term Seaway GICs at high rates of interest had them terminated prematurely. The three-year GIC at 13¼% which I had taken out on Dec. 31, 1982, would normally have not matured until the end of 1985. Instead, by forcing Seaway into liquidation, the CDIC was able to pay off the certificate half way through its term.

As it happened, interest rates were a lot lower in mid-1984 than they had been when the original Seaway investment was made. Instead of getting 13¼% on my money for the 18 months to the end of '85, I was only able to reinvest at 10¾%. The result was a loss of about $600 in interest compared to what I would have made if Seaway had stayed in business.

So even though your principal may be fully protected by CDIC coverage, your interest entitlement won't always be. It's something to keep in mind when you're making decisions on where to put your money.

Also keep in mind that if the financial institution where you keep your money should run into trouble, you may not be able to get access to your funds for several weeks, even though they're insured. It never hurts to have another account at the bank or trust company across the street to use in an emergency. You never know!

Remember, take nothing for granted. There's too much turmoil in the financial world right now to take any more risks than you need to. You can never protect yourself completely from the unexpected. But the good wealth builder will do everything possible to minimize risk and protect his or her asset base. Knowing the ground rules of deposit insurance is an essential part of that process.

CHAPTER 17

Understanding Mutual Funds

I 'VE MENTIONED mutual funds several times in the past two chapters. You may understand what they are—but don't feel bad if you don't. For a lot of people, the term "mutual fund" is something like the word "empathy"—they feel they *should* know what it means but they aren't absolutely certain.

So if you're a bit vague about mutual funds and how they work, you've got lots of company. I learned that a couple of years ago when the firm I was working for launched two mutual funds of its own. An employee meeting was held to explain the exciting new venture to everyone. Shortly after it began, the person chairing the meeting asked if there was anyone in the audience who did *not* know what a mutual fund was.

Predictably, no hands were raised at first. Then one daring lady raised hers. Another hand went up, then another and before long it was apparent that almost half the people in the room did not know what a mutual fund was. And would you believe that the main business of this particular company was financial education?

That meeting was a real eye-opener for me. I knew that only a relatively small percentage of Canadians invest in mutual funds. But I had assumed that just about everyone knew what they were all about. Now I know better—which is why I'm devoting this chapter and the next to explaining what mutual funds are and how people without a great deal of money to invest can use them as one of the early steps towards building wealth.

A mutual fund is simply a pooling of money for investment purposes. When you buy into a fund, you're really buying two things: a diversified portfolio in a particular investment area, and professional investment management. In effect, you're getting a small stake in many different investments. The value of your stake will move up or down depending on how well the investments held by your fund perform.

The type of investments you hold will depend on the kind of fund you buy—and you may be surprised at the choices available. There are several hundred mutual funds in Canada and thousands in the United States. None are the same—they differ in investment philosophy, the timing of their sales and purchases, the nature of their holdings, their volatility, and in numerous other ways. That's what makes picking a good mutual fund so difficult. Out of all the choices available, how do you know where to begin?

I'll offer some guidelines on how to choose a good fund in Chapter Eighteen. For starters, let's take a look at some of the different types of funds currently available and some of the basic terms used.

Mortgage Funds

We took a look at these in Chapter Fifteen, in the discussion on RRSP investments. Most mortgage funds are investments in first mortgages on Canadian residential real estate—in other words, you're helping to finance other people's family homes. As we've already seen, these funds are relatively safe and rarely lose money. However, the return on your investment is modest.

Some mortgage funds go beyond the single-family residential market to invest in industrial and commercial properties, as well as apartments. The London Life Mortgage Fund is one of these and its track record has been remarkably good—it was either first or second in performance in its category every year between 1981 and 1986. That's consistency—something to look for in making a fund selection.

BOND FUNDS

These funds invest in bonds and debentures issued by governments, municipalities, utilities, and private companies. They're also known as *income funds* or *fixed income funds* because of the income they generate through regular interest payments. Many people think of bond funds as being dull and ultra-conservative. They're certainly more stable than equity funds. But they can have major swings in their performance, depending on what's happening with interest rates. For example, the units in Central Trust's Bond Fund went from a loss of 8.9% in 1980 to a gain of 38.5% in 1983, according to statistics compiled by the *Financial Times of Canada* and published in their *Mutual Fund Sourcebook*. That's a swing of over 47%. So don't make the mistake of assuming bond funds won't have much price movement. They'll do very well when interest rates are dropping because bond prices rise in that situation. Conversely, when interest rates are rising you're best to stay well clear of bond funds.

CANADIAN EQUITY FUNDS

These mutual funds specialize in Canadian stocks, and they're very popular among investors, especially when things are hot in the stock market. They're an easy way for people who know little or nothing about stocks to get in on the action with minimal risk. But that doesn't mean they're safe. When the stock market is strong, as it was in the early to mid 1980s, a well-managed equity fund can produce spectacular results. Holders of Trans-Canada Equity Fund received returns on their money of 20.8%, 22%, 21.8%, and 44.6% during the four years from 1983 to 1986. What does that mean in real dollars? Well, let's suppose you'd invested $1,000 in Trans-Canada on January 1, 1983. And we'll assume you paid their maximum load fee (the mutual fund industry's term for sales commission), which is 8.75%. By the end of 1986, your original $1,000 investment would have grown to $2,368.52—a pretty impressive performance. If you'd established a regular investment program and put in $1,000 at the start of each of those four years, your $4,000 investment would be worth $7,254.45.

But not all funds did as well. During the same period, investors in CGF Venture Fund had returns of 15.3%, 12.1%, 4.8% and -27.1%. That means if you'd invested $1,000 in the fund at the beginning of 1983, paying a 9% load fee, the value of your holdings at the end of 1986 would be down to slightly under $900. If you had put in $1,000 each year, your total assets at the end of 1986 would be worth $3,036.58. In both cases you would have lost money; in fact, the value of your fund units would be less than half what it would have been had you chosen Trans-Canada.

That's why choosing the right fund is so important. A top performing mutual fund will build your wealth much faster than a mediocre or poorly performing one.

Don't assume any equity fund is safe from losses, though—not even the best performers. And the losses can sometimes be heavy. Even a top-ranked fund like Trans-Canada fell 24.7% in value in 1982, a disastrous year for the markets. And that wasn't the worst performer by any means; if you'd put $1,000 into AGF's Growth Equity Fund in 1981, you would have had less that $600 left a year later. Nine other funds did even worse than that. When the stock markets crashed in October, 1987, virtually all equity funds took a beating. Some lost more than 30% of their value within a few days.

So you can make a lot of money in equity funds—but you can lose as well. Treat them with caution.

AMERICAN EQUITY FUNDS

As the name implies, these funds specialize in U.S. stocks. Again, they can have spectacular advances in bull markets, sometimes increasing in value over 50% in a year. But they may be battered when the market collapses, as they were in the October, 1987 crash.

INTERNATIONAL EQUITY FUNDS

These became the hottest thing in mutual funds in the 1980s. They invest in stocks from all over the world that the managers see as having high potential. Best known is the Templeton Growth

Fund, founded by the guru of investment fund managers, John Templeton. Its track record is a model of consistency; only twice in the 14 years from 1974 to 1987 did the fund's units lose money and in only one other year was the gain less than 10%.

Some international funds specialize in a particular country or region of the world, such as Investors Japanese Growth Fund and the Global Strategy Europe Fund. One of the most exciting in the early 1980s was AGF Japan Fund, which was designed to give Canadians a chance to participate in Japan's economic miracle. Those with the foresight to buy in did wonderfully well; $5,000 invested in the fund at the end of 1980 would have been worth over $24,000 by the end of 1986. Unfortunately, this is one I missed out on.

SECTOR FUNDS

These are funds which specialize in a particular type of stock—health care, energy, food. Sector funds became immensely popular in the U.S. in the mid 1980s, with some mutual fund companies, such as the Boston-based Fidelity Group, offering dozens of them. They haven't yet caught on in a big way in Canada, although more are appearing. Examples include AGF's Canadian Gas and Energy Fund, the Natural Resources Growth Fund, and TechnoFund, which specialized in high-tech companies.

The problem with Sector Funds is that they have an even greater boom or bust propensity than the more broadly based stock funds. This is because if the particular industry in which the fund invests goes into recession, there's nothing to take up the slack. The record of Royal Trust Energy Fund reflects this: down 33.1% in 1982 when the country was gripped by recession and the National Energy Policy; up 15.3% in 1984 as the Conservatives took office and there was renewed optimism in the oil patch; down 23.6% in 1986 as the international price of oil collapsed; up 45.3% in the first quarter of 1987 as the oil price recovered and renewed signs of inflation appeared.

That kind of performance is typical of Canadian sector funds. They're really for more advanced investors who understand market timing and know when to move in and out.

Precious Metals Funds

This is a type of sector fund that specializes in such precious metals as gold, silver, and platinum. These funds may hold the metal itself or shares in producing companies. I've singled them out for particular mention because every wealth builder should own some gold related assets and this is a good way of doing it.

Balanced Funds

These funds hold a variety of securities—stocks, bonds, debentures, mortgages. The investment mix will vary depending on the fund managers and general economic conditions; when interest rates and inflation are rising, for instance, they may reduce their bond holdings and add gold. You would expect these funds to be somewhat more stable than ordinary equity funds, but even they are not immune to heavy losses in poor markets.

Dividend Funds

These funds specialize in providing maximum dividend income, usually through investments in preferred shares. The swings in these funds don't tend to be as violent as in regular equity funds, and the best ones have a respectable track record.

One of the best performers in recent years was the Viking Dividend Fund, which is sold through Eaton's financial centres. Most of us don't normally think of a department store as a place to make investments, but this particular fund's track record may change a few minds. The fund has a low load charge (3.5% maximum). If you'd invested $1,000 at the beginning of 1983, it would have been worth $2,120.65 at the end of 1986. Not quite as good as the Trans-Canada Equity Fund, but not far off. A $1,000 per year investment over that period would have been worth $6,054.84 at the end of 1986.

Money Market Funds

These are simply a place to park your cash for a temporary period. They invest in high-grade, short-term notes, such as Treasury bills, banker's acceptances, certificates of deposit, etc. They are the safest type of mutual fund you can buy; no properly managed money market fund should ever lose money. As you might have guessed, the corollary of that is a low return on your investment. Your return will be something close to current short-term interest rates—although, as with any other mutual fund, an astute management group can turn in an above-average performance.

One of the most consistent performers over the years has been the Bolton Tremblay Money Market Fund, which charges a maximum 2% sales commission. Fron 1983 to 1986, annual returns were 13.4%, 8.7%, 11%, and 9.5%. As you can see, not spectacular, but certainly respectable, especially given the safety of these funds.

Many investors use money market funds as a safe haven in uncertain financial times. A good example is the big run-up in the stock market of the mid-1980s. By the middle of 1987 many people were becoming nervous. They had big profits in their equity funds; they didn't want to risk losing them if the stock market plunged, as it did a few months later. When you have those kinds of concerns, it's a good time to consider switching into a money market fund. Your profits will be protected and you'll be getting a decent return on your money while you wait for the economic storms to clear.

Real Estate Funds

These funds are relatively new in Canada—in fact, none has a track record long enough for us to get a clear idea of whether this is a good or bad choice for investors.

These funds hold a variety of real estate related investments, including office buildings, apartments, shopping centres, medical buildings, and retail stores. While the concept seems good for those who would like to hold real estate in this way, the absence of a proven track record suggests a cautious approach.

Those are the types of funds available to you. As you can see, they cover a broad range of investing options. Before we move on to consider how to use them most effectively as wealth builders, there are a few more terms you need to understand.

Front-end Load Funds

As I've already explained, a load fund is one that charges a sales commission. Front-end load means that commission is paid at the time of purchase. For example, if you wanted to invest $1,000 in Industrial Growth Fund, you would have to pay a maximum commission of 9%. So you'd end up with only $910 worth of fund units to your credit.

The important point to remember about front-end load funds is that you should rarely, if ever, pay the maximum quoted fee. It's like buying an appliance; if you don't get a discounted price it's probably because you haven't shopped around. Most front-end load funds post a maximum sales charge of 9%. But even small investors don't usually have to pay that. I rarely pay more than 4% commission on a load fund, even if I'm only investing $1,500. A good broker will save you a lot of money in this area. You should also find out the name of the company that manages the fund and phone them; some sell units direct to the public without any sales charge at all.

Back-end Load Funds

These are mutual funds that don't charge you anything when you buy, but hit you for a fee when you decide to cash in. They're quite common in the U.S. but something of a rarity in Canada. The best known is probably Industrial Horizon Fund, which was launched with a great fanfare of publicity early in 1987. It charges a 4½% redemption fee if you cash in your units during the first year. That charge drops by half a percentage point a year, so that after you've held the fund for nine years, it vanishes. The idea, of course, is to discourage people from redeeming their fund units. If you plan to buy and hold for a long time, that's fine. But if you plan to move your money around, back-end loads are an inhibiting factor.

Management Fees

Every mutual fund has a management fee structure, usually expressed as a percentage of the total fund assets. So if a fund has $100 million in assets and charges a 1.25% annual management fee, the managers would receive $1.25 million a year for their services. This money comes out of the fund's holdings before distributions are made to investors and goes directly to the fund's managers. That means you may never be aware the money is being taken out. But those fees are cutting into your profits so you should consider them when you make your mutual fund investment decisions.

Sometimes part of the management fee also pays for the expenses involved in running the fund, which can be quite high. But more often these expenses are an extra charge on fund profits.

Although management fees are common all funds, the amount the managers take can vary significantly. For example, London Life Equity Fund charges a 0.975% fee for its management services. Guaranty Trust, on the other hand, charges 2%. Both charge expenses directly to the fund.

The *Mutual Fund Sourcebook* of the *Financial Times* has developed something called a Management Expense Ratio which takes all fees and expenses into account and shows you how much it actually costs to run a fund. The costs can range from less than 1% to about 3%. When you're dealing with hundreds of millions of dollars, that can mean a big difference in the fund's profit, and therefore in your return on investment. That's why it's a good idea to do some checking before you buy.

VOLATILITY

This is a term you must understand before you choose a mutual funds investment strategy. A fund's volatility is simply a measure of how likely it is to move sharply in response to what's happening in the stock or bond market. The most volatile equity funds will tend to score the best gains in a bull market and the worst losses when there's a market crash. A fund with a lower volatility rating will be more stable—the ups won't be as exciting; the downs won't be as gut-wrenching.

If you're investing for the long term, you'll probably want a fund with a low volatility rating. That means your chances of losing a substantial part of your investment will be lower in the event of a sudden decline in the market.

On the other hand, if you choose a mix-'em-and-move-'em fund strategy—one in which you keep switching from one fund to another in an attempt to take advantage of the hot areas— you'll probably want to look at more volatile funds. Just pray you can get out before the market goes down.

As you might expect from what you've read so far, the funds with the highest degree of volatility tend to be the sector funds— those that specialize in particular areas of the economy, such as gold, energy, and natural resources. The international equity funds also tend to rank high on the volatility list.

The least volatile funds are the money market funds, which are about as stable a mutual fund investment as you'll find. Mortgage funds are close behind.

RRSP/RRIF ELIGIBLE

The federal government has imposed some pretty tight restrictions on the type of investments you can hold in a Registered Retirement Savings Plan (and in Registered Retirement Income Funds—RRIFs—which are taken out after retirement). If you're buying mutual funds for your RRSP, you have to take this into account.

If a fund is listed in the paper as RRSP-eligible, that means you can hold it in your plan without restriction. If it's shown as being of limited eligibility only, then you have some problems.

While you can hold limited RRSP-eligible funds in your plan, they are considered to be foreign investments. As such, they can't exceed 10% of your plan's book value (the prices at which you purchased the securities, not their present resale value). So if your RRSP has a book value of $10,000, you can't hold more than $1,000 worth of foreign securities in it.

Typically, limited-eligibility funds will be those which specialize in foreign investments, such as U.S. or international equity funds. If you're considering any of them for your RRSP, be careful.

Specialized funds, such as those involved in mortgages, gold, and real estate, are usually RRSP-eligible. But it's always good policy to double-check before you buy.

NET ASSET VALUE

This is the value of each unit of a fund at any given point in time. Sometimes you'll see two net asset values shown, one of which is labelled "fully diluted." That simply means that all potential shares have been taken into account, for example, those that might be issued as a result of people exercising warrants (which allow for purchase of shares at a specific price for a certain time) or convertible bonds (bonds which can be exchanged for stock at the owner's request).

OPEN-END FUNDS

These are mutual funds which continue to issue new units from their treasury. In other words, there's no limit on the number of units that can be held by the public. Most mutual funds fall into this group. Holders of units in an open-end fund can cash them in at any time for their current net asset value.

CLOSED-END FUNDS

These funds sell a fixed number of shares at the outset; after that purchasers can only buy them from another investor, normally on the stock exchange. So only a limited number of shares exist and that number never increases. Closed-end funds haven't been very popular in recent years because, for reasons no one seems able to adequately explain, they tend to trade at a discount to their net asset value. That means you can buy them on the stock exchange for less than they're really worth—something that doesn't happen with open-end funds. As a result, some closed-end funds have been converting to open-end in order to improve the return to investors. Two of the best known funds to do this are Guardian-Morton Shulman Precious Metals and Guardian Pacific Rim, both of which changed over in 1987.

Those are all the basics you need to know for starters. Now that the homework is done, let's get on to the fun part—finding some mutual fund strategies that will make you money.

Building Wealth With Funds

CHAPTER 18

T HE FIRST MUTUAL FUND I ever bought was AGF Special Fund. Perhaps it would be more accurate to describe it as the first mutual fund I was ever sold; it's a time-worn but still true cliché in the industry that most mutual funds are sold, not bought. That should immediately put you on your guard when it comes to mutual fund purchases.

It was the late 1960s. My father had recently passed away, leaving me a small amount of money. Most of it went towards the downpayment on our first home in west-end Ottawa. But there was a bit left over and I decided to try my hand at investing.

Mutual funds go through cycles of public favour and disfavour — cycles which, not surprisingly, tend to coincide with what's happening in the stock market. In the late '60s, funds were hot — in fact, they would never be as desirable again until the roaring bull market of the mid-1980s.

I can't remember exactly how I became involved with AGF (which has since become one of the leaders in the mutual funds industry in Canada). I do recall their sales literature: it was full of impressive looking graphs and terrific performance claims. In that regard, nothing much has changed over the years.

I had $1,000 available, quite a bit of money at that time, especially since I was making less than $15,000 a year. With the great track record the AGF funds had already established, I figured I couldn't lose. And the salesman who sold me the fund did everything he could to reinforce that impression.

Sigh. If only I'd known. . . . It didn't occur to me then that the fact the stock market was at one of its periodic highs might indicate this wasn't the best time to buy. Mistake number one. Nor did I worry about the 9% front-end load. The salesman assured me I'd earn it back within months, and the record of the fund was so good to that point his argument seemed perfectly logical. Mistake number two.

You can guess what happened. The market went into a tailspin a few months later. I watched in horror as the value of my fund units dropped. It never occurred to me to take advantage of the lower price and invest more. Mistake number three.

The value of my holdings fell by around 25% (including the front-end load) before bottoming out. I almost panicked and cashed in my units at one point, but I held on. The units finally recovered their original value and, with great relief, I sold them in February, 1973. Mistake number four.

My net profit after holding the fund for about four years was $23.63. Not exactly a sterling performance.

But if I'd held on at that point, this would be a different story. If I had not drawn out the money—nor invested any more—the units in AGF Special Fund which were worth just over $1,000 when I sold them in 1973 would have increased in value to over $12,500 by July 1987.

Mind you, it would have taken strong nerves to hang in. The fund dropped by 18.5% in 1974 and by another 3.9% in 1975 before turning around and recording a series of spectacular gains which included profits of over 70% in 1981 and '83.

But that's the way mutual funds work. Either you pick a good one with solid management and stay in it over the long haul or you trade in and out of them like stocks, trying to catch the hot ones on the way up. More experienced investors can try that route; I wouldn't recommend it if you're just starting out.

The 1980s saw a huge revival of interest in mutual funds, or *investment funds* as they're also called. Sales of new units hit record levels both in Canada and the U.S. as small investors sought to use the funds as a way to participate in the booming stock and bond markets.

The hot markets were a major force behind the fund industry revival, but there were others as well. The growth of RRSPs has created a huge pool of investment money in Canada, an increasing portion of which has been directed into mutual funds. As well, investors are becoming more sophisticated. They want a better return on their money than a savings account or a GIC offers, especially when they read reports of big money being made in the markets. Perhaps the most important element of all in the fund industry revival was performance. Some mutual funds did remarkably well during the 1980s, with growth rates that once seemed unattainable to the ordinary investor.

We've already looked at some of them, but here's a couple more from the *Financial Times Mutual Fund Sourcebook*.

MD Growth Investments Equity Fund is a special fund open only to members of the Canadian Medical Association. If you're a doctor and you're not in it, you should be. It's a no-load fund with a great track record.

Let's suppose you'd invested $1,000 a year in this fund during the decade from 1977 to 1986. That's a total investment of $10,000.

By the end of 1986, the value of your units would have reached $47,855.72. That's real wealth building.

Or, let's suppose that at the beginning of 1982 you began a program of investing $1,000 a year in RoyFund Equity, a no-load fund which you can obtain through branches of the Royal Bank. The first year would have been a disaster—your investment would have fallen in value by one third. But if you'd resisted the natural temptation to pull out your money and head for the hills and instead stuck with your program for five years, your total investment at the end of 1986 would have been worth $9,435.94. Your total contributions would have amounted to $5,000, so even with that serious first-year loss your investment would have increased in value by almost 90% over the five-year period.

That performance tells you why I recommend a patient and conservative mutual fund strategy for beginning wealth builders. Funds will have their ups and downs, that's inevitable. But if they're solid and well managed, they'll pay off in the long run for those who set up a regular investment program and stick to it through good times and bad.

This doesn't mean you should never withdraw your money or switch funds. If your particular fund is consistently not meeting the industry average for its group, you should certainly move to one that is doing better. But don't pull out just because of one bad year, especially if the whole fund industry is going through a difficult time. If anything, that's the time to increase your contributions, to take advantage of low unit prices.

Enough of the preliminaries. Now let's get into some specific strategies you can use.

CHOOSING A FUND

Your initial choice of a fund is critical. You want to get involved with a company with a good track record, strong prospects for the future, a good reporting program and strong management. How do you find the right one?

1. *Assess the economic climate.* If possible, avoid buying into a fund just when it's about to go through one of its periodic declines. If interest rates appear to be on the way up, don't rush to buy a bond fund; you may be able to pick it up six months from now at 10% less. If the stock market appears to be peaking or is in a clear-cut bear phase, stay away from equity funds. Again, you'll probably be able to buy them more cheaply in six months.

This doesn't mean you should try to outguess the markets every step of the way. But for your initial fund purchase decision, at least give it a try.

If you're not sure just what's happening, start with a money market fund and watch for awhile. You can switch into some other type of fund when you're more comfortable.

2. *Check out the fund's performance.* Spend a couple of hours with the *Financial Post* or *Financial Times*, reviewing their mutual fund performance tables. You're looking for a combination of good results and consistency. If a fund has shown a solid record of growth over the past ten years, the odds are in your favour that will continue—although, of course, nothing is guaranteed. The tables will tell you how the fund has performed over the past year, three years, five years, and ten years.

Look closely at the pattern of the average annual compound rates of return. If they're highest over the ten year period and declining as the time span gets shorter, it could be a warning that the fund isn't performing up to earlier standards. I prefer to see an improvement in the performance pattern. For instance, in July, 1987, *Financial Times* reported that the Cundill Value Fund, an international equity fund that was one of the high flyers in the late '70s and early '80s, had achieved an average compound rate of return of 24.1% over ten years. But the average return over five years was down to 23.3%, and over three years was only 17.4%. That type of pattern would cause me concern as a first-time investor.

On the other hand, Cambridge Growth Fund, a load fund that invests in Canadian stocks, recorded an average 18.3% return over ten years—not a bad performance but not up to the standard of the Cundill Value Fund. But the five-year average was 28.1%. And the three-year average was an astounding 32.7%. This would appear to be a fund that, as of mid-1987, was on an upward surge. That type of pattern should strongly appeal to the first-time fund investor.

3. *Don't buy a new fund.* That may sound harsh, especially since the market is teeming with new and exciting investment funds. But stop and think a moment. When you purchase a new fund, what exactly are you buying? There's no track record to guide you. You have no clue as to the fund's performance. It could go gangbusters, but it could also be a dog.

When you buy a new fund, you're usually buying hope. New funds are often heavily promoted to the investing public; the Industrial Horizon Fund and the Hume Funds are recent examples. Promotion doesn't mean the funds aren't good. But hype is a poor substitute for a proven performance record when it comes to making a selection.

4. *Give preference to no-load funds.* (But don't automatically eliminate the front-end load options.) If you're just starting out and don't have a lot of money to invest, expensive front-end loads can be a real drain on your assets. Load funds also tend to lock you in; the high up-front charges make many people reluctant to switch to something else if the fund fails to perform to expectations.

That a fund charges a front-end load does not guarantee its success by any means. But it is true that of the top ten performing mutual funds in the decade from 1977-86, according to *Financial Times* rankings, eight were available to the general public—and all eight were load funds. In fact, only two no-load funds made the top 20—CA Mutual Accumulating Fund and RoyFund Equity.

Since all of the top performing funds during that period were equity funds of one type or another, you'd obviously be severely restricting yourself if you went the equity route but limited your choices to no-loads. But if you decided in favour of some other type of fund—say a mortgage fund or a bond fund—it would be a different story. There are a number of excellent no-loads among the top performers in those groups.

If you do decide on a load fund, remember to shop around for the best price. Very rarely should you have to pay the full commission charge; brokers will often sell them for less than half the maximum quoted fee. And remember to check with the fund company itself to see if it will sell you units directly with no commission charge.

One final word on load versus no-load. Never, never pay a load charge to get into a money market fund. There's not enough variation in their performance to make it worthwhile. For instance, the Bolton Tremblay Money Fund had a slightly better track record than the AGF Money Market Fund during the three-year period from 1984-86. But the Bolton Tremblay fund charges a maximum load of 2%. The AGF fund is no-load. Once the 2% load is factored in, it turns out you'd have been slightly ahead putting $1,000 a year into AGF over that period, even though on the surface it didn't appear to perform quite as well.

Also, money market funds are useful for switching money in and out of, depending on market conditions. If you plan to use the fund that way, you don't want to be stuck with paying a sales commission every time.

5. *Choose a fund that meets your objectives.* If you're like most Canadians, your number one priority is safety of capital. If that's the case, start with funds that hold relatively safe investments—you can check which ones they are in the previous chapter. Stay away from the speculative funds. They may have more growth potential but they're also higher-risk.

You should also consider your financial requirements over the next few years. For instance, if you think you may have to cash in soon for retirement or other needs, a low volatility fund with a minimal risk potential becomes an even greater priority. In these circumstances, a mortgage fund would be a good option. With a high volatility fund you run the risk of being caught in a downturn just when you need the cash.

The portfolio-building strategy outlined for your RRSP in Chapter Fifteen is equally valid here if you're just starting out. Begin modestly, protect your capital base, and only add higher-risk funds to the mix as you progress.

6. *Find out the costs.* There can be all kinds of fees associated with mutual funds beyond the front-end load. Some charge you to switch from one fund to another in the same family. Some funds have a one-time set-up or registration charge. Some funds levy a cancellation charge if you pull out. There can also be administration fees, withdrawal fees, certificate fees, and more. Be sure to ask before you sign on.

7. *Ask about the reporting system.* Most funds will send you a quarterly performance report, but check.

8. *Inquire about the fund's managers.* They should be solid people with a good reputation in the financial community. A knowledgeable stock broker can help you here; he or she should know the background of any major fund manager. The management team is extremely important in your selection of a fund; they're the people you're trusting to look after your money. Some are very good, with proven track records. Others are mediocre or unknown quantities. Ask yourself which type you prefer.

Managing your funds

Making the initial fund selection is only the first step in using mutual funds to build wealth. From then on, it becomes a matter of skillful financial management if you're going to make the most out of your investments. Here are some guidelines that may help as you move forward.

1. *Diversify.* Just as you wouldn't consider putting all your money into one stock, don't stay with just one fund. Introduce more funds into your portfolio as soon as possible, preferably different types. This allows you to spread your risk—if you only hold equity funds and the stock market falls, you're going to take a beating. A basic mutual fund portfolio would include an equity fund, a bond or mortgage fund, a gold fund and a money market fund. This combination gives you stock market participation, an inflation hedge in your gold fund, an interest play in the bond/mortgage fund, and what amounts to a cash position in the money market fund. Once you have that structure in place, you can add extra funds if you wish.

Don't go to the other extreme and over-diversify, however. Building a large mutual fund collection is not a good strategy. The more funds you have, the more work that's involved in monitoring them. And the more difficult it is to maintain a regular investment program.

2. *Establish a fund investment plan and stick to it.* As we've already seen, regular contributions to a well-managed fund will pay off over the long haul. One term for this is *dollar-cost averaging*; that simply means putting a specific amount of money, say $500, into a fund at regular intervals. In this way the cost of your units is averaged out over the years to somewhere between the fund's high and low points.

3. *Never turn your back on your money.* Monitor the performance of your funds on a regular basis and compare the results with others in the same group. That's easy to do; just check the quarterly reports in the financial papers. Pay particular attention to the average for the group, which you'll find at the end of each section. If you discover you're in a fund that continues to underperform the average for more than six consecutive quarters, it may be time to consider a switch to one with a stronger record.

4. *Avoid leveraging.* During the mid-1980s, when the stock markets were going crazy, borrowing to invest in mutual funds became the rage. I know of people who took out huge mortgages on their property to invest in mutual funds, with hopes of making a big killing.

The attractions are obvious. Not only were you in a position to increase your return on investment, you also got a tax break to make the prize even bigger.

So widespread did the practice become that in 1986 an estimated 30% of all mutual fund sales in Canada were paid for with borrowed cash. That amounted to something in the order of $800 million. The situation finally reached the point where the Ontario Securities Commission, the watchdog of the investment industry in the province, felt obliged to issue a warning about the dangers of borrowing money to invest in funds.

As I discussed in Chapter Twelve, there's nothing wrong with borrowing to invest. In fact, it can be a smart decision in the right circumstances. But timing is critical because, as we've seen, leveraging magnifies your risks. If you borrow to buy equity funds when the stock market is high and the economy then turns sour, you could end up in serious financial trouble. That's probably why John Templeton, the dean of fund managers, offered these words of advice on a visit to Toronto in mid-1987, a time when the markets were high: "Do not have heavy debts against investments in mutual funds."

The tax consequences of borrowing to buy funds must also be considered. When Finance Minister Michael Wilson announced his tax reform proposals in June 1987, he increased the risks involved in this type of leveraging by reducing your potential after-tax return.

Let's look at how a leveraging strategy worked with a mutual fund purchased in 1986, when the market was so hot, and what would happen today as a result of tax reform. (As I write this, the tax reform measures haven't been passed into law, so any references to them are based on the assumption they went ahead as outlined by Mr. Wilson in June 1987.)

Suppose that in January 1985 you had set aside $5,000 which you wanted to put into a fund. But then you talked to a fund representative or read an article about leveraging. As a result, you decided to borrow an additional $20,000 at 13%, increasing your total mutual fund investment to $25,000.

Over the next three years, your money grew at the rate of 15% a year—and that's a modest performance by the standards of that period. At the end of 1987, you sold and took your profits. Instead of the profit of just over $2,600 you would have received if you hadn't borrowed, you now have a profit of over $13,000. You had to pay the interest on the loan, though, which was $2,600 a year, or a total of $7,800 for the three years. But those interest costs were tax deductible, so if you were in a 50% bracket you'd have saved half of that, making your after tax cost $3,900.

That made your real profit from the whole deal $9,100 ($13,000 minus $3,900 interest). That profit was a capital gain, and we'll assume your lifetime exemption shielded it from tax. The result: A whopping 182% return on your original $5,000 investment—compared to a 52% return if you hadn't borrowed. Pretty good, right? You can see why people rushed to try it.

Now let's suppose you did the same thing today. All the numbers are the same, and fund produces the same return. We'll assume that, as a result of tax reform, your combined federal and provincial rate is 43.5%.

Look what some subtle rule changes do to your profits. First, the government changed the way in which taxable capital gains are calculated. In the past, 50% of gains were tax-free, 50% were subject to tax. In 1988, two thirds of your capital gains became subject to tax. In 1989, 75% of gains are taxable.

There were also changes made to the rules governing your interest payments. As a result of tax reform, you now have to deduct the cost of your borrowed money from the amount you can claim against your capital gains exemption. I've illustrated the effects of these changes below, assuming 75% of capital gains are potentially taxable:

	1985 Investment	Today's Investment
Your money	$ 5,000	$ 5,000
Borrowed money	20,000	20,000
Total at risk	25,000	25,000
Value after 3 years	38,022	38,022
Capital gain	13,022	13,022
Tax-free portion	6,511	3,256
Taxable portion	6,511	9,766
Interest cost (gross)	7,800	7,800
Interest cost (after tax)	3,900	4,407
Interest cost deduction from taxable capital gains	0	(7,800)
Allowable capital gains exemption	6,511	1,966
Taxable capital gains	0	7,800
Tax at 43.5%	0	3,393
Net profit	$ 9,122	$ 5,222
Return on investment	**182%**	**104%**

See what's happened? When you leveraged your mutual fund investment in 1985, you walked away with a net profit of $9,122. As a result of the tax changes, the same manoeuvre today would net you only $5,222. That's still more than double the $2,600 profit you would have had if you hadn't borrowed the $20,000. But you have to take a close look at whether the risks involved are still worth it.

That's because while your potential rewards have been cut, your risks have actually increased a bit. Let's suppose the fund lost 15% a year in the two instances we've looked at. What happens?

	1985 Investment	Today's Investment
Your money	$ 5,000	$ 5,000
Borrowed money	20,000	20,000
Total at risk	25,000	25,000
Value after 3 years	15,353	15,353
Loss	9,647	9,647
Interest cost (gross)	7,800	7,800
Interest cost (after tax)	3,900	4,407
Net loss	**$13,547**	**$14,054**

As you can see, tax reform has slightly increased your potential loss in this situation. And remember, the only way you can get a tax break for those losses is if you have some capital gains to offset them. Capital losses aren't deductible from any other income.

Had you not borrowed at all, by the way, your loss in this situation would have been limited to about $1,930.

You can see how tax reform has eroded the advantages of leveraging on both sides of the equation. On the one hand, your profit potential has been reduced. On the other, your loss potential has been slightly increased.

The combination makes leveraged mutual funds even more risky for the beginning wealth builder. My advice is to stay away, at least until such time as you've acquired more investing experience and have a clearer understanding of the risks involved.

5. *Consider fund "families."* One of the more popular investment innovations in recent years has been the growth of mutual fund families. These consist of separate mutual funds run by the same company—the AGF funds and the Industrial group of funds managed by MacKenzie Financial are examples.

These families offer investors the ability to switch their assets from fund to another at minimal cost. This is a useful privilege, especially as you become more experienced in money management. There may be times, for example, when you want to protect profits made in equity funds by switching part or all of the assets into a money market fund. If you're operating within a fund family, this type of transfer can be arranged quickly and easily, usually with just a phone call.

Fund switching is really a game for more seasoned investors. But even beginners may wish to do it occasionally when clear-cut situations present themselves.

Mutual funds are a good way to start an investment portfolio and you should consider them carefully when you feel the time is right. Just remember, they're like any other investment. You have to select them carefully, monitor them regularly, and treat them as long-term holdings. If you follow the strategies I've outlined and do your homework carefully, mutual funds should add considerably to your wealth over time.

Who's Afraid of the Stock Market?

I T'S HARDLY NEWS that Canadians are ultra-conservative when it comes to money. Traditionally, we simply haven't been risk takers. We have a fascination for people who are—E.P. Taylor, Roy Thomson, Conrad Black. But given a choice, most of us would opt to bury our money in the backyard rather than put it into a risky investment, even though that investment might have major growth potential.

That element in our national psyche probably explains why, until very recently, only about half as many Canadians as Americans owned stocks, on a proportionate basis. According to a 1983 study carried out by the Toronto Stock Exchange, less than 15% of Canadians owned stock in one form or another. The TSE called that "worrisome" and said that something had to be done to encourage people to overcome their "undue concern with risk, and their lack of understanding about stock investment."

Well, something *was* done. The mid-1980s saw the stock markets take off into the stratosphere. It was almost impossible not to make money; just about every major stock increased substantially in value. The impression of other people getting rich while they stood still made a big impact on many stockless Canadians.

The federal government added to the incentive to get into stocks by introducing a $500,000 lifetime capital gains exemption (later reduced to $100,000 under tax reform).

Many provincial governments also got into the act, offering residents tax breaks which would encourage them to invest in stocks of companies located in their provinces.

As a result, by the time the TSE completed its 1986 survey, over 20% of the adult population were shareholders. TSE chairman Donald Page described that increase as "dramatic" and said that "Canadian ownership of equities now rivals the level of shareownership in the United States".

So buying stocks became a fashionable thing for new investors to do. As long as the bull market stayed hot, that was well and good. But it didn't take long for the bear market that followed the October, 1987 crash to send newcomers into mass retreat, licking their wounds as they went.

The plain fact is that many novice stock buyers probably shouldn't have been in the market at all. They were attracted by tax breaks and dreams of a quick buck; they knew virtually nothing about what they were getting into. As Andrew Sarlos, one of Bay Street's most canny money managers, observed at the height of the bull market: "Many of these people probably don't even know that stocks can go down. They think up is the only direction that exists."

Well, stocks *can* go down—sometimes a lot, as we learned yet again on that traumatic Black Monday. Sure, there are great profits to be made. But there is also large loss potential for the naive or the unlucky.

Don't interpret this as a suggestion that stocks are to be avoided at all costs. That's not the case. It's more a matter of priorities. There are other places where you should direct your money first. Then, when the time does come to venture into the stock market, you should do so cautiously and with a clear understanding of what you're getting into.

Let's pause for a moment here and review the priorities a good wealth builder should have in place.

Number one is the family home—acquiring one and paying down the mortgage.

Number two is an RRSP, because the tax breaks make it a unique wealth-building vehicle.

Number three are some interest-bearing investments, like CSBs, TDs, and GICs. These enable you to gain some feel for money management without putting your capital at undue risk.

Number four are mutual funds. You're now adding an increased element of risk to your assets, in the hope of generating better returns. But your risk level is still relatively low, especially if you use the plan I outlined to build a mutual funds portfolio.

Number five would be bonds, mainly because I think they're easier for most people to understand and be successful with than are stocks. As I said in Chapter Ten, the key to profitable bond investing is getting the interest rate trends right. There are many more variables when it comes to investing in stocks.

Let me be clear here. I'm not suggesting you have to complete each stage before you move on to the next. It isn't a case of paying off the family home before you set up an RRSP. You should be gradually developing a range of assets as you go.

Rather, the above list should be used as a guideline on how to progressively add different assets to your holdings. Which brings me back to stocks.

I would not suggest the beginning wealth builder get involved with the stock market directly until he or she has had some experience with more basic types of investments. I would especially recommend holding one or more equity-based mutual funds for a period of time. This can be an excellent way to learn about the stock market, especially if the fund has a good reporting system. The Hume Funds are among the best in this regard; they publish a periodic newsletter which discusses the buy and sell decisions made by the fund managers and the rationale behind them. This kind of information will provide you with invaluable insights into how the professionals make investment decisions. You have to take the time to read and digest it, however; too often mutual fund investors simply throw away their reports unread. What a waste of potentially valuable information.

Your reports will also provide a summary of the fund's holdings, usually as of the end of the last quarter. This gives you an opportunity to see how professional money managers deal with diversification by spreading their risk among a variety of stocks in various market sectors. You'll also receive information on how much of the fund's holdings are in cash. Watch that percentage closely; the higher it is, the more nervous the fund managers are about general market conditions—and the more nervous you should be too if you're thinking of striking out on your own.

As you approach the point when you feel you may want to go into the stock market, pay even closer attention to the financial press. Watch the investments section in the *Financial Times* to see what the brokers are recommending. Pick some of the stocks that sound pretty good and start developing your own phantom portfolio. Make notes on what the recommendation predicted would happen to the stock's price and see which ones pan out over a period of time.

The phantom portfolio stage is extremely important for the first-time stock market investor. Make your selections carefully; pretend you're really putting your money at risk. Track the performance of your stocks at least weekly. Make sales when you think it's appropriate and note the gains or losses. Add new stock when it appears a buying opportunity has presented itself.

Judge the results realistically. If you're consistently losing money in your phantom portfolio, analyze why. Is it because the entire market is down? If so, are your stocks doing better or worse than the index average? If you're doing better, be encouraged—your stock picking instincts are good. It's just a question of honing your market timing instincts.

As you're monitoring your phantom portfolio, tune into what's happening to the markets generally, especially the Toronto Stock Exchange and the New York Stock Exchange. Read the daily reports in the financial section of your newspaper on what the indexes are doing. Find out whether the market is in a bull (advancing) or bear (declining) phase. Develop a sense of what the financial professionals are saying and thinking. In mid-1987, for instance, there was a great deal of nervousness arising from the fact the markets were at near-record highs. Fears were being expressed that a major downturn was in the offing, perhaps even the start of a bear market after five years of steady gains—fears which turned out to be well-grounded. Ask yourself whether you would want to begin a stock investment program in that kind of climate.

There is, of course, no perfect time to buy stocks. But some periods offer better prospects for gains than others. Ironically, it's not always the time when euphoria is sweeping the market when the best profits can be made. In fact, undue optimism may be the harbinger of disaster, as the 1929 crash demonstrated. Long-time stock market watchers know that times when doom and gloom is everywhere can be the most rewarding of all. Everyone has heard stories of how fortunes were made by those with the courage and the foresight to buy stocks like General Motors when they were at their low point during the Great Depression. But there are more recent examples of cashing in on a doomsday scenario.

In mid-1982, for instance, there was serious concern that North America was tumbling into another depression. The economy was in a tailspin. Long-established companies were closing down. Those firms that survived were chopping staff right and left in an effort to reduce overheads. Middle-class families who had never before faced serious financial difficulties suddenly found themselves in real trouble as salaries were frozen and second jobs lost. In a phrase, things were in a helluva mess.

The stock market responded accordingly. Prices of top quality shares were way down. There was fear they would fall even lower, perhaps to levels seen in the '30s.

That's when smart investors bought. They picked up shares of Torstar Corporation, publishers of the Toronto Star, in the $8 to $10 range. Five years later, in mid-1987, they were trading at around $35. They bought Lac Minerals, the big gold producer, for less than $5 a share. By mid-1987, those shares were selling for over $40. Imperial Oil stock could be had for a bargain price of between $20 and $25 a share. Five years later it was worth over $75.

Obviously, the first-time investor is going to have difficulty deciding exactly when to jump in. The temptation is to enter the market when enthusiasm is high. You tend to get swept away in the psychology of the moment—the madness of crowds can cast a spell on all of us.

But you must exercise patience. Your first stock purchase is a critical one in the wealth-building process. If you get badly burned, it may turn you off the market for years, perhaps forever. It's happened to others. If that should occur, you'd be cutting yourself off from one of the most exciting, and most lucrative, wealth-building techniques around. That's why it's so important to give yourself every opportunity for success the first time out.

Here are some thoughts that may help you in the initial timing decision.

1. Be patient. Wait for the right moment to make a purchase. Don't rush.

2. The best possible time to enter the market is after a lengthy downturn, when indexes are showing signs of starting to move up and the economy seems to have bottomed out.

3. Don't enter when stocks are at an all-time high. They may move higher, sure. But your risk potential is much greater in that situation.

When you do decide to go in, move cautiously. You will have put some money aside for stock investment at that stage; don't invest it all at once. Get a feel for what you're doing. Talk things over with your broker (more on that in the next chapter). Explain your strategy, and get him or her on-side.

I strongly suggest that you begin by assembling a modest portfolio of top quality blue chip stocks. There'll be a temptation not to go this route, for a couple of reasons. First, blue chip stocks tend to be expensive. Beginning stock investors often feel more comfortable with $5 stocks than with $50 ones. And there's the nagging feeling that it's easier for a $5 stock to double than for the $50 stock to reach $100. Well, t'aint so. It's the value and performance of the company that's important. And when you buy a premium-priced blue chip stock, that's what you're getting.

The other tug away from the blue chips will be the stories of huge profits made from penny mining stocks. It's true, that does happen occasionally. But for every penny stock that strikes it rich, 100 others will fail. There are times when playing the penny stocks can be fun and maybe even profitable. But not when you're just starting out.

But blue chips, you may be muttering. Boring.

Think so? Try these on for size. At the beginning of January 1987, you could have bought shares of Ford of Canada for $154 each. By the end of July they were trading at close to $200—a gain of almost 30% in just seven months. IBM shares were going for $167 Canadian in early January. Seven months later they were over $215—a gain of just under 23%. You could have purchased Shell Canada for $26 at the start of the year. By the end of July it was trading around $47—up an astounding 81%!

The point is there's plenty of action in blue chip stocks—and a lot of money to be made. So don't be lured by the siren call of cheap shares or highly touted juniors. Stay with the big boys, at least at the start. If you time your market entry properly, you'll reduce your chance of a major loss first time out—and you may find yourself with a tidy profit faster than you expected.

Don't put all your money into a single stock. If you haven't got enough cash to buy shares in four or five companies, hold off until you do. No mutual fund manager would dream of putting all his or her assets into one stock, no matter how good its prospects. Too risky. You're in the same position. No matter how good a stock may appear to be, don't let everything ride on it.

Spread your initial stock selections across several market sectors. Don't load up in one area, such as oils or gold. We've already discussed the high volatility rate of sector mutual funds, those which concentrate in a particular area. Don't create a similar situation for yourself in your stock selections.

Here's an example of how you might go about starting a stock portfolio. Please note that I'm *not*, in any way, recommending you purchase the particular stocks mentioned. I'm only using them as examples of companies in different sectors.

For starters, you should decide which sectors of the economy you'd like to be involved with financially. There's a broad range of choices: the forest industry, mining, real estate, oil and gas, banks, steel, breweries, high technology companies, financial services, management companies, communications firms, pipe-lines—the list goes on and on. The Toronto Stock Exchange lists 32 sub-indexes that allow you to track the current performance in each of the main sectors; the financial section of your newspaper should carry them.

Some sectors do better than others at certain stages in the business cycle. For instance, natural resource stocks tend to perform best in the late phases of an economic boom. Stocks of consumer products firms, by contrast, will perform best in the early stages, when interest rates are low and consumer confidence is recovering from a just-ending recession.

If you have a good broker, he or she should be able to advise you as to what sectors appear to offer the best prospects at the time you're ready to enter the market.

Let's say, for example, that after reviewing the situation you decide you want to begin with investments in the management, communications, integrated oils, and bank sectors. Your next step is to review the major blue chip companies in those areas to see which appear to have the best growth potential. Try to narrow the selection down to three in each group.

In the management sector, you might find that your choice comes down to Brascan, Power Corporation and Canadian Pacific. Among the integrated oils, Imperial, Shell and Texaco may look like the best bets. In the communications sector, Maclean-Hunter, Thomson Newspapers, and CHUM Ltd. may seem attractive. Among the banks you may settle on Toronto-Dominion, Bank of Montreal and CIBC as the leading candidates.

Now comes the toughest part of all: choosing which stocks to actually buy.

Ask your broker to supply you with research reports on the companies in those sectors his or her firm is recommending.

Read them over carefully—broker research reports are written in a language all their own; if they appear to be damning a stock with faint praise ("appears to have overcome recent difficulties"; "may have long-term profit potential"), avoid it.

Look for such things as a steady improvement in earnings in recent years. Check the price/earnings radio (the ratio between the price of the stock and the earnings per share) and see how it compares with others in its group. In general, a low price/earnings ratio is good; as long as the company is sound, a low p/e ratio suggests the stock price is not overvalued in comparison to similar firms.

See what the brokerage firm has to say about dividend payouts. A stock with a good dividend and a solid payment history will tend to hold up better in a market downturn.

Finally, see how strong the brokerage house is in its buy recommendation. Is the report giving the stock lukewarm approval, or is the tone one of genuine enthusiasm?

Also, read the financial press carefully for any references to the companies you've selected. Is there a new scare on loan defaults by Third World countries? If so, see which of the banks could be most affected and take that into account when you make your decision. Watch for new earnings reports on the firms in which you're interested. See if anything unusual is happening.

While you're doing all this, track the prices of the candidate stocks in the paper and see how they're performing. If there's any sign of weakness, ask your broker if there's any particular reason for it. It may be just a case of profit-taking, in which case there's a buying opportunity for you.

Once you've done your homework, start buying. But remember, do so gradually. You don't have to place all your orders in the same day. You may spread your initial purchases over a month—perhaps even longer if you're nervous about the general state of the market. In the meantime, keep a close watch on what's happening to the companies you selected for purchase. A new report or a sudden price run-up may affect your decision. If so, don't be afraid to change course and switch to your second choice.

Finally, a word about selling. Some people never sell. They consider themselves to be in the market for the long haul, through good times and bad. So they buy a stock and hang on to it through its peaks and valleys.

This kind of long-range investing approach is perfectly valid and can be very profitable. At the beginning, there's nothing wrong with taking the long perspective with stocks, just as you would with mutual funds.

You may reach a stage, however, when you find you want more action in your stock portfolio. I certainly did.

The reality, of course, is that no stock, no matter how solid and blue chip, is going to rise forever. When the market falls, as it inevitably does, so will the bluest of the blue chip stocks. I found I didn't like going through the gut-wrenching process of watching my profits get wiped out and having to wait for months, perhaps years, to rebuild them.

As I became more knowledgeable about investing, I found myself selling more frequently. And sooner rather than later. Now, I very rarely hold a stock for more than two years. I take my profits (or my losses) and move on.

In doing so, I've missed some opportunities. Stocks that I've sold for a 50% profit would have produced a 100% return if I hadn't let them go. But I've also sold a stock for a 50% gain and then watched as it fell back to my original purchase price.

Just remember: nobody ever went broke taking a profit. Once you've developed a feeling for the market, consider adopting a more aggressive approach. When you buy a stock, set a profit target for it. When it reaches that point, collect your earnings happily and don't worry about leaving some money on the table for the next player.

And, although you don't want to think about losing money, you should also set a loss target. If the stock drops to that level, dump it out. I admit, locking in a loss is the hardest decision a wealth builder faces. You always cling to the hope it might come back. Don't fall into that trap.

This is obviously a different approach from my earlier advice on mutual funds, which was to hold them for the long haul if you're a beginning investor—assuming you've exercised care in your selections.

That's because mutual funds have some built-in safety factors. They represent a diversified portfolio, so you don't have all your money in one investment the way you do with a single stock. And they're managed by professionals who, if they're any good at all, should be able to minimize the impact of a market downturn and profit from the recovery.

With a single stock, however, you're out on a limb. The price may be dropping as a result of a general decline in the market. Or it could be because of serious problems within the company. Unless you know why—and have good reason to believe a turn-around isn't far off—you're better to limit your loss and get out.

I speak from experience here. Let me tell you my classic story about holding a stock too long.

The company was called Nu-West. It was an aggressive, western-based real estate firm that rose to prominence in the Alberta economic boom of the 1970s. I bought 1,000 shares in the late '70s at about $8, on the recommendation of a broker friend.

The stock performed wonderfully well. Within a year it was trading at over $13 and I was delighted. Prospects for the company still looked great. But, applying my rule of taking profits when the target is met, I decided to sell. Because I had 1,000 shares, though, I compromised. I only sold half. I've been kicking myself ever since.

Alberta's economic miracle came to a sudden end. Nu-West, which had borrowed heavily to finance its growth, found itself in deep trouble. The stock began to tumble. But did I sell? No way. I stupidly sat and watched it as it dropped through $10, then $8, then $6.

How could you be so dumb, you ask? Good question. You find yourself applying different rationalizations along the way. When it fell to $10, I dismissed it as a temporary price correction. The company was going through a tough period. But Alberta and Nu-West would come back. Anyway, I had the profit from the initial 500 shares; I could afford to wait out the downturn.

When the stock hit my original purchase price of $8, I clearly should have dumped it. That would have protected my profit from the 500 shares already sold. But I held, still expecting a rebound.

By the time the stock was down in the $4 range, I knew I'd made a bad mistake. But at that point I figured it couldn't drop much lower. All the downside potential was gone. Hah!

Nu-West finally ended up trading for around a quarter a share. That's right, 25¢! And would you believe I still had those lousy 500 shares? Looking back on it. I wonder where my mind was at that point in time. About the only good thing in the whole experience is that it gave me a genuine horror story to tell all you emerging wealth builders.

Incidentally, I still have that stock. There's no point selling it now. I figure I might as well hang on in the hopes that one day management will be able to restore the company to profitability.

So let me say it again. If your stock drops to your loss target—which should probably be set at 15% to 25% below your purchase price—get out. Don't ride the stock down and watch your losses mount. Salvage what you can and live to fight another day.

The stock market is like anything else in life—the more you know about it, the less afraid of it you'll be. Stocks are tricky and potentially dangerous investments. But they can also be immensely rewarding—if you approach them carefully and intelligently.

Your Broker is Your Buddy— Sometimes

S INCE I ENDED the previous chapter with a horror story, let me begin this one with another.

During the winter of 1985, I was keeping a close watch on the stock of a small company based in London, Ontario. The name of the firm was Cableshare, and it had developed what appeared to be revolutionary new method of selling merchandise. It was a shop-at-home technique called Touch 'n Shop, and I had been knocked out when I went to a demonstration of the technology.

The system was based on interactive video discs. It operated by using cable TV and a touch tone phone. People who were hooked up to it could browse through thousands of items of merchandise, watch demonstrations, do price comparisons among several stores, and place orders for home delivery.

Some of the applications were highly innovative. You could plan a vacation to Bermuda by calling up videos of various hotels on the island, with details of their available services and price ranges. If you wanted to look for a new home, Touch 'n Shop could select all the current listings in your price range within your preferred area and bring up photos of home interiors and exteriors on your screen. You could select those that really interested you for a visit and eliminate the rest. The system even contained a mortgage payment calculator which would work out the carrying costs of any house on the basis of the downpayment you planned to make.

Like I said, knockout stuff!

Moreover, Cableshare was 37% owned by J.C. Penney, the huge U.S. retailing giant. They were handling the marketing of this exciting technology, which meant it had an excellent chance of making big inroads in the States.

This was all still in concept stage, of course. Cableshare wasn't making any profits at that point, and there was no guarantee enough people would be willing to change long-time shopping habits to make it profitable.

So the stock was a pure speculation. But I thought it was a pretty good one.

I felt it was priced a bit too high, however, so I watched it over a couple of months. I'd made up my mind that if went below $6, I'd buy.

On March 5, 1986, that happened. The stock slipped to $5.75 a share. I phoned my broker. The nightmare began.

My broker was out of town. But he had an assistant, and he'd told me previously that any time he wasn't available I could safely place my orders with her.

So I did. I asked for 1,000 shares of Cableshare, at a price of $5.75 or better. She acknowledged my order and our conversation ended.

Now I should explain something at this point. I'd dealt with this particular broker for several years prior to this incident. We had grown into a rather casual relationship; he never phoned me back on an order unless there was a problem. If I didn't hear from him, I automatically assumed all was well and a few days later a confirmation of the trade arrived in the mail. Sloppy. I don't do it any more. You're about to find out why.

For the next couple of days, I checked Cableshare prices in my morning scan of the TSE listings. It continued trading at $5.75 on fairly large volume. So it never occurred to me there may have been some difficulty filling my order. I assumed I owned 1,000 shares of the company.

Then the stock started to move. It quickly rose to over $7. In the meantime, I noticed I hadn't received my confirmation slip. So I called. And that's when it all hit the fan.

The assistant told me she'd only put in a "day" order. That's a stock order that automatically expires at the end of the day unless it's renewed. I'd never used day orders, only what are called open orders, which means they're valid until filled or cancelled. My broker knew that. The subject had never come up in my brief conversation with the assistant so it never occurred to me that she might do otherwise.

But she did. At the end of that particular day, the order expired automatically with only 100 shares purchased.

I was livid. I don't think I've ever been so angry in my life. The stock was now trading at $7.50, which meant I'd been done out of a profit of almost $1,600 by the error. Bad enough, certainly. But there's more.

When my broker got back, he tried to placate me. He said the stock was still a good buy at $7.50 and I should pick up the other 900 shares at that price. But after having carefully watched the stock and waiting for just the right moment to buy, I was too angry to do that. No way was I going to pay out $1,600 when I should have had the shares at $5.75.

Well, Cableshare really started to move. When it reached $9 in about a month, I decided to dump my 100 shares and take a 40% profit. The fact was, I was so disgusted by the whole affair I just wanted it out of my portfolio.

That upward move turned out to be just the beginning. By early June—just three months after I had placed my buy order— the stock was trading at over $60 a share! That's right, $60. If my order had gone through as I'd intended and I'd held on during the rise, my original investment would have been worth over $60,000 at that point—a ten-fold return.

I still have bad dreams about it.

This is a rather lengthy story, but it's an important one because it contains several lessons about dealing with brokers.

Lesson one: Just because you've been dealing with a broker for a period of time, don't take anything for granted.

Lesson two: Whenever you place an order, make sure all the details are clear. And if you intend it to be an open order, say so.

Lesson three: Ask your broker to call you back with verbal confirmation that a transaction has been completed. If you haven't heard from your broker by the end of the day, you place the call.

Lesson four: Don't let your emotions get in the way of a good investment decision. My broker had tried to persuade me to buy more Cableshare at the higher price but I'd been so angry I refused to listen. That ended up costing me far more than the original botched order.

A good stockbroker can be worth his or her weight in gold to you. A good broker can provide sound advice on when to buy and sell and what stocks are appropriate for you at any given point in time. He can provide you with research reports prepared by his company. She can advise you of hot new issues that are about to hit the market and make sure you get some. He can tell you about good tax shelter offerings—and bad ones. In short, a good broker can make you a lot of money—just as a bad broker can lose you a lot of money through bad advice, ignorance, or account churning. (Churning is a commission-generating technique practiced by unscrupulous brokers. It involves encouraging clients to buy and sell more than necessary. Since each transaction generates a commission, the more activity there is in an account, the bigger the pay-off for the broker.)

Obviously, the trick is to find yourself a good broker. And believe me, it's not easy. It took me years.

There are five key points to look for when it comes time to select a broker. I call them the Five P's: Personality, Philosophy, Patience, Prudence, and Profits. Let's look at each.

Personality: It's extremely important to find a broker with whom you feel comfortable and whose personality meshes with yours. After all, you're embarking into a new area about which you know very little. You'll probably feel somewhat intimidated at the outset. You need a broker who will relate to you, guide you along, take a little more time explaining things and generally make you feel good about what you're doing. You don't want someone who's going to leave you feeling brow-beaten and nervous.

I remember when I was out searching for a new broker some years ago. I was given the name of a real fireball at one of the largest brokerage houses in the country— a man who'd made fortunes for his clients. I called for an appointment and went to see him.

The meeting was a disaster. The fellow talked faster than a machine gun. He showed no interest in my needs or concerns; instead he monopolized the time by pontificating on his own views on investing. At the end of the meeting he handed me some documents to read and told me if I was interested in becoming one of his clients to call. Needless to say, I never did. He was undoubtedly brilliant, and I happen to know he's still doing very well for his clients. But the personality fit just wasn't there. I like to talk freely with my broker, and not be subjected to ego tripping whenever I call.

So be sure you're comfortable with the personality of any prospective broker before you sign on. If you're not, keep looking— there are plenty of others out there.

Philosophy: There are almost as many different investing philosophies as there are brokers. You'd better find one that thinks more or less like you do, or you're going to end up being very unhappy.

Some brokers believe in taking big risks because when they pay off, the returns are spectacular. Others prefer conservative investments with modest growth potential but low downside risk. Some brokers believe in building solid, long-term portfolios. Others genuinely think that the active trader stands the best chance of profiting. There are brokers who put a great deal of emphasis on proper diversification of your holdings. There are others who pay no attention to that at all, focusing entirely on the strength of individual stocks and not worrying whether you have too much concentration in a particular sector. And the list goes on.

Before you talk to any broker, you should decide what your stock market approach is going to be. If you decide you want to begin with conservative stocks in a well-diversified portfolio, with a view to turning them over as profit objectives are met, then you should look for a broker who shares that philosophy. Otherwise, you and your broker are going to be in a constant state of turmoil and indecision.

Patience: As a beginning stock market investor, you *must* find a broker who has the patience to work with you. That means he'll devote a little more time than you might otherwise expect to explaining new terminology, discussing possible trades, and outlining alternatives. A little hand holding is going to be needed at the outset; make sure you find someone who's prepared to do it.

Prudence: You want a broker who's going to treat your money as if it were his or her own. That means someone who is careful, who assesses the risk in any situation and makes sure you know about it before you go in, and who generally keeps his or her eyes open for potential trouble, such as a major market correction. If a prospective broker gives you the impression of being a little too much of a high flyer, pass. He or she is unlikely to bring the caution and prudence you need to the relationship.

Profits: The most important P of them all. A broker may have all the other virtues I've outlined, but if he or she can't make money for you, forget it. In the end, it's performance that counts. If you end up with a bunch of dogs in your portfolio, any good rapport you may have established with your broker is going to collapse pretty quickly in any event.

Of course, you're really not going to know how effective a broker is in generating profits until you've dealt with him or her for a while. But there are ways of testing the water first. When you're interviewing, ask what he or she is recommending to clients and why. Then track those stocks for a while and see how they do. You might also ask for some examples of past successes—with trading slips to back up any claims, of course.

One broker I know has a sign on his wall that pretty well sums it up: "Our clients don't come to us so they can sleep well. They come to us so they can eat well."

Those are the Five P's to look for. Now, how do you go about conducting your broker search?

To begin with, allocate some time. You should select a broker as carefully as you would a doctor, dentist, or lawyer. That means doing some proper research and having some interviews. Don't decide you're too busy and grab the first broker who can talk in coherent sentences; you'll regret it later.

Next, give some thought to the type of brokerage house you want. A bigger firm will have a number of advantages: a larger research department and better opportunities to participate in new issues are just two. A smaller firm will probably track fewer stocks but may monitor the ones it does more closely. And you may get more personalized service.

Once you have some idea of the type of brokerage house you'd prefer, you can begin the search for a specific broker. Start by asking friends and acquaintances for recommendations. Whom do they use, are they happy with him or her, why or why not? Don't just get a phone number to call. Do a little probing. See how well their brokers fit with the Five Ps.

If you can't come up with any good leads this way, your task is obviously going to be more difficult. But you should still be able to locate the right person.

Contact several brokerage firms in your area. Start the conversation by inquiring whether they're actively interested in small retail accounts. Some houses concentrate on institutions and very large individual investors only; you'd be wasting both their time and yours to go any further with them.

The method of dealing with prospective new clients varies from one brokerage firm to another. But typically, when you phone for the first time, you'll be connected with the broker of the day. That chore is rotated among all the brokers in the office, so the person you get depends strictly on the luck of the draw.

Give the broker of the day some good background. Explain your position, the amount of money you plan to invest at the outset, and provide an idea of the type of person you want to work with. If the broker you're talking to doesn't feel you and she would make a good fit, she should suggest another name for you to contact. But it doesn't always happen that way. New brokers just starting out are sometimes so hungry for clients that they'll jump through hoops in an effort to persuade you that they're exactly what you're looking for. If you're uncomfortable with the broker of the day but are still interested in the firm, call back, ask to speak to the manager, and explain your concerns. If he's sincerely interested in you as a prospective client, he should come up with one or two other names for you to contact.

If you find a broker who comes across well over the phone, arrange to set up a meeting. You might even consider taking him to lunch; you'll often pick up a lot more insights after a second glass of wine than you will by spending twenty minutes in the broker's office.

Obviously, you want to concentrate on seeing how well he measures up to your Five Ps. But get some nuts and bolts information as well. Ask for copies of the firm's research reports. Find out their commission structure. Get a sample of the reports they send clients and determine how frequently you'll receive them. While your comfort and confidence level in the broker is the most important element in your decision, these are all factors to take into account in making a final choice.

So now, let's assume you've done it. You've made a selection, signed all the necessary papers to set up an account, and you have a broker of your very own. Your first reaction may be a new sense of status ("I spoke to my broker today, and she said . . . "). Your second one may be a sense of disappointment (How come she never calls?). The third one will likely be elation or despair, depending on how well your first investments perform.

Whatever your feelings about the broker, remember you haven't gotten married. There's no lifetime commitment involved. In fact, you've really only completed the first step in the broker selection process.

You may have picked a crackerjack. On the other hand, the guy could be a dud. You won't know for sure until you've worked with him for a while. Here are some of the things to watch for:

Attentiveness: A good broker should call you periodically with suggestions—good suggestions. He should review your account with you regularly, maybe once a quarter. He should return your phone calls promptly. He should advise you when orders are filled and if there are any problems. He should ensure you're on the firm's mailing list for research reports. All of these things tell you he's interested in you and your business. If he's not performing up to standard, you should discuss it with him and, if matters don't improve, look elsewhere.

Churning: I've already explained what churning is. If you begin to feel that's what your broker is doing, switch in a hurry.

New issues: Brokerage houses are involved in underwriting new stock issues. This means the firm purchases new securities from a company and then resells them to institutions and the general public. The underwriting function can be a mixed blessing for you as an investor. Sometimes a new issue can produce spectacular profits in no time. I bought units which consisted of one share and half a warrant in a Quebec-based shipping company called Socanav when they were issued at $5 in the fall of 1986. Within weeks they were trading on the Toronto Stock Exchange for $7.50. Needless to say, I was more than happy with a 50% gain in that short space of time.

More often, however, new issues bomb. I've seen them drop 25% from issue price in the first day of stock exchange trading. That's not the type of investment you need.

The problem here is that when you come right down to it, your broker is a salesperson. If her firm is underwriting a stock, she has a genuine conflict of interest. She has to help move the stock out—and the less attractive the issue, the more of it she's likely to be called upon to sell. On the other hand, she has an obligation to you, as a client, to make the best recommendations possible. The two don't always coincide.

As a result, you may find your broker constantly trying to sell you new issues of dubious quality. That's a situation you don't need and shouldn't tolerate.

During your first meeting with your broker, you should clearly state what relationship you wish to establish regarding new issues his firm underwrites. You may say you don't want to hear about any of them—the conflict of interest is too serious. You may ask him to advise you of all of them, so that you can make your own decisions. Or you can ask to be advised only of those he genuinely believes are potential winners—and make it clear that his track record on these particular calls will be of special interest to you as you evaluate the business relationship.

If, as you work with the broker, you feel you're not being well served on new issues—either because you're not being offered a crack at the good ones or he's pushing too many duds—talk it over with him. If things don't improve, consider moving your account elsewhere.

Performance: No broker is going to be right all the time—infallibility is the exclusive prerogative of only one Being in the universe and He doesn't happen to be in the brokerage business. So don't expect that every recommendation you receive is going to turn to instant gold. What you do have a right to expect is a reasonable batting average. Your broker's suggestions should be profitable more often than not, and the net result of all gains and losses should be decidedly in your favour.

I keep a scorecard on which I track all stock trades. I note the source of each recommendation, and how it turned out. That way I can easily see how my brokers are doing. If I find a situation in which performance is starting to lag, I'm much more cautious about accepting recommendations from that particular broker.

When you're dealing with your broker, remember you're in a give-and-take situation. Your broker's only income results from the commissions which your account generates. If you're not doing a lot of trading, you won't be contributing much to his or her take-home pay. That's all right, certainly at the outset. But recognize the situation and don't impose unduly on his or her time. Do your own homework, read the research reports that come in, and generally keep informed. When you do need input, make sure it's for matters of substance—not trivial issues. If your broker is good, he or she will appreciate your discretion and be more prepared to spend a few extra minutes when you do call.

Finally, a brief word about discount brokers. As you read the financial pages or watch TV, you'll see advertisements for a number of firms offering to handle your stock trades for a fraction of the cost charged by the full-service firms. Some of the leading names are Green Line Service (operated by the Toronto Dominion Bank), Disnat, and Marathon Brown.

There's no gimmick here. The discounters are for real. You can actually have your trades done for as much as 75% or 80% off the rate you'd pay at a regular broker. You may wonder, then, why I don't recommend you do it.

The reason, in a word, is advice. The discount brokers are strictly order takers, nothing more. You tell them what you want and they'll execute the trade for you at a bargain price. That's terrific—if you know exactly what you're doing. If you don't you're asking for all sorts of trouble.

Allan Robinson, who writes a column on stocks in the *Report on Business*, once described a letter from a reader which makes the point more strongly than I ever could The reader had purchased 1,000 warrants of Gulf Canada through the TD Bank's Green Line Service. The warrants offered an opportunity to acquire an interest in all of Gulf's holdings, which extended well beyond oil and gas. But they had to be exercised by July 1, 1987. The reader failed to recognize the significance of that date—and because he had purchased the warrants through a discount broker, he had no one to advise him. As a result, he allowed the deadline to pass without exercising his warrants—and lost $20,000!

That's why I firmly believe that if you're just starting out, you need the hand holding of a regular broker. Even if you have some firm ideas of what you want to buy, it's always useful to have someone to bounce them off. You need good research reports and advice on when to take a profit and run. The discount brokers don't provide it.

Once you've developed some experience in the stock market, you can consider opening a second account with a discount broker to handle those trades you don't feel you need advice on. But until then, I suggest staying away. Remember the old adage: you get what you pay for. Brokers are no different.

Keeping Some For Yourself

L ET ME BEGIN this chapter with a question. How much of every
dollar you earn do you think goes out in taxes?

I'm not just talking about income tax here. I want you to
consider the whole range of taxes you pay: sales taxes, property
taxes, gasoline taxes, liquor taxes, tobacco taxes—everything.

Take a moment to think about it. Write down your answer on
a piece of paper.

Ready? Okay. According to a recent calculation prepared by
the Bank of Montreal, the average Canadian is handing over
about 41¢ of every dollar earned to our various levels of government. Put another way, you get to keep only 59¢ of every dollar.

When you've recovered from that shock, think about this: the
average American pays his governments only 25¢ of every dollar
earned. The other 75¢ stays in his pocket.

That's one big gap. If you look at it in percentage terms, it
means it's costing you about 64% more in taxes than the average
American pays. If you've ever wondered why the United States is
so attractive to many successful Canadians, there's a large part of
the answer.

The plain fact is that the tax burden in this country is stifling.
British Columbia's Fraser Institute has its own unique way of
driving home that point to Canadians. Every year the Institute

204

calculates what it calls Tax Freedom Day—the day when you've worked long enough to pay off all your tax obligations and can start enjoying your money. You'll be depressed to learn it almost always falls in late June—and sometimes even in early July.

If you're looking for someone to blame for this mess, start with the politicians. They've allowed government spending to get completely out of hand—with the result that our national debt is atrocious. Until they screw up the courage to make some real spending cuts, the situation is just going to get worse.

What does the debt level have to do with high taxes? Well, in 1970, the total cost to the federal government for interest payments to service the national debt amounted to just 6% of Ottawa's revenues. By the 1988-89 fiscal year, the cost of interest payments on the debt had risen to over 30% of total revenues. That's $30 billion a year in debt charges alone—and the total is still rising.

There are only two ways to deal with a situation like that—cut spending or raise taxes. So far, the politicians have cringed at the idea of any serious cost cutting. So, while the tax system gets rearranged, the amount we pay continues to go up.

This onerous tax burden is extremely significant to the aspiring wealth builder. Clearly, the more the government grabs in tax, the less that's available for investment and wealth building. And so, by extension, the longer it's going to take to achieve your wealth objectives.

That's why minimizing the tax bite has to be part of the basic strategy of every wealth builder. It's not much good making all the right investment decisions if the government is going to turn around and grab a big chunk of your profits back from you.

Unfortunately, it's becoming increasingly difficult to protect your money from the long arm of government. Ironically, the Progressive Conservatives under the leadership of Brian Mulroney (who from a philosophical point of view should have been encouraging wealth creation) have been the major culprits in closing off the escape hatches. From the moment they were elected in 1984, the Tories began systematically closing down tax shelters, introduced a minimum tax, eliminated many deductions and exemptions, cracked down on legitimate tax avoidance, and generally played havoc with traditional tax planning strategies.

The Conservatives also hit us in a more furtive way when they put an end to full indexing of personal exemptions and tax brackets in May 1985. That meant we were no longer protected against the first 3% of increase in the cost of living. Indexing only cut in after that. So if inflation rose 5%, the adjustment for tax purposes would only be 2%. This formula has been extended to the tax credit system introduced with tax reform.

Most people don't understand the full implication of this. It's too technical and the numbers seem to small to worry about. But in fact, this subtle change could end up costing middle-income taxpayers thousands of dollars in the years ahead.

Let me illustrate. Suppose you live in Ontario, have a taxable income of $27,000 a year, and support a spouse and a couple of kids. Let's say that for the next five years, inflation increases at a rate of 3% a year. Your pay increases just keep pace, no more, no less.

And the end of five years, you've stood still financially. Your salary went up—your taxable income is now just over $31,000 a year. But since prices went up at the same rate, your money isn't buying any more than it was before.

But look what happened to your tax bill! I've illustrated the result below, assuming the provincial tax rate at 50% of the federal rate and not allowing for any surtaxes:

	Now	5 Years Later
Taxable income	$ 27,000	$ 31,300
Federal tax payable	4,590	5,663
Provincial tax	2,295	2,832
Total tax	**$ 6,885**	**$ 8,495**

Look at that result closely. Your buying power hasn't gone up one cent. But your tax bill is $1,610 higher! Now do you think that indexing change was insignificant?

Every Canadian taxpayer is being hit by this change. The amount will vary, of course, depending on your income and which province you live in. But unless your income is so low you don't have to pay tax, you're going to be giving the government a lot more money in the years ahead. The Conservatives have managed to build an automatic tax increase into the system that will hit you progressively harder each year, probably without you even realizing it.

The tax reform program introduced by Finance Minister Michael Wilson in June 1987 was the last straw in the Tories' money grab. It knocked the props from under all sorts of valuable tax-saving techniques. It's true that federal tax rates were lowered in the process. But, on balance, the wealth builder fared very poorly.

So, unfortunately, I can't offer as many tax-saving tips as I could have a few years ago. There are some left, though—and because they're so precious, you should do everything possible to take advantage of them. In this chapter, I'll deal with some tax-saving ideas that are applicable to your general income. In Chapter Twenty-two, I'll discuss those that relate strictly to your investments—the heart of your wealth-building activities.

Let's start with some basics. The first step in reducing the amount of money the government grabs from you each year is to do some tax planning. This doesn't have to be overly complicated, at least at the outset. It's really just a case of organizing your affairs so that you attract less tax than you otherwise might.

For example, you should estimate in January how much your maximum RRSP contribution is likely to be for the next calendar year. Divide the total by 12 and budget that amount each month to be set aside. That way you won't be caught short when RRSP time rolls around (which, inconveniently, falls shortly after Christmas, if you haven't already noticed). Many people fail to make their maximum RRSP contribution, and so don't get the full tax break, because they didn't put enough money aside during the year. Basic, perhaps, but important.

Your start-of-the-year tax planning should include a careful review of the income of all members of the family, including the children, to see if there are any income-splitting opportunities available. Obviously, any time you can switch income from a higher tax bracket to a lower one you're going to come out ahead. I briefly discussed some income-splitting ideas in Chapter Five; you may wish to go back and review them. Generally, income-splitting opportunities are greater if you have a family business, whether on a full or part-time basis. That allows you to employ several members of the family and split the business income between them in the form of salaries or dividends. It doesn't have to be anything elaborate. I know of a woman who runs a small catering business from her home, specializing in hot and cold hors d'oeuvres for private parties. She and her daughter handle the food preparation, her teenage son does the deliveries, and dad keeps the company books. All of them get paid according to the amount of work they do, effectively dividing the company's revenue among four people for tax purposes.

Another factor to take into account in your tax planning is when you receive income. If your only source of revenue is a weekly pay cheque, there isn't much you'll be able to do here. But if you have some income that allows for some flexibility in when you receive it—commissions, bonuses, and dividends from a family company are examples—you may find it advantageous to defer some of it until the next tax year. You have to stay on top of the latest tax developments to make that decision, of course. But, as a good wealth builder, you'd be doing that anyway. As an example, after the tax reform program was announced in June, 1987, tax planners calculated that in many cases people would be better off deferring some income until 1988, when maximum rates would be lower. You would have had to work out whether that was true in your own case—but people with flexible income who took the time to do so ended up saving hundreds of dollars.

Your start-of-the-year tax planning should give consideration to the nature of your investments and the type of income they're likely to generate. I'll go into this in more detail in the next chapter but it's important it be on your checklist.

If you plan to purchase any tax shelters, you should work out just how much money you can effectively shield from Revenue Canada by doing so. Be sure to take account of the Alternative Minimum Tax in the process. I haven't explored the subject of tax shelters in depth in this book because most beginning wealth builders won't need them yet. But if you're an exception, be sure to plan things out carefully before you commit any money.

Your tax planning review should include a close look at any outstanding loans you may have. Remember, you can only deduct interest costs on loans incurred for investment or business purposes. If you have any consumer loans outstanding, you should see if there's any way they can be made tax deductible. For instance, you might own some Canada Savings Bonds which are worth more than the outstanding balance on your consumer loan. Sell whatever is necessary to pay off the debt, then take out a new loan to replace the CSBs when the new issues comes out at the end of October. Your debt load is exactly the same—only now the interest is tax deductible.

Here's one more idea for your start-of-the-year exercise. Do a preliminary calculation of your income tax for the previous year. If it turns out you have a refund coming—especially if it's a large one—you need to do some careful thinking.

A large tax refund may be gratifying. But what it really means is that you've been providing the government with an interest-free loan for many months. That's money that could have been earning more cash for you, even if you'd only held it in a daily interest savings account.

Frankly, I don't like loaning money to the government free of charge and I doubt many people do. If Ottawa wants to borrow from me, let them do so with CSBs or Treasury bills and pay market rates of interest.

Usually this abusive practice results from Revenue Canada setting the source deduction levels too high—in other words, more than necessary is taken off your weekly pay cheque. Unfortunately, there's not a lot you can do about that except write your MP to complain and copy the Minister of Finance. But there is a little known procedure which can be used in certain situations to lessen the withholding tax and thus reduce the amount of the interest-free loan you so graciously give Ottawa each year. I can't guarantee it will work for you. But I've made it work for me on occasion, so it is possible.

Revenue Canada has a provision which allows you to apply for a reduction in the withholding at source if you expect to receive a large refund next year. It's not widely publicized and the rules on who can get it are somewhat vague. There's also a fair amount of bureaucratic hassling involved. And it only works if you're having tax deducted at source from your income. But it's available if you want to try it. This technique is only effective if you make use of it at the beginning of the tax year, however. That's why it's essential that you consider it in the context of your overall tax planning strategy.

Here's how it works.

Look over your tax plans for the year ahead and see whether there's anything in them that would entitle you to make a claim of this type. Some examples: advance payments to an RRSP (you'll need to provide a receipt), alimony or child support payments, rental or investment losses, substantial charitable donations, and investments in legitimate tax shelters. If any of these apply, you have a case.

To get things going, write a personal letter to the chief of the source deduction department at your district taxation office. Explain why you want your source deductions reduced and include the necessary documentation to substantiate your claim. Be sure to provide all the basic information the tax people will need, such as your social insurance number and the name and address of your employer.

There's a buzz phrase you should also include in your letter— "undue hardship"—as in "Not obtaining this tax relief would cause me undue financial hardship." This kind of tax break is supposedly reserved for those who would be seriously hurt financially if it were not granted. But the tax people tend to be quite liberal in their interpretation of that term, so don't let it deter you.

Your letter will be reviewed and you may get a phone call from someone at Revenue Canada with further questions. Don't panic if that happens; it's just routine. If your request is granted, you'll get a letter to that effect and your employer will be advised. Your exemption will be increased, less tax will be withheld at source, and presto, you'll have more money to spend—or save—each month. Of course, you won't get a big tax refund a year later—but that only means you've managed to eliminate that interest-free loan to Ottawa.

So much for general tax planning. Now let me give you a few ideas on how you might save some money when the time comes to complete your return.

I'll begin with some advice you may not like: prepare your own tax return. About half the people in the country have someone else do their tax form. Often, the work is done by street corner tax preparation services who charge relatively modest fees. Once again, you get what you pay for.

Most tax preparation firms provide decent training for their staff. But even with this training, the person who does your return will not normally be a high powered tax professional. More likely, it will be a housewife or student who's picking up some extra cash with part-time work. Their knowledge of the tax laws and regulations may be very rudimentary. And, at the low fees they charge, they're certainly not going to devote a lot of time to studying the intricacies of your particular situation and looking for unusual ways to save you money.

The only person who will be truly motivated to spend the time to save your tax dollars is you. That's why I strongly urge you to devote the hours necessary to learning the tax rules and completing the returns for yourself and the members of your family. If you wish to have them double-checked later by someone else, fine. But do the planning and thinking yourself.

What should you look for? Here are some ideas.

Every year, thousands of people lose out on money that is rightfully theirs by failing to take advantage of all the tax credits and deductions available to them. That's not so surprising because with all the tinkering that's been going on with the tax system, it's almost impossible for the ordinary person to keep track of what's permitted and what isn't. Your best bet is to be aware of the most common errors or omissions others make in completing their return—and then be sure you don't do the same thing.

One of these is the equivalent-to-married credit, which I'll refer to as ETM for short. In fact, some tax experts contend it wins top prize as the most overlooked tax credit available.

Essentially, this provision allows unmarried or legally separated people to claim what amounts to a married tax credit if they support a dependent who lives with them. The dependent can be an offspring or some other related child under age 18, a parent, a grandparent, or some other relative if he or she is infirm.

Single parents very often miss out on this one by claiming the child credit instead of the ETM. That can be a costly mistake. For example, a divorced woman with a young child can obtain a tax credit worth $850 in 1988 by claiming the ETM on her return. If she claimed the child credit instead, it would be worth only $65.

Technically, the dependent is supposed to be living with you but Revenue Canada has been somewhat relaxed on this point. For instance, if you qualify for the ETM but your child attends boarding school, you can still claim the credit as long as the child lives with you when school's not in session.

But remember, you're only allowed one ETM credit. If you're a single parent with two children, only one qualifies. The other gets the standard child tax credit.

By the way, if you've read this with dismay because you could have made an ETM claim in the past but didn't, contact Revenue Canada. You're allowed to go back three years to claim money to which you were rightfully entitled.

Another area of the tax return that gives many people fits is spousal transfers. And no wonder. The rules were hard enough to understand under the old system. Take this explanation from the 1986 general tax guide, for example: "Line 1 should equal the amount that would be Total (D) in Area IV of Schedule 4, if your spouse were to complete Schedule 4." How is anyone supposed to make sense out of that? I can't blame people for giving up in despair when they're confronted with bureaucratese like that.

Unfortunately, tax reform complicates these transfers even more, unless the government has a change of heart by the time you read this. But if your spouse has a low income and is any one of disabled, over 65, attending school, or receiving a pension cheque, you'd better learn the rules.

As of 1988, the old age and disability tax credit are each worth $550. The maximum tuition and education credit is $600. The most you can claim for a pension credit is $170.

If your spouse qualifies for any of these but can't make use of them, you can claim them. A typical example would be an older couple living on pension income. The wife is over 65 and receives just over $3,000 a year in pension money as her only income. She won't be liable for any tax, but she has tax credits available for $720.

Her husband can make use of those credits, but the formula isn't easy. He must first calculate the value of the eligible credits. Then he has to calculate his spouse's net income and subtract $6,000. In the example we just looked at, the result would be zero, but let's say it was $1,000 for purposes of this calculation.

He multiplies the $1,000 by 17%, giving a result of $170. That amount is then subtracted from the total value of the eligible credits to find out how much can be transferred.

I'm sorry that's so complicated, but I didn't make the rules. The point is, this tax reduction method is frequently overlooked, so be sure you determine whether you can take advantage of it.

One other point before I leave transfers. Unused tuition and education credits and the disability credit can also be transferred to a supporting parent or grandparent. So if you have a child in university who can't make use of these credits, claim them yourself.

Another frequently misunderstood tax credit is the one relating to medical expenses. An estimated 500,000 Canadians claim this credit each year. But many of those aren't getting as large a tax break as they should. And there are thousands of others who could be making a claim but don't know how to structure their tax affairs to do so.

The basic rules are fairly well understood. You can only claim those medical and dental costs which exceed 3% of your net income. That means if your net income works out to $30,000, only those costs in excess of $900 ($30,000 x 3%) are eligible. Your tax credit is 17% of the eligible amount. Either spouse can claim all the medical expenses incurred by the family. And the expenses can cover any 12-month period that ends in the tax year for which you're filing the return.

So much for the basics. Now here's some angles to look at.

First, you can include any premiums paid to a private health insurance plan as part of your medical expenses. That means if you belong to a group plan at work and pay all or part of the premium yourself, you can add that amount to your medical costs. Just ask your employer to tell you what your share was.

Second, it isn't automatic in two-income families that the higher earner should claim the medical costs. In fact, it's the contrary. As a result of tax reform, it will usually be advantageous for the lower-income spouse to do so. The 3% rule means that the lower-income person will have a larger deduction to claim. And the way the tax credit is structured, it doesn't matter what tax bracket the claimant falls into. The value of the credit will always remain 17% of the eligible amount.

Let me give you an example. Let's take a two-income family in which the wife has a net income of $40,000 a year and the husband, who works part-time because he's studying for a degree, has $20,000. They have eligible medical/dental bills totalling $1,500.

If the higher-income wife should make the claim, the return would look like this:

Net income	$40,000
Exempt medical expenses (3%)	1,200
Eligible expenses	300
Tax credit (17%)	**$ 51**

If the lower-income husband makes the claim, however, the result changes significantly:

Net income	$20,000
Exempt medical expenses (3%)	600
Eligible expenses	900
Tax credit (17%)	**$ 153**

As you can see, by a simple reorganization of the way in which the medical expenses are claimed, this particular family saves over $100 in taxes.

Third, you can use a split claim for children if it's advantageous in maximizing the medical tax credit. It used to be that only one parent could claim for a child. But in 1987, Revenue Canada changed the rules, allowing parents to divide children's claims between them if it made sense to do so. The claim can be split in any way that makes sense—50/50, 75/25, even 90/10. The income received from family allowance payments is to be divided between spouses for tax purposes on the same basis.

We've already seen that it makes sense in most cases for the lower-income spouse to claim the medical costs. But if some of those costs relate to the children, a spouse can only do that if he or she is claiming them on his or her return. In the case of the lower-income spouse, that might not always be the most advantageous route to go.

But now Revenue Canada has made it possible to have your cake and eat it too. As long as a spouse claims any portion of the child credit on his or her return, he or she can take the full medical deduction. It doesn't have to be pro-rated between them. So the lower-income spouse could, if desired, claim only 10% of the child credit—but *all* the medical costs relating to that child.

Let's look at another area: disability. If you or anyone in your family is disabled, you know that the impact goes far beyond the physical and mental anguish involved. Any kind of serious disability involves a severe financial strain as well. As I mentioned earlier, we have a daughter who is profoundly deaf. She's done remarkably well in overcoming her handicap and is living a reasonably normal life. But there has been a lot of expense involved in making that possible: costly hearing aids, a captioning decoder so she can enjoy TV, special equipment to enable her to use the telephone, an alarm clock that shakes her bed to wake her, just to mention a few.

Until recently, however, she was not considered to be officially disabled for income tax purposes. In that regard she was in exactly the same position as people suffering from mental retardation, or severe cardiorespiratory failure, or a variety of other debilitating conditions. The expenses were all there—but the tax relief wasn't.

But now the government has changed the rules. The disability tax credit has been extended to thousands of people who couldn't use it before. Under the revised guidelines, you're considered to be disabled if you have a severe impairment that markedly restricts you in the activities of daily living.

You have to have your doctor complete a form which confirms you or a family member falls into this new, broader definition. But the reward is considerable; the disability tax credit is $550. As I mentioned before, this credit can be transferred to a spouse or supporting parent or grandparent if desired.

Although the change got a fair amount of publicity when it was announced, many eligible people are probably still not aware of it. If you think anyone in your family should be claiming it, request Form 2201 from Revenue Canada and get your doctor to fill it out.

These are only a few examples of frequently overlooked claims and strategies. There are many more—in fact, entire books have been written on the subject. If you want to explore the possibilities in greater depth, I suggest you get hold of one. You should also consider subscribing to a newsletter on the subject; *The TaxLetter*, published by Hume, is the best one I know of.

Taxation is a complex area, but one that any aspiring wealth builder should spend some time studying. After all, why give the government any more than you absolutely have to—especially when the system seems to make it almost impossible for you to win? You *can* win, though—if you arm yourself with the facts.

Tax-Efficient Investments

I T'S NO ACCIDENT that the basic building blocks in my wealth program are a home and an RRSP. It just so happens they're the most effective tax shelters still around.

To build wealth effectively in Canada, given our high tax rates, you have to construct your plan in a way that minimizes the impact of taxation on your money. Every dollar you are required to hand over to governments is one less dollar that's available to you for investment and growth.

The younger you are, the more important this becomes. I've already stressed the significance of compounded growth in an investment program, but let me remind you of it again in a tax context. Let's say you're 25 years old and you plan to be financially independent by the time you're 55—that's 30 years from now. Assuming you were able to invest for an average 10% return per year, every $100 in extra taxes paid today means you will have $1,745 less in your investment portfolio at age 55. (Those compounded interest numbers always seem astounding, but they're correct. If you don't believe me, try it yourself on a calculator.)

That's why I lay such stress on developing a wealth-building program that is shielded from taxes wherever possible, with your home and your RRSP as starting points.

The family home allows you to build tens, maybe hundreds of thousands of dollars in equity over the years, entirely tax-free. There's no ceiling, no restrictions. The capital gain you make on your principal residence doesn't even come under the $100,000 lifetime exemption limit. It's over and above that. And by using devices like the home equity line of credit, which I described in Chapter Twelve, you can gain access to that tax-free money whenever you want. It doesn't have to remain locked away until the house is sold.

As for RRSPs, I don't have to reiterate their wealth-building power. Just keep in mind that it's all made possible because they're tax sheltered until it comes time to take the funds out.

After the home and the RRSP, however, your tax-sheltered choices start to thin out. But there are still some techniques you can use to keep money out of the hands of Revenue Canada and in your own pocket.

The first is to take full advantage of the $100,000 lifetime capital gains exemption.

When Michael Wilson originally announced the capital gains exemption plan in 1985, it looked like an absolute bonanza for wealth builders. We were all eventually going to be allowed half a million dollars in tax-free gains with few restrictions.

Unfortunately, tax reform watered down the plan considerably. The lifetime limit has been capped at $100,000 (a fifth of the original exemption) in all instances except for the sale of farm property or shares in a privately held small business. In those cases, the $500,000 limit remains.

As if that weren't enough, some new rules have been introduced which will cut further into the value of the exemption. One of these is the provision which increases the taxable portion of capital gains from 50%, where it stood at the end of 1987, to $66\frac{2}{3}\%$ in 1988 and 75% in 1990. This rule is a two-edged sword. It appears to increase the value of the exemption itself. But it means you'll be paying more taxes once you pass the $100,000 mark.

Here's how it happens:

	50%	66⅔%	75%
Gross capital gain	$ 1,000	$ 1,000	$ 1,000
Non-taxable portion	500	333	250
Taxable portion	500	667	750
Amount of tax saved as a result of exemption (assumes 43.5% rate)	218	290	326
Tax on gains over exemption limit	**$ 218**	**$ 290**	**$ 326**

See what's happened? By changing the taxable portion of capital gains, the government has theoretically increased the value of the exemption. In reality, though, as long as you haven't reached the $100,000 maximum, it doesn't matter how you juggle the numbers. But once you pass that mark, you're going to be hit harder than before. In fact, if you're skilful enough to earn $300,000 or more in capital gains over your lifetime, you'll wish the government had junked the exemption entirely but left the rest of the rules the way they were. Here's why, using the 75% rate that comes into force in 1990:

	Tax Reform Rules	Old Rules with No Exemption
Lifetime capital gains	$ 300,000	$ 300,000
Exemption	100,000	0
Gains subject to tax	200,000	300,000
Non-taxable portion	37,500	150,000
Taxable portion	162,500	150,000
Tax at 43.5%	$ 70,688	$ 65,250

For most people, $300,000 worth of capital gains over a lifetime looks like an impossible dream. Even $100,000 may appear unachievable. But the thoughtful wealth builder will realize that the combination of inflation and compounding over many years will make those numbers appear much less daunting ten or 20 years from now than they are today.

Of course, the rules of the game will probably change many times during that period. But as they stand right now, truly successful wealth builders will recognize that the rules as they existed before Michael Wilson started tinkering with them gave a much better break to investors who hit it big.

The other major change tax reform brought to capital gains was the provision that investment losses have to be deducted before the amount eligible for the capital gains exemption is calculated. These include such costs as interest on money borrowed to finance the investment. I explained in Chapter Eighteen how this can significantly reduce the amount of capital gains actually eligible for the exemption, thereby making borrowing to invest less attractive than previously. You need to keep this in mind in your investment planning.

Even with all these hedges, however, the $100,000 capital gains exemption offers a third opportunity (after your home and RRSP) to build wealth tax-free, and you should certainly do everything you can to take advantage of it. The main vehicles for achieving this goal should be stocks, bonds, and mutual funds. (Gold and real estate are two other methods you'll want to consider as you become more experienced in wealth building. I haven't dealt with them in this book because of their more specialized nature).

The desirability of accumulating capital gains is one reason why I've stressed the importance of diversifying your investments as you move forward. Too many people never get beyond GICs and CSBs, neither of which normally have any capital gains potential (there have been occasional exceptions with both, but they're rare). At some point, you need to add investments with capital gains potential to the mix, following the plan I outlined in earlier chapters. That $100,000 lifetime exemption is there for the taking; don't pass up the opportunity to use it.

And if you're entrepreneurial and think you'd like to start your own small business, remember you can still get up to $500,000 tax-free when you sell it. Now there's a good incentive to get you going!

Aside from becoming familiar with the possibilities for tax-free wealth building, you should also get acquainted with devices you can use to reduce the tax payable on your investments.

The most important is the dividend tax credit. In fact, once you've exhausted the capital gains exemption, dividends are the most tax-effective way to receive income.

A lot of people have either never heard of the dividend tax credit or have only a vague idea of how it works. Believe me, it's worth the trouble to find out.

There are two philosophical reasons for this particular tax break. One is to encourage more Canadians to invest in our own industries. The other is to recognize the fact that when companies pay dividends on their stocks, that money comes out of after-tax profits. In other words, corporation income tax has already been paid on that money. The dividend tax credit goes some way (although not all the way) towards ensuring that money isn't taxed twice.

Like the capital gains exemption, the dividend tax credit has been watered down over the past few years. As a result, it's nowhere near as valuable as it once was in reducing tax. But it's still better than nothing and you'd be smart to take advantage of it.

Here's how it works. Let's assume you own shares in Bell Canada and you received $100 in dividends last year. You're going to end up paying less tax on that money than if you'd received it as CSB interest. But you're going to have to jump through some mathematical hoops in the process.

As a first step, you'll have to *gross-up* your dividend income. Grossing-up is one of those little tax wrinkles Ottawa dreams up to complicate our lives but, believe me, it's much harder to explain than it is to do. It involves increasing your dividend income artificially for tax purposes to an amount that approximates the before-tax income received by Bell Canada. The purpose of this strange exercise is to enable Ottawa to then give you credit for the tax Bell already paid on that income before the dividends were distributed to you and other shareholders. The idea is to avoid double-taxing the same money.

For the 1987 tax year, the gross-up amounts to $133\frac{1}{3}\%$ of the actual dividends you received. So in this case, your grossed up dividend for tax purposes will be $133.33 ($100 x $133\frac{1}{3}\%$).

For 1988 and beyond, assuming the tax reform proposals go through intact, the gross-up will be 125% of dividends. So a $100 dividend will be grossed-up to $125.

Still with me? Sorry it's so complicated, but it's vitally important to understand.

Now let's assume you're in the 26% federal tax bracket—the middle range. The federal tax payable on your dividend income is calculated on the grossed-up amount. So, staying with this example, you'd owe $34.67 in the 1987 tax year ($133.33 x 26%) and $32.50 in subsequent years ($125 x 26%).

Now for the good part. You get a credit that you can deduct from your tax payable. This dividend tax credit is supposed to reflect an amount roughly equivalent to the tax Bell Canada has already paid on that income.

For the 1987 tax year, the dividend tax credit is $16\frac{2}{3}$% of your grossed-up dividends. So, using our Bell Canada example, your credit would be $22.23 ($133.33 x $16\frac{2}{3}$%). Your actual tax payable on that $100 of dividend income would therefore be $12.44 ($34.67 minus the $22.23 credit).

For 1988 and beyond (again assuming the tax reform proposals go through) the dividend tax credit drops to $13\frac{1}{3}$% of the grossed-up total. So in this case, the credit would be worth $16.66 ($125 x $13\frac{1}{3}$%). Your actual tax payable would be $15.84 ($32.50 minus $16.66) As you can see, this makes dividends somewhat less attractive from a tax point of view. But they're still better than equivalent interest income, as the following example shows. I've used the tax reform plan for 1988 and after to illustrate the difference.

	Dividends	Interest
Amount received	$100.00	$100.00
Gross-up	125.00	100.00
Gross federal tax payable (26% bracket)	32.50	26.00
Dividend tax credit	16.66	0
Net federal tax	15.84	6.00
Provincial tax at 50%	7.92	13.00
Total tax payable	$ 23.76	$ 39.00

As you can see, the tax advantage of dividend income over interest is considerable. That means that you could select dividend-paying investments, such as preferred shares, which actually appear to have a lower return than an interest-bearing alternative, and still come out ahead after tax.

Suppose, for example, you had $2,000 to invest. You were faced with a choice between a solid utility stock paying a 6% dividend and a one-year GIC paying 7¼%. The GIC might look like the better alternative. But is it once you've taken taxes into account? Let's take a look.

	Stock (6% Dividend)	GIC (7¼% Interest)
Annual return	$120.00	$145.00
Gross up	150.00	145.00
Gross federal tax (26% bracket)	39.00	37.70
Dividend tax credit	(20.00)	n/a
Net federal tax	19.00	37.70
Provincial tax @ 50%	9.50	18.85
Total tax payable	**28.50**	**56.55**
After-tax return	$ 91.50	$ 88.45
Percentage return after tax	**4.6%**	**4.4%**

As you can see, you're better off after-tax choosing the stock even though at first glance it would appear to pay a lower return.

Now here's a point that's extremely important for beginning wealth builders who are not yet earning a lot of money. *The lower your income, the more tax-efficient the dividend tax credit becomes.* Let's look at the same example again, but this time assume you're in the lowest federal tax bracket (17%).

	Stock (6% Dividend)	GIC (7¼% Interest)
Annual return	$120.00	$145.00
Gross up	150.00	145.00
Gross federal tax (17% bracket)	25.50	24.65
Dividend tax credit	(20.00)	n/a
Net federal tax	5.50	24.65
Provincial tax @ 50%	2.75	12.33
Total tax payable	**8.25**	**36.98**
After-tax return	$111.75	$108.02
Percentage return after tax	**5.6%**	**5.4%**

As you can see, the percentage of after-tax return on your investment increased significantly in both cases in the lower tax bracket. Also, the gap between the actual net revenue received from the two investments widens—in the 26% bracket, your after-tax dividend income was $3.05 more than the after-tax income from the interest-bearing investment. In the 17% bracket, that difference widened to $3.73. Once again, that might not seem like a lot. But applied to larger amounts and spread over several years, it adds up.

What all this means is that you must take the tax consequences into account in assessing your investment alternatives. Examine the before-tax rates of return, find out your tax bracket, and calculate the probable after-tax results. If they're relatively close, or even if there's a slight advantage for the interest-bearing alternative, you may still decide on the dividend-paying stock. That's because shares carry the possibility of capital gain, which many interest-bearing investments do not.

There's a downside risk there, of course. Even a blue chip stock with a solid record of dividend payments can drop in value in a falling market. But if you select wisely, and avoid buying when the market is at its peak, you can minimize that risk.

If you do go the dividend route, don't overdo it. You can't use a dividend tax credit to generate a refund; the best you can do is to reduce your taxable income to zero. And if you're in a high income bracket, the Alternative Minimum Tax may come into play. If you make over $40,000 a year and have a lot of dividend income, check this potential booby trap carefully.

One other caveat. If you're considering investments within an RRSP, the after-tax calculations won't apply because all the income is tax sheltered. In that case, go for the investment with the best total return.

That's about it for tax-efficient investments. The old $1,000 investment income deduction, which used to be a great place for sheltering modest interest and dividend payments, is gone, swept away in tax reform. That's a real loss for beginning wealth builders because it provided an opportunity to start accumulating an investment base tax-free.

Incidentally, one result of the demise of that deduction has been to change the strategy in reporting income on compound interest investments, like Canada Savings Bonds. You're allowed to declare the interest yearly if you wish, but you must do so at least once every three years, even though you haven't actually received the cash. In the past, the standard route was to declare your compound interest every year, with the idea of sheltering it under the $1,000 investment income deduction. Now you're better off to allow it to accumulate, and declare it only every three years. Since you're going to have to pay tax on it anyway, you're better off delaying the day of reckoning for as long as possible.

I wish I could offer more ideas on how to protect your money from big government but there's been a systematic attempt in recent years to reduce the tax-sheltering opportunities available. So let me summarize the list of the top four tax-efficient investments for starting wealth builders:

Number one: Your home. Unlimited capital gains potential. Does not effect lifetime capital gains exemption.

Number two: Your RRSP. Tax-free growth for as long as the plan is in force. Funds are taxable at your marginal rate when withdrawn.

Number three: Capital gains. Tax-free up to $100,000, except for the sale of farm property or a small business, where the limit is $500,000.

Number four: Dividends. Not tax sheltered, but the dividend tax credit makes them the most effective type of investment income once the capital gains exemption has been exhausted.

There they are. Good luck.

It's Hard to
Get Good Help
These Days

D ON'T BE SURPRISED if there comes a time when you want to throw up your hands and scream for help. It's a natural reaction. Starting and maintaining a wealth-building program isn't easy. And even though I've tried to provide both general guidelines and specific examples in this book, you'll undoubtedly run into a situation at some point that isn't covered here. It's to be expected; everyone's personal circumstances are different. The question is: Where do you turn for good advice?

When the time comes to ask this question, you might be consoled that you're not alone. It's the question I am asked most frequently, on hotline shows, in question periods after speeches, or in my mail. And it's not an easy one to answer.

Where you go for help depends to a large extent on the nature of your problem. You shouldn't go to a lawyer or bank manager for investment advice, for example, although a great many people do. They aren't trained to deal in matters like that. Your broker is not usually the best person to ask about a tax problem, for the same reason. Nor is your insurance agent normally the best source of impartial advice on an RRSP.

Going to the wrong expert for advice is not just an unproductive way to spend your money. It could actually end up costing you a bundle, as a result of improper counselling.

I once received a call from an Ottawa businessman which both flattered and shocked me. He had heard me talking about money on CBC radio and, acting on no more knowledge than that, asked if I'd undertake to manage his money for him.

"How much?" I asked.

"About one million dollars," he replied.

My immediate reaction was that it was a put-on. But as we talked further, it turned out it wasn't.

The man's story was a prime example of how financial advice from the wrong person can be disastrous. He had spent most of his adult life developing what became a very successful business. About a year prior to his phone call, he had sold it and walked away with just over a million dollars. Like many successful business people, he knew virtually nothing about investing; his whole life had been devoted to making his business a success. So when he suddenly found himself with more cash than he'd ever dreamed of, he didn't know what to do with it.

So he turned to a financial expert for help. In this case, it was his accountant, the man who'd helped him in business matters and looked after his tax returns for many years. Unfortunately, the accountant might have been terrific at financial statements but he was no investment expert. Faced with the prospect of finding somewhere to place a million dollars, he chose the safest, most conservative route possible—he put all the money into Treasury bills.

Now, this was at a time when interest rates were at their lowest point in a decade while the stock markets were in the midst of their biggest run-up since the 1920s. But because all the money was in T-bills, the businessman didn't get any part of that action. His return on the million dollars was about 7% over that year. Sure, the money was safe. But he would have liked to have done a little better than that.

I wasn't in the money management business at that time, but I gave him some names of people he could contact. I also strongly suggested he do so without delay. The poor investment advice he'd received had already cost him many thousands of dollars; the faster he rectified the situation the better off he'd be.

That's why it's so important to seek advice from the right qualified person.

Some people think that's their bank manager. Not so, unless the advice you're looking for relates to borrowing or to one of the specific products offered by the bank. The *Bank Act* puts tight restraints on the type of financial advice bank personnel can give. And when they have strayed beyond the bounds, the results haven't always been auspicious. In one case a few years ago, two widows actually ended up suing their bank after the manager had approved loans for them to invest in a speculative cattle deal. When it collapsed, they lost everything. They launched legal action, claiming they hadn't been properly advised — and the courts agreed with them.

Lawyers tend to be another favourite source of financial advice, perhaps because of a misconception that since they're highly educated they must know about handling money. Most of them don't; they only know about law. There are some exceptions, of course, but if you want to use a lawyer for financial advice, make sure he or she has knowledge in the area.

Insurance agents are another favourite source of advice. But keep in mind, their main interest is in selling you their products. If the financial plan seems to put heavy emphasis on the things they're selling, a small dose of suspicion might be in order.

Too often, people in search of financial help find they've inadvertently set themselves up as a target for a sales pitch on a dubious investment, tax shelter, insurance policy, or something similar. If an insurance agent or mutual fund salesperson is doing the planning, you'd better be on guard.

One of the newest professions in Canada is financial planning, and more and more people are turning here for help. There are some excellent financial planning services available — but be very careful. Although there's been a lot of talk, there are still no regulations governing the operations of financial planners in this country. As a result, anyone, qualified or not, can hang out a financial planner sign. Their fees can vary widely, and there's no guarantee that the highest fee will produce the best results. To complicate matters further, many self-styled financial planners are not that at all. They're well-trained salespeople who use financial planning techniques to build a case for selling you their products.

My personal experience with financial planners has been limited to two occasions, neither of which was encouraging. I described one of these in Chapter Sixteen when I told you about the recommendations that caused me to put money into Greymac Trust and Seaway Trust just before the Ontario government closed them down.

The company making those suggestions was a well-known and highly reputable Toronto firm which was being paid a lot of money for its services. Yet even that wasn't enough to protect me from bad advice. That same company, by the way, also recommended that I make some major insurance purchases, including a disability insurance program that would have cost several thousand dollars a year to carry. When I questioned this, I discovered that the firm—which, remember, was being paid a lot to advise me—was also an agent for the insurance company in question and stood to receive a commission if I agreed to the proposal. The recommendation may have been perfectly valid. But, given that kind of conflict-of-interest situation, it was hardly impartial.

My second experience with financial planners came a few months later, when I was searching for a tax shelter in an effort to protect some money from Revenue Canada. I asked my banker for some suggestions; he had high praise for the thoroughness and integrity of a particular firm. Fortunately, I had no problems with them. I purchased my tax shelter without a hitch. But I *could* have had trouble—I was just lucky. The company also suggested that I buy a number of other investments, many of which they had developed and promoted themselves. A couple seemed tempting. But in the end I decided against them. A few months later, I read in the paper that the financial planning company was in trouble—and that people who had bought some of the investments I turned down were in danger of losing a great deal of money. After I breathed a sigh of relief that it wasn't me, I began to pay closer attention to what was happening in the financial planning community.

I wasn't left with a high confidence level. Unfortunately, experiences such as mine are not uncommon. There have been far too many cases of financial planning abuses, ranging from bankrupt firms leaving investors dangling in the wind to so-called personal financial security programs that are nothing more than cleverly disguised sales pitches for mutual funds.

This does *not* mean that all financial planners are bad. Far from it. There are lots of good ones out there and the Canadian Association of Financial Planners is making a determined effort to establish standards for the profession. And there are plenty of positive stories to go along with the negative ones.

One that I came across recently involved a Vancouver woman whose husband died suddenly. She was left with a fairly sizeable inheritance, but had no idea how to handle the money in a way that would allow her to keep her home and maintain her lifestyle. So she contacted a financial planner. He put together a comprehensive program that included recommendations for investments that would provide her with the cash flow she needed. He also showed her some of the techniques we looked at in Chapters Twenty-one and Twenty-two for reducing her tax liability. His work wasn't cheap—she was charged $1,200 for the plan. But she came away with a sense of security and the feeling she had received excellent value for money.

So there are good financial planners out there—quite a few of them. The trick, of course, is finding them. I can't offer a fail-safe method of doing that, but I have some tips that may help.

First, (and it's good policy in anything you do) ask friends and relatives for their input. See if any of them have ever worked with a financial planner. If so, get all the details: the kind of work they had done, the cost, their degree of satisfaction, any problems or concerns they may have had. The best guarantee of a good choice is the endorsement of someone you know and respect.

I also suggest you contact the Canadian Association of Financial Planners. There's a chapter in every province or you can write to their national office at Suite 59, Box 24, First Canadian Place, Toronto, Ontario, M5X 1K2. They'll send you a roster of all certified financial planners in your province which will include information on their rates and how they're paid. That's especially useful because it will enable you to identify which planners are involved in insurance, mutual fund, or tax shelter selling.

When you're making a selection, I suggest you try to find a planner who charges on what's called a fee-for-service basis. That simply means you'll be paying the person for his or her time—and that nobody else will. By that I mean the planner will not be relying on commissions earned by selling you something in order to make a living. Obviously, planners who earn even part of their income from commissions are less likely to give you unbiased advice.

The Association's roster contains all the information you need to identify the income source of a planner. For instance, one roster entry may read: "Fees—none". Then it will go on to say something like: "Licensed to sell the investment funds of . . . " At that point it will list the name of whatever company the planner represents. You know immediately from that type of listing that this planner's main concern is going to be in selling you mutual funds. If that interests you, fine. But just understand the planner's perspective and realize that the "free" plan he or she prepares for you is going to be heavily weighted to the company's products.

In contrast, another roster entry might read: "Fees—$110 an hour. The company is not licensed to sell any financial products."

That's your classic fee-for-service planner. There are no hidden interests at work.

When you contact the Association, also request their Consumer Guide to Financial Planning. This brochure will give you some suggestions on what to look for in a financial planner and some questions to ask before you made a decision.

Fee-for-service planners are *not* cheap. After all, the good ones are well-trained people who probably have years of experience in some type of financial work and who may have completed a long and complicated course. The Association says you should expect to pay between $50 and $200 an hour for a good one. A bare bones, computer-generated plan will run you about $150, and that won't include any follow-up help. A full-scale, custom tailored plan will cost between $500 and $5,000, depending on how complicated your financial affairs are. At those prices, be certain you really need the advice before you go.

Even though a planner is billed as being fee-for-service, double check by asking whether he or she accepts commissions from any source. Full disclosure up front will put you in a better position to evaluate the objectivity of the program that's prepared for you.

Major chartered accounting firms that charge on a fee-for-service basis are your best bet for top quality, independent advice. But don't go to them unless you've got a lot of money. The minimum cost for them to sit down with you will likely be upwards of $2,000. Unless you've got several hundred thousand dollars you don't know what to do with, you're better to look elsewhere.

Some trust companies are starting to move into the financial planning field and you may want to consider that option. They aren't inexpensive, but they won't be as pricey as the big accounting firms.

There are also a lot of independent operators out there, with varying degrees of skill.

With all those choices, it's important that you interview any prospective consultant carefully before proceeding. Ask about background and experience, what courses he or she has completed and whether they belong to a recognized industry association. Ask for references and follow up by contacting them. Satisfied clients are the best indicator of competence.

While you're at it, get a sample of the type of report you'll be receiving. Look it over carefully and make sure you'll be able to understand it. Also decide whether you'll be able to implement the recommendations yourself or will need the planner's help on an ongoing basis. If the planner is going to have to decipher and implement it for you later, your costs will be much higher.

During the interview, consider your reaction to the planner. You should feel comfortable with the person and come away with the feeling he or she is really interested in your problems. If you don't end the interview feeling enthusiastic about working with the planner, you'd better look elsewhere.

Also, try to find out just what the person's strengths and weaknesses are. Don't expect a planner to be an expert in everything. Just because he can put together a terrific tax strategy that will save you thousands of dollars doesn't necessarily mean he should be advising you on what stocks to buy. For that kind of specialized advice, an investment counsellor might be more appropriate.

While you're interviewing planners, they'll be interviewing you. They'll want to know whether you have a clear idea of your needs and objectives. They'll be trying to get some idea of your priorities—whether your emphasis is on establishing an income flow as opposed to saving taxes, for example. Your plan will be much easier to prepare and more tailored to your needs if your goals and the time frame for achieving them are absolutely clear.

They may also be trying to assess what type of person you are. Financial planners in the United States have faced an increasing rash of lawsuits from disgruntled clients claiming they were badly advised. If the planner feels you're the type who might try something like that if things don't go well, he or she may reject your business.

Once you've made a selection, do yourself a favour by not wasting the planner's time. Remember, every hour spent on your project is costing you money. So do some advance preparation to make the task as easy as possible. Don't show up with a shoebox full of unsorted documents, dump them on the planner's desk, and ask him to make sense out of them. Believe it or not, I know of cases where just that sort of thing has happened. Avoid it, unless you're prepared to pay for the extra hours it will take to piece together the whole mess.

You'll minimize your costs by summarizing all the relevant information on a sheet of paper and making copies of the important documents before your first planning meeting. Be sure to take along copies of pay slips, your latest tax returns, mortgage information, a list of your assets, a summary of your liabilities (including up-to-date information on the interest rate being charged on any loans you may have) and anything else you think may be useful. All of this will be a tremendous help to the planner and will get things moving quickly.

There are six things you should expect the planner to do for you:

1. Clarify your current financial situation. You should receive a clear snapshot of where you stand right now in terms of your income, assets, debts, and taxes, among other things.

2. Identify your objectives. What do you want and in what time frame?

3. Assess your financial problems and identify any difficulties which stand between you and your goals.

4. Produce a written report containing recommendations and alternative suggestions.

5. Assist you with the implementation of the report.

6. Review your plan with you periodically and keep it up to date.

When the report is done, don't accept the recommendations unquestioningly. Review the final plan with a critical eye to see if it truly meets your objectives. Make sure you're comfortable with any investment recommendations and that you fully understand the direction and details of the program. If some of the advice contradicts what you've read in this book, ask why. Don't listen to idle speculation; you want—and deserve—well-reasoned arguments.

And remember, the plan isn't etched in stone for the rest of your life. Your goals may alter. Economic circumstances may change, dictating a different investment strategy. Tax rules will inevitably be tinkered with. You should review any financial plan at least once a year, either on your own or with the help of an expert.

Obtaining a comprehensive financial plan from a competent person is definitely a good idea if you're at all concerned about how to proceed. It will help focus your priorities and provide direction and discipline.

But just be sure you use the *right* person. And if he or she tries to use the business relationship to sell you something, run.

Now It's Up to You

I 'VE DONE AS MUCH as I can.

The preceding chapters should give you two of the three essential ingredients you need to begin a lifetime wealth-building program.

You have the basic knowledge—the information you need to acquire before you start. By now, you should understand such key concepts as risk and return, compounded growth, income splitting, leveraging, tax sheltering and diversification. I hope you've grasped the relationship between interest rates and bond prices, understood the difference between constructive and destructive debt, and mastered the implications of the dividend tax credit. And you've come to grips with the fundamentals of mutual funds, stocks, term deposits and mortgages.

The second ingredient in the mix is technique, and you are now acquainted with that as well—at least as much as you need to get started. You know how to set up and carry out a program for purchasing a home and paying off the mortgage quickly. You know how to accelerate the wealth-building process by keeping a large portion of your investment money out of the government's hands. You're aware of the basic techniques for setting up and managing an investment portfolio. You know how to improve the odds that the mutual fund you select will outperform most of the others on the market. You know where to look for professional help, and what criteria to apply in the process. And you know what sources to tap regularly for relevant information.

As I said, two of the three essential ingredients: knowledge and technique.

But it's like baking a cake. If *all* the ingredients aren't there, in the right proportions, it will end up a disaster. Leave out the egg, or the sugar or, heaven forbid, the flour, and even your dog will turn up his nose at it.

And I can't provide that third essential ingredient. Only you can. If you can't, or won't, then I'm sorry to tell you the time you've spent reading this book will be wasted.

What is this magical final ingredient?

Motivation.

Let me repeat, because it is so essential.

Motivation.

Even more specifically, *motivation to action*.

It's not just a matter of genuinely wanting to acquire wealth. Most of us do. That's why lotteries have become such an integral part of our social fabric.

But lotteries are relatively painless. A buck or five gives you a crack at millions. Never mind that the odds are better you'll be struck by lightning; there's always a chance. After all, someone has to win!

And, who knows, maybe you'll get lucky. But the more likely result is that you'll throw away thousands of dollars on useless tickets over the years.

Wealth building, by contrast, is *not* painless. As I said at the beginning of this book, it requires dedication and hard work. The necessary motivation isn't just the desire to acquire wealth. It's the commitment to actually *do* something about it. If you don't have that, the cake will never get baked.

On the other hand, if you *do* act, the chances that you will succeed are a heck of a lot better than if you just keep buying lottery tickets. No guarantees, of course. But life doesn't offer many of those anyway.

Consider this, though. Suppose you were offered a $10,000 bet. The idea would be to pick which of two people would have accumulated the most wealth 20 years from now. One of them will spend $50 a week on lottery tickets over that time. The other will use that same $50 a week to set up a dedicated wealth-building program. Which one do you want?

If you chose the lottery player, you might luck out. But he or she had better win the big one because if the wealth builder manages only a 10% return each year, he or she is going to be sitting with over $150,000 in assets when the time comes to declare the bet winner. I know which one I'd pick.

In Chapter Two, I offered what you may have felt at the time was a rather facetious bit of advice. I told you to *begin*. Now I'm saying it again.

All our lives are full of unrealized good intentions. We all have books we intend to read, trips we're someday going to take, people we mean to tell we love, sensations we'll eventually get around to experiencing, projects we'll start tomorrow. A thousand events waiting for a beginning.

Add wealth building to that list, and I can almost guarantee it won't happen. And years from now, it will end up on another list we all have: the "If only I'd . . . " list.

You *must* make a start. Now!

Let me tell you one more story.

Every aspiring writer dreams of one day producing a novel. I was no different. All through the early years of my journalistic career, I told anyone who would listen about how I would someday write a novel that would dazzle the literary world. My poor wife must have heard the boast a thousand times; it's wonder she didn't divorce me.

But the years went by and there was no novel. The intent was always there. But there was never any time. There was always another election campaign to cover, or some new international flare-up to write about, or a fascinating new political figure to profile. The novel would have to wait.

And then I turned 40. Everyone has a different reaction to that event; mine was pretty traumatic. I suddenly realized I was an overstressed, overweight male entering the coronary belt. While my health was good, I'd seen too many friends and acquaintances suddenly stricken to feel comfortable. And the thought kept going through my mind: what if I died tomorrow? My last thought might well be that I'd never accomplished the one thing I'd set my heart on since I was a kid. I'd never written that novel.

That's what it took to motivate me to action—the realization that my life was probably more than half over and it was time to put up or shut up. There still wasn't any time—but I *made* time. I got up before six every morning and wrote for a couple of hours before leaving for work. I spent evenings and weekends hashing over plot, characters and dialogue with my friend and co-author Tony Aspler.

The books that were eventually published didn't exactly rock the North American literary establishment to its foundation. But that didn't matter. I had done what I really wanted to do. The novels were there on my bookshelves, all the evidence I needed of the achievement of my personal objective.

But it only happened because I finally stopped dreaming and began. And it was tough at first. Six pages of manuscript one day, four the next, five the next. Putting together more than 400 pages seemed like an impossible objective. But as I plugged away at it, the file folder got thicker. And then, one day, I was done. The novel was finished.

Wealth building works in very much the same way. Ten dollars here, twenty there, maybe a hundred occasionally. It seems at the start you'll never get anywhere. But if you have the self-motivation to begin and the determination to stay with it, you'll eventually start to see the results. And then one morning you'll wake up and you'll have it. Not a pile of money, because, remember, money is only a means to an end. No, what you'll wake up to is the ultimate satisfaction of knowing you've achieved what you set out to do: that you've created a life for yourself and your loved ones that offers all the material and spiritual rewards you've ever dreamed of.

That's real wealth!

Good fortune!

INDEX

Cableshore, 193-96
Canada Deposit Insurance
    Corporation, 29, 80, 135,
    140, 148-49, 150, 155
  protected assets, 151-52
  unprotected assets, 154-55
Canada Pension Plan, 117, 120-21
Canada Savings Bonds
  GICs vs., 78-79
  gift idea, 38
  investment in, 19-21, 23, 68-70,
      74, 84, 106-107, 154, 220
      225
  minimum interest guarantees,
      72-73
  RRSPs and, 132, 139
  trading up, 68-70
  true bonds vs., 86, 88
  See also: Bonds
Canada Trust, 98
  Canada Trust Investment Fund,
      143-44
Canadian Association of Financial
    Planners, 231-32
Canadian Commercial Bank, 151
Canadian dollar. See Foreign
    Exchange
Canadian Tire, 93
Capital, 8
  banks and, 26
  preservng, 22.
  See also: Assets
Capital gains. See Taxes, capital gains
Central trust
  Bond Fund, 159
Child Tax Credit,
  investing, 23
Children
  costs of, 32-33
  financial benefits of, 33-35
      Family Allowance, 33-34
  over 18, 35
  teaching about money, 37-41

Citibank, 93
Collectibles
  as assets, 13, 132
Commodity futures, 132
Credit. See Debt
Credit cards, 92-102
  American Express, 94-95
  cheques vs., 101-102
  effective use of, 95-100
  interest, 97-100
  Mastercard, 95, 98
  status cards, 96-97
  user fees, 95-96
  Visa, 92, 93, 94, 95, 98
Credit unions
  banks vs., 27-29, 80, 111, 153-54
  Guaranteed Investment
      Certificates and, 74-75, 79
  term deposits and, 74-75, 79
Crown Trust, 150
Debit card, 101. See also: Credit card
Debt
  consumer debt, 8, 103, 104-105, 209
  home equity line of credit, 113-15
  investment debt, 12, 103, 105-15,
      176-79, 209
  banks and, 110-11
  loans, types of, 111-112
  personal line of credit, 112-113
Deposit insurance. See Canada
    Deposit Insurance
    Corporation
Disinflation. See Inflation, disinflation
Dome Petroleum, 45
Equity. See Real estate, equity
Family Allowance
  investing, 23, 33-34
Financial planning. See Investment,
    advice; RRSPs, self-directed;
    Taxes, tax shelters
Financial Post, 7, 80, 142, 145, 171
Financial Times of Canada, 7, 57, 80,
    141, 142, 145

INDEX